Writing at Work

About the Authors

Edward (Ted) L. Smith is a communication consultant and trainer for government organizations and Fortune 100 companies. A former professor of English, he taught courses at the University of Michigan and the University of Texas, Austin, in oral and written communication from 1976 to 1985.

Ted's special expertise is the simplifying of technical information intended for nonspecialist audiences. In addition to teaching and publishing in this area, he has served as an award-winning consultant to various organizations on producing "user-friendly" documentation. Ted has conducted writing seminars for IBM sites around the U.S., Canada, and Europe, winning several "Star Quality" teaching awards for his work there. He has also taught courses on technical and business writing for Motorola, Hughes Aircraft, Schlumberger, 3M, the Continuum Company, Liant Software, Seton Medical Center, National Technological University satellite television programs, and many Texas state agencies—including former Texas Governor Ann Richard's office.

Stephen A. Bernhardt is professor of English at New Mexico State University, Las Cruces, where he teaches technical and business communication at both undergraduate and graduate levels. Widely published in leading journals, he is currently president of the Council for Programs in Technical and Scientific Communication (CPTSC); chair of the Research Advisory Panel of the Society for Technical Communication; former vice president and secretary of the New Mexico Coalition for Literacy; editorial board member of the Journal of Computer Documentation; and former director of two National Workplace Literacy Demonstration Projects, funded by the U. S. Department of Education. He has served the Association of Teachers of Technical Writing for several years, both on its executive committee and on its editorial advisory board of its journal *Technical Communication Quarterly,* to which he frequently contributes. He has also consulted and provided training to employees of IBM, Motorola, Hughes Aircraft, and other organizations. As senior consultant for Scientific Services, Franklin Quest Consulting Group, he recently spent a year working full time within the pharmaceutical industry in Switzerland, England, and Italy, helping coordinate the production of large documentation sets using global teams and technologies.

Writing at Work

PROFESSIONAL WRITING SKILLS FOR PEOPLE ON THE JOB

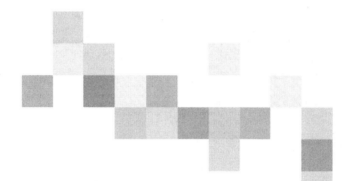

EDWARD L. SMITH

Edward L. Smith & Associates

STEPHEN A. BERNHARDT

New Mexico State University

McGraw Hill

New York Chicago San Francisco Lisbon London Madrid Mexico City
Milan New Delhi San Juan Seoul Singapore Sydney Toronto

The *McGraw·Hill* Companies

Library of Congress Cataloging-in-Publication Data

Smith, Edward L., 1951–
    Writing at work : professional writing skills for people on the job / Edward L. Smith,
Stephen A. Bernhardt.
        p.   cm.
    Includes index.
    ISBN 0-8442-5983-7 (paperback)
      1. Business writing.   I. Bernhardt, Stephen A.   II. Title.
HF5718.3.S654   1996
808′.06665—dc21
                                     96-46402
                                        CIP

    13 14 15 16 17 18 19 20 WFR / WFR 0

ISBN-13: 978-0-8442-5983-3
ISBN-10:   0-8442-5983-7

McGraw-Hill books are available at special quantity discounts to use as premiums and
sales promotions, or for use in corporate training programs. For more information, please
write to the Director of Special Sales, Professional Publishing, McGraw-Hill, Two Penn
Plaza, New York, NY 10121-2298. Or contact your local bookstore.

This book is printed on acid-free paper.

Contents

unit one
"Professional writing is *appropriate* to the situation." **1**

unit two

"Professional writing is grammatically *correct*." **39**

unit three
"Professional writing uses punctuation to show what *is*—and what is *not*—important." **119**

unit four

"Professional writing uses a *clear* and *concise* vocabulary." **173**

unit five

"Professional writing is appropriately *active* and *personal*, rather than passive and impersonal." **247**

unit six

"Professional writing *emphasizes* what is important—and downplays what is *not*." **291**

Preface

Most people would agree that writing is one of the most essential skills in business. Writing is an important way in which a business presents its public self; it is also a means by which individuals within a business communicate. And writing is often the yardstick that we use to evaluate others' performance and that others use to evaluate ours.

In spite of the central role of writing in business, most people would also agree—somewhat guiltily—that writing is something they dread. Writing takes too long, and the final product doesn't match the effort.

Most people think that, to become a good writer, they need to learn a thousand incomprehensible, little rules—all the rules they never quite learned in English class. We don't think so. We see remarkable agreement among good writers and good writing teachers about what contributes to a strong, effective, clear style.

This book gives you some principles to help make writing less nerve-racking and, perhaps, less mysterious. Understanding these principles won't automatically make you a *great* writer, but putting them into practice in your daily or weekly writing will make you a *better* one.

Who This Book Is For

We have written *Writing at Work* for several audiences. The first audience is people in a business environment who write as part of their job and would use this book in a self-study situation to improve their writing. Some might be full-time writers (including report, proposal, and documentation writers). Others might write as part of their job but not consider themselves full-time writers. These people might include administrative assistants, accountants, managers, line supervisors, test engineers, researchers, systems programmers, marketers, or product developers. If you are in this audience, you will appreciate the clear presentation of the six principles of writing that can help you to write better on your own. You will also appreciate having the exercise answers at the end of each chapter so that you can get immediate feedback on your choices in the exercises.

The second audience for *Writing at Work* is also in a business environment, but instead of working through this book on their own, the people in this audience might be attending a short class on improving writing skills. If you are in this audience, we imagine that you will appreciate the short, modular chapters of the book. During class discussion, you will have the chance to expand upon the book's content by drawing on your personal expertise and writing experiences. We encourage you to supplement the exercises by analyzing real documents produced by members of the class.

The third audience for this book is university students, either in an undergraduate- or graduate-level professional writing class or in a tutorial writing center. For those of you in this audience, we imagine that you will profit most from focusing on the specific aspects of grammar and style you wish to improve and especially from seeing familiar principles for effective writing applied to documents in a real business and technical environment.

What This Book Is *Not*

Many people take courses on writing—in either a business or an academic setting—because they want to improve the overall logic and structure of their documents. This book will not directly help you do that, because it is aimed at a lower level of organization—that of the paragraph and the sentence. While we look at sentences in the context of paragraphs and, occasionally, larger documents, this book is not primarily a *rhetoric* text; that is, we don't discuss strategies for organizing larger documents.

Other people take writing courses or pick up writing books to learn the rules: where to put commas or how to choose between confusing words like *affect* and *effect*. Though we discuss principles for accurate and effective grammatical usage, we don't intend this book to be a *handbook*. An exhaustive treatment of rules is outside our scope. This book is not really a reference book; rather, it is a guide to be read and applied step-by-step. (We do, however, include a glossary with definitions of the grammatical and writing terms printed in **bold** throughout the book.)

We encourage you to develop a file of good examples of the various types of written communication in your specific field. Such a file might be of more use to you than the sample documents in any of the rhetoric texts recommended in the appendix of this book. You should feel free to borrow from those examples when you produce written documents. Creativity in professional writing doesn't mean reinventing the wheel each time you sit down to write.

How to Use This Book

This book contains six principles for effective writing at the sentence and paragraph level (see the list in Chapter 1, pages 10–11). The principles are cumulative, moving from the most general principles of good writing (appropriateness), to principles of grammatical correctness (usage), and finally to principles of effective and appropriate choice (style). Each principle is the subject of one of the six units in the book, each of which contains several short chapters on related topics.

Traditional writing books often treat grammatical topics—for example, parts of speech or punctuation—as *ends in themselves*. Here, we deal with those topics as *means to an end*. We won't overwhelm you with a slew of grammatical terms but rather offer you a limited set of essential terms and principles that will help you to see how your sentences work. The various grammatical topics we discuss are all grouped beneath the umbrella of our six principles for effective professional writing. You will find important terms **boldfaced** the first time we use them in text and explained in the glossary at the end of the book.

As we mentioned earlier, we envision that this book will be used for independent study and for classroom use. What follows are some suggestions for using the book in these two different situations.

On Your Own

We intend for you to work through this book sequentially—reading the chapters, working through the exercises, and checking your answers against those provided at the end of each chapter.

Unit One provides the context for the approach to good writing taken in this book. This is an important unit, but if you are eager to begin working on grammar exercises immediately, you can jump to Units Two and Three, which deal with grammatical correctness and punctuation usage. Some of the material in these units may seem elementary, but it builds a necessary foundation for the latter units on effective style. If you are contemplating skipping the discussion in any of the chapters in these units, we suggest that you first try doing the chapter exercises to assure yourself of your command of the topics covered.

The longer exercises contained in the section "Putting It All Together" at the end of each unit allow you to synthesize all that you have learned in that particular unit. These exercises will stretch your skills and remind you that sentences and paragraphs always exist within a larger context:

Sentences refer to other sentences; paragraphs connect to other paragraphs. Further, every document is presented within a complex work situation and needs to be negotiated.

In Unit Four, we cross the (admittedly fuzzy) boundary between grammatical *usage* and effective sentence and paragraph *style*. Here, the choices you are asked to make are not between correct and incorrect usage but between appropriate and inappropriate words, clear and unclear reference. Most real decisions you make in writing fall into the category of style, where you are choosing appropriate sentence strategies rather than simply correcting errors. Unit Five concentrates on active and personal style, including detailed discussion of passive and active voice. Unit Six shows you how to create emphasis through sentence structures and visual design, with the final chapter summing up the marks of a professional style.

However you proceed, we urge you to make good use of your time in working through the written discussion and exercises. When material is simply review for you, read quickly and use the exercises as a quick check on your understanding. When material is new to you, read the chapters thoughtfully and work the exercises carefully. Before moving to a new chapter, let the principles you have learned sink in. Consciously practice those principles in your everyday writing. The payoff will come not by working through the book quickly, but by working with it attentively and selectively, and then applying what you have learned to your own writing.

Notes for an Instructor

We have used this book in a corporate setting as the text for a five-day, all-day course on improved writing skills, covering two units the first day and one unit the remaining four days.

If you use the book in this way, you will want to summarize much of the discussion of each unit in short lectures based on the chapters, devoting the major portion of class time to the exercises and individual or group corrections. Following is a suggested class schedule:

Day	Syllabus
Monday morning	Unit Two on correctness
Monday afternoon	Unit Two (continued)
Monday evening	Unit One (to be read at home)
Tuesday morning	Unit Three on punctuation
Tuesday afternoon	Unit Three (continued)
Tuesday evening	Catch up on previous exercises (to be done at home)

Wednesday morning	Unit Four on vocabulary
Wednesday afternoon	Unit Four (continued)
Wednesday evening	Chapter 24 on achieving a professional look (to be read at home)
Thursday morning	Unit Five on active and personal writing
Thursday afternoon	Unit Five (continued)
Thursday evening	Chapter 25 on a professional style (to be read at home)
Friday morning	Unit Six on emphatic structures (Chapters 21–23)
Friday afternoon	Unit Six (concluded)

The above plan assumes you are teaching the course in a corporate setting. If you are using this book in an academic setting, you can easily spread the individual chapters over an entire semester.

In an academic setting, you could also supplement this text with other materials, perhaps case studies or a business communication rhetoric. (See the list of books in the appendix for possible choices.) Our book will give your students good coverage of style; you need to decide how to enhance their abilities to choose appropriate rhetorical strategies. Interesting assignments may be the best way to do so, precluding the need for a supplementary text. You may wish to supplement the exercises in the "Putting It All Together" sections with additional documents for analysis, to which you can apply the "Checklist for Professional Writing" found in Chapter 25.

Acknowledgments

Many people helped us in creating and testing the material in *Writing at Work,* and we would like to take time to thank them.

We first acknowledge our debt to the works of Joseph Williams and Richard Lanham. Both scholars take a grammatical approach to style, as demonstrated in their books: Williams's *Style: Ten Lessons in Clarity & Grace* and Lanham's *Revising Business Prose.* Our indebtedness to Williams's book will be especially apparent in the latter chapters of *Writing at Work.* Teaching his book with our particular audiences, however, showed us that there was a need for a work with coverage of both grammar and style, aimed less at academic audiences and more at business ones. This realization inspired us to write *Writing at Work.* We acknowledge our intellectual debt to both writers and recommend their works enthusiastically.

Because *Writing at Work* grew out of our experiences teaching writing in professional settings, we would like to thank the various audiences in those settings for their review comments in helping us to polish the contents in this book:

- Our colleague, Lucia McKay, who taught the material many times both at IBM and Motorola, making copious notes and suggestions.
- Steve's colleagues at New Mexico State University and Southern Illinois University, especially Stuart Brown, Paul Meyer, and Bruce Appleby for their helpful advice.
- Ted's students in professional writing classes at Motorola, Hughes Aircraft, SEMATECH, and IBM sites around the country—especially Jeannette Emery and Dennis O'Neal at IBM Tucson, Sandi Wilson and Ann Dixon at IBM Bethesda, Kay Paff at IBM Manassas, and Steve Hughes at SEMATECH in Austin.
- Graduate students in Steve's professional writing classes at New Mexico State University, who not only worked through the materials as a course text but also offered careful review comments along the way. Special thanks to Bev Kolosseus, Cheryl Nims, Karen Luces, RoMay Sitze, Becky Sellars, and Melody Munson-McGee.

We also want to thank Midge Bernhardt: first, for her hospitality during Ted's trips to Las Cruces to work on the manuscript with Steve; second, for assembling the glossary and index; and finally, for her gentle but persistent encouragement to us to complete the manuscript.

Finally, we thank John Nolan, Marisa L'Heureux, and Heidi Hedstrom at NTC for believing in the manuscript and for their expert editorial assistance in creating this final version.

"Professional writing is *appropriate* to the situation."

Although very few people write full-time as a profession, many people find that writing is a large part of their chosen field. If you are one of these people, you may well have been surprised when you first started working by how much writing you do on the job: memos to coworkers and managers, electronic mail sent to a distribution list, forms to complete, letters to customers, weekly or monthly status reports, yearly appraisals—and those are only the generic writing tasks that almost everyone tackles! There are also specific writing tasks to be performed in almost every profession: lab reports, investigation results, marketing materials, conference papers—and the list goes on. By offering useful principles and practice in developing your professional style, this book will help you gain confidence so you can write whatever is needed in your job.

In Unit One, we try to place the elements of a professional style in various *contexts*. Chapter 1, "Writing on the Job," discusses the importance of good writing in a work setting. Chapter 2, "A Model of the Writing Process," places the principles of good writing in the context of your own writing process. We think you will gain control over style by understanding how you gather and organize ideas, draft text, revise for large concerns, and edit for correctness. Finally, Chapter 3, "Real Rules, Nonrules, and House Rules," looks at the status of writing rules and makes some valuable distinctions for those who are confused about what rules are important to follow. Chapter 3 urges you to recognize the real rules of grammar and to distinguish these rules from individual preferences for certain expressions and from company-based guidelines on style or punctuation.

This book is about principles, not rules. That's an important distinction. Rules imply rigidity and right vs. wrong choices; principles imply flexibility in solving problems for which there are no neat solutions. Though there are definitely cases of right vs. wrong choices in writing, we think writing is often a problem-solving activity where you look for a *good* solution, not the *only* solution. Keeping that distinction in mind while you work through this book will help you in completing the exercises and checking your answers to the suggested answers in the back of each chapter. Maintaining a distinction between principles and rules when you write on the job should make writing more enjoyable, since you will be in control as you weigh your choices and take control of your own professional style.

chapter 1

Writing on the Job

In This Chapter

This chapter introduces in a general way the topic of writing in business settings. It argues that you need to understand your writing situation and to be as clear as possible about your purpose and audience: why you are writing and to whom. The chapter offers a model of the writing situation—the Communication Triangle—and previews the general principles for good writing that are taken up throughout the book.

The Place of Writing in Business

Writing is important to business. Estimates of the time people spend writing in a normal workday run upwards of 25 percent. Some researchers believe this may even be a low estimate, since people typically don't consider time spent planning their writing to be actual writing time. If we count both the time spent writing and the time spent reading what others have written, the figure is closer to 40 percent. That is a lot of time, and it represents a significant business expense.

Poor writing is bad business. It slows down the communication process, causes confusion, and encourages mistakes. Most businesses are inundated with paperwork. There is just too much paper around—reports are too long, memos too frequent, correspondence too burdensome. When the writing is not only lengthy but bad—filled with mistakes, poorly organized, unclear—writing becomes a hindrance rather than a tool for doing business.

But good writing is *more* than just a tool for doing business; it is itself a business product. In the widely heralded information economy, written information (whether in hard copy or electronic form) is often the commodity that is being traded. Product documentation, feasibility studies, product brochures, test reports—these all represent business products just as much as manufactured goods do. Companies have huge sums wrapped up in their information products.

Individual Writing in Business Settings

Good writing is also important at the individual level. The memos and reports that employees write serve the interests of the company, but they also serve as a primary means of individual evaluation. No one may ever say outright that you will be evaluated on your written reports or memos, but all too frequently nobody knows what you did until you put it in writing. Thus writing serves as a key means of job evaluation and plays a large role in decisions concerning promotions and merit raises.

Writing serves to establish and maintain an employee's role within a company. The impressions formed of you as a worker, especially by higher-ups who are not in your immediate work setting, are often based on what you write. And the higher one moves within an organization, the more important and time-consuming writing becomes (both writing and reviewing the writing of others).

Yet the importance of writing is often not acknowledged. Researchers who look at the workplace find that many employees feel uncomfortable with their writing. Most employees feel they spend too much time writing, that their writing is weak in one of a dozen ways, that they really need to brush up on the principles of good writing. Employers will complain that they see weaknesses in the writing of others, perhaps lamenting that colleges don't do a better job of training students in essential communication skills. They will also admit that their own writing could be improved.

Many employees do not define themselves as writers or define writing as their work. They say they are test engineers, or biologists, or sales representatives, or accountants; yet these workers spend much of their time writing, and many of their work activities are directly aimed at producing some written product. Many employees attempt to keep writing in a subordinate position, as something they have to do but would rather not. They see writing as a necessary evil associated with their jobs. Writing is a foe, not a friendly tool, a tool closely related to success within the organization.

The Need for Writing Training

It is ironic that the importance of good writing is not more directly confronted in business settings. We acknowledge the need for training in new methods of accounting, or in management by objectives, or in using new data-processing tools, yet we don't often recognize the need for training in writing. Perhaps this situation is changing: a recent survey of Fortune 500 executives noted that poor reading and writing skills were the number one cause of employees being terminated within their first year. And the same survey identified training in writing and communication skills to be the top priority for the workforce.

Writing is complicated business. Writers need a special language to work with, special techniques for editing others' written language, and special concepts for understanding what makes writing clear, forceful, and effective. Instead of working to gain these specialized competencies, many employees assume they can simply pick up what they need to know as they use the language.

This book is an attempt to bring the importance of writing to the surface—to talk explicitly about good writing. As an employee, you need to know what counts as good writing, how writers think and work, and how readers respond to your writing. You need to recognize and control grammatical trouble spots and to have a language for doing so. And you need a few terms and some special skills to describe how sentences work, so you can control language and use it effectively.

The Importance of Purpose and Audience

The real key to good writing is a well-developed sense of **purpose** and **audience.** Good writing will follow once a writer decides exactly what needs to be accomplished and who can accomplish the task. And often a clear sense of purpose and audience will prevent problems of grammar and word choice at the sentence level. Very often the most important improvement a writer can make in a piece of weak writing is to state clearly at the beginning what the writing is intended to do and who is likely to be affected. A clear, up-front approach cues readers to the whole situation. Being direct and up-front lets readers know why they are reading and what to expect.

The worst kind of writing has no clearly stated purpose or targeted audience. You might read a memo and wonder: "Am I supposed to do something? What is this writer's point? Why am I being told these things?" And often this kind of writing may have annoying errors or unfocused sentences, problems that indicate the writer's uncertainty (or even lack of thought) about purpose and audience.

Even though much of this book is concerned with the sentence-level choices we make as writers, we want to emphasize here the importance of making those choices in the larger context of thinking about purpose and audience. When you shape a piece of writing around a clearly defined purpose and audience, you give yourself a tool for deciding what to include and what to delete, what to emphasize and what to downplay, and how to order your arguments and evidence. A sharply defined sense of purpose and audience will also guide you toward an appropriate strategy and tone. With a clearly defined purpose and audience, you can begin writing to specific individuals with a clear sense of what you would like them to do. You then have a yardstick for editing and revising that lets you measure how well you are communicating your purpose to your audience.

Multiple Purposes, Multiple Audiences

Most work environments are complicated places, and purposes for writing reflect these complications. A writer will have an obvious purpose for writing, but behind the stated purpose may lie hidden motives of personal advancement, empire building, or efforts to change or influence the organization.

For example, suppose you are a supervisor who has a problem with employees using the office photocopier for personal business. If you decide a memo is the best way to handle the situation, this gives you an obvious purpose for writing. But behind the obvious purpose of stopping unauthorized uses of the machine are other, secondary purposes that make the memo a complicated business. You do not wish to alienate those who haven't used the machine for unauthorized uses. Nor do you wish to make a contest of the problem, challenging people to use the machine without being caught. And you certainly don't want your employees to get the idea that the office will be patrolled by a photocopy police squad. You would simply like cooperation from your employees; you want them to recognize the reasonable nature of your request to stop using the machine for unauthorized copying.

Most writing situations are like this—complicated, multifaceted, somewhat touchy in their interpersonal complications. It takes some clear thinking about strategy to determine exactly what purpose or purposes your writing will serve.

Nor is it a simple matter to define an audience. Your memo ostensibly will go out to those in your office with access to the photocopy machine. Yet there may be other, secondary audiences who will see your memo. Perhaps your manager will review your files to evaluate your work. Perhaps you will end up having to discipline an employee who continues to use the photocopier for personal use, so your memo becomes a legal document used as evidence in the proceedings against the employee. Suddenly, new purposes and audiences open up for your "simple" memo. The words you wrote with your initial purpose in mind may suddenly prove inadequate to the new demands on them.

You often cannot predict where a memo will end up or into whose hands it will fall in addition to those named specifically at the top. Every time you decide to copy a memo up or down the organizational hierarchy (and this happens frequently with electronic mail), you risk appearing to go over someone's head or appearing to be insensitive to office politics. Often the tone and approach that are right for the primary audience—perhaps a close supervisor—are totally wrong for the secondary audience—perhaps a manager up the line.

Writing has a permanence that speaking lacks. Once you commit an idea to a paper, it has a life of its own. It ends up in files where you don't expect it, and it may show up at the wrong time. Before you write, your first step must be to decide whether to write at all—whether your purpose might not be better realized by telephone or face-to-face communication.

A Communication Model of Writing

To understand writing tasks many writers find it helpful to visualize the communication situation as a triangle (see Figure 1.1). In this **Communication Triangle,** the message—what is actually being communicated—is surrounded by those features that shape the message. At one corner is the writer, the one who usually has some purpose for sending a message. The writer sends the message to some reader or audience—represented at a second corner—who has some reason for reading the message. Finally, in the third corner is the subject: what the message is about. So the writer, the audience, and the subject are closely related, like three corners of the same triangle.

There is more to this representation, however. Note that the writer and reader are connected by one side of the triangle. They don't exist in isolation but are directly tied in some relationship, represented by the connecting side. Every time you write, you establish some sort of relationship between yourself and your audience. You try to get them to do things for you, or you do the things they have asked you to do, or you do things together. As a writer, you can assume a role of either asking or telling someone to do something, of either cajoling someone into cooperation or threatening them with undesirable consequences. In other words, you don't simply send messages about the world when you write—you impose a relationship on the receiver of the message. It is in this touchy place of imposing relationships where writers often fail, for the writer's sense of appropriate relations is often at odds with the reader's sense.

The other sides of the triangle represent the writer's understanding of the subject and the reader's understanding of the subject—two understandings that are rarely equal. Sometimes writers get so close to their subjects—they have such thorough understanding—that they begin to have trouble imagining what their readers don't understand. They begin

Figure 1.1 *The Communication Triangle*

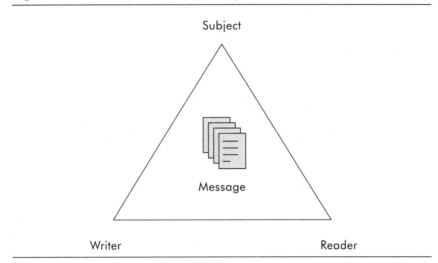

using **jargon, acronyms** (like ADCOM or UNIX), and insider language that their readers have trouble understanding.

The relation between the reader and the subject is especially tricky because it involves not only the reader's *actual* understanding of and attitude toward the subject but also the writer's *estimate* of that understanding and attitude. You know the feeling of reading something where the writer seems to know much more than you do. And as a reader, you are sometimes alienated by a writer who patronizes you by assuming that you know less than you really do.

Surrounding the whole triangle is the very messy, complicated world that influences the written text. Deadlines, budgets, outside issues that compete for your attention—all influence your shaping of the message. How messages are produced and delivered, what the reader's frame of mind is, whether a reader actually reads the message—everything in the situation that surrounds a message helps determine its success.

The Communication Triangle can remind you of the complexity of most writing situations, with its key elements at each corner and the connections between these elements. Writing often feels like a balancing act, trying to achieve an appropriate balance between appearing too bossy or too undecided; between writing as an expert or writing to be fully understood (even by novices); between relying on what readers know and deciding what they need to be told. The triangle, with its geometry of perfect balance, offers you a metaphor of good writing.

Becoming a Good Writer

No book can teach you how to analyze your particular writing situations. To be a good writer—one who responds to the situational demands of particular purposes and audiences—you need all your analytical skills. You need to be firmly in control of your work situation, understanding what needs to be accomplished and what are efficient strategies for achieving your goals. You need to be a psychologist, understanding what motivates people and what alienates them. You need to be a manager, responsive to how duties and roles are assigned within your organization. And you need to be a politician, one who understands how to get competing groups to work harmoniously.

To be a good writer, you also need confidence. You need to trust your insight, to believe you have good ideas worth conveying. If you are insecure about the quality of your ideas, anxious about your authority, hesitant about your ability to solve problems through writing, you will produce writing that is obscure, riddled with jargon, impenetrable, and confusing. Many insecure workers try to hide behind their writing, creating smokescreens that obscure and confuse. Confident writers tend to have a clear purpose, and they are willing to put that purpose up front where readers can see it. They know that readers benefit from sharing a clear sense of purpose with the writer.

Confident workers can be confident writers—they can see problems clearly and offer solutions that will stand on their own merits. Good writers take responsibility, confident they have ideas others will respect and respond to. Good writers recognize that most business situations are already complicated and don't need language that further complicates matters. Good writers appreciate prose that is lean and efficient, that works hard, and gets the job done without a lot of wasted words.

The problems of the vague, stuffy, bureaucratic style that are covered in this text tend to show up in the writing of employees who are new to an organization, who are insecure with their positions, or who are uncomfortable with their own authority. The principles we recommend for a vigorous, direct, active style will only feel comfortable if you are confident of the quality of your work and secure in your position within your organization. In many ways, your writing style announces who you are. By choosing to write in a strong, confident style, you can project an image of assurance, of thoughtfulness, and of competence.

Six Principles of Good Writing

This book offers you six principles for developing a clear, strong style:

1. Professional writing is *appropriate* to the situation.
2. Professional writing is grammatically *correct.*

3. Professional writing uses punctuation to show what *is*—and what is *not*—important.
4. Professional writing uses a *clear* and *concise* vocabulary.
5. Professional writing is appropriately *active* and *personal,* rather than passive and impersonal.
6. Professional writing *emphasizes* what is important—and downplays what is *not.*

Each of these six principles is the topic of one of the units in this book (hence the six units). Understanding and following these principles will be of little help, however, if you are not firmly in control of your work, comfortable with your authority, and confident of your ideas. The principles won't help if your goal is to hide behind words or evade responsibility.

If, however, your goal is to be understood, to present ideas confidently, to use writing as an effective way of getting things done, then this book can help.

chapter 2

A Model of the Writing Process

This chapter describes a process approach to writing. It urges you to consider how you approach a writing task, encouraging you to be aware of what steps you go through as you plan, draft, revise, and edit. The assumption here is that you can gain control over your writing by being aware of how you work and by being able to articulate a structured approach to a writing task.

The chapter describes how expert writers typically behave and invites you to consider doing likewise. Certainly, different writers have different composing processes, and the point is not that everyone should use the same process. You may find ideas here that offer a different approach to composition than the one you typically follow. Consider trying new processes to see if they can be productive and efficient for you.

Planning, Drafting, and Rewriting

Many people think that good writers sit down at a typewriter or word processor and let a document flow letter-perfect onto the page or screen. Although they themselves can't do this, they believe that if they were truly good writers they would be able to do so.

In fact, good writing involves a great deal of planning up front before you begin to write, as well as revising and editing after you finish a draft. The best writers are those who allot time before and after drafting to include these vitally important activities.

It is convenient to speak of the writing process as having three stages: **planning** (or prewriting), **drafting** (or composing), and **rewriting** (revising and editing) (see Figure 2.1). Identifying these three stages suggests that writing is a process that unfolds over time and that it is useful to distinguish where you are in the process. If you can think in terms of

Figure 2.1 *The Writing Process*

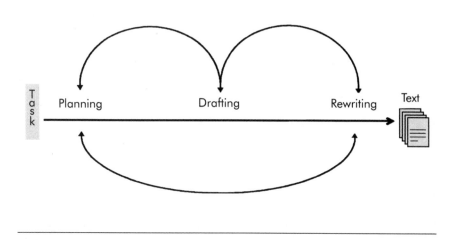

stages, you can avoid thinking that you must produce perfect text while planning and drafting, and you can control the tendency to edit picky little details when you should be concentrating on the ideas and the overall structure of the document.

In the process of producing a successful document, you generally work through each of these stages. Depending on the importance of the document, the amount of time you have to produce it, and your writing experience, you may shortcut some of the activities in each stage. Nevertheless, when you're involved in any of them, you are truly engaged in *writing*.

The Planning Stage

Chapter 1, "Writing on the Job," stressed the importance of having a clearly defined purpose for writing and of adapting your writing to a specific audience. But purpose and audience are only two of the things you need to think about in the planning stage, before you begin to write. You need to think generally about the situation in which you are writing—not just your immediate reason for writing but the larger political and social situation. What has happened that calls for you to communicate at all? Why have you chosen to do so in writing? Where will your readers be when they read your document, and what will they be doing with it?

You also need to think about the type of document you are going to produce—what it typically looks like and how it is typically organized. An internal memo is formatted and organized differently from a piece of external correspondence. You need to think about the **medium** in which the document will be produced—handwritten, typed, printed, or sent through electronic mail. Each of these has a different look and a different impact on the reader. You also need to think about what your likely sources of information are and how broad a scope your document will cover. Finally, you need to know how much time you have to produce the document. Time constraints shape all stages of the planning and writing process.

Creating an Outline

Once you have given some thought to these considerations, you need to continue planning by gathering your information and creating a rough outline. Your outline needn't be formal—you can just jot down the main points you want to make and then, indented beneath each point, sketch a few subpoints or supporting pieces of evidence. Many people find it helpful to create diagrams that show the major points and their connections. Others like upside-down tree structures that show the hierarchy of the document. All the outline really needs to show is the order of points you're going to make, with some indication of which points are more important than others.

These planning activities take time. One thing research tells us is that good writers will spend up to *half* of their total writing time in planning. Again, the amount of time you spend on these planning activities will depend on the importance and length of your document. If you have written similar documents before, you will probably finish your planning faster.

Once you have thought about audience and purpose, gathered your information, and sketched out an outline, you're ready to begin drafting. But before you begin, notice the approach taken here. We're suggesting that you shape your document from the *outside in* (some writers call it *top down*). We're not suggesting you start with sentences on a page and try to build up a successful document word by word and sentence by sentence; instead, you're beginning with external considerations and letting your decisions there dictate the shape of the document you ultimately produce.

The Drafting Stage

Another popular misconception about writing is that good writers write it right the first time, without having to go back and change anything. But while good writers may produce *pretty good* drafts the first time (and experience helps here, especially previous experience in the type of document you happen to be writing), nobody gets it perfect the first time.

In fact, good writers typically go back and make lots of changes in their documents. But what good writers know is a technique that lets them get a first draft done very quickly. We will share it with you here: *Good writers separate drafting from rewriting.* That means they don't try to get it perfect the first time; instead, they try to get their material down on the page or screen *before* they worry about cleaning it up.

This simple technique can save you a lot of time, because it allows you to postpone editing and criticizing your writing until you get some ideas roughed out on the page or screen. It is also the best cure for writer's block, which generally stems from allowing an overactive self-editor to interfere with simply getting words on paper.

There's a good analogy here to building a house. After you lay the foundation for a house—which is essentially what you do in the planning stage of writing—you don't frame one panel of the house, install your wiring and plumbing in the panel, frame in a window, insulate the panel, sheetrock and wallpaper the inside, brick the outside, and then stand back and admire the beginnings of your house. For one thing, you would be lucky to have all the seams and corners match in the final product. For another, it would be unbelievably expensive to keep calling in your various subcontractors to finish off one panel at a time: they would all be there every day!

And yet many people try to draft in just such an inefficient way. They work on one paragraph or section at a time, polishing off that section until they are satisfied enough to go on to the next section. No wonder such writing is so agonizing for its writers and so choppy to its readers. And on top of being agonizing, such a method of writing is wasteful, because the one paragraph that you spend a long time polishing may end up in the scrap heap when you decide to rewrite. There are better strategies for drafting, which we outline below.

Suggested Strategies for Producing First Drafts

Below are some suggested strategies for producing a first draft of a document. Like the activities listed in the planning stage earlier, these strategies are only suggested ones. You may not always follow all of them or follow them in the same order. But we believe they will help you get a first draft (of whatever kind of document you are writing) done more quickly.

1. You might start by putting your outline on paper or on a computer screen with spaces left between the headings for the text you will later write. Then try grafting your text onto the outline. The outline provides the skeleton for fleshing out your text; so when you get

blocked in one section, the outline can serve as a reminder of other sections to work on.

2. For shorter documents, try to get your whole draft done in one sitting, as quickly as you can. For longer documents, see if you can complete a whole section at one sitting. Remind yourself that you're not after perfection but thorough coverage of your material.

3. Start writing the part that you feel you know the best. There's no obligation to start at the beginning; in fact, the introduction is often the *last* thing you should write. After all, how do you know what you're going to say until you have said it?

4. If you are writing in one section and get an inspiration for another section, quickly jump to that section, write yourself a brief note (perhaps surrounded with square brackets so you can easily search for them later), and then jump back to where you left off.

5. Force yourself to keep going forward, not backward. This is hard, but if you can kick that editing demon off your shoulder while you draft, you may be able to keep up with the composing voice that dictates what to write. (The editing demon tends to quiet the composing voice.) You will be surprised by how much you have to say about your topic.

6. When you get blocked (and everyone does sometimes), try jumping to another section and begin drafting there. (Remember those bracketed notes you left for yourself?) If that doesn't help, go back to the top of your document and read down through what you have already written. That often gets the creative juices flowing again.

7. If you are still blocked, you might seek out a colleague and tell him or her what you are trying to write. You will often talk through the block and find yourself saying *exactly* what you want to write. It's often a good idea to tape record these sessions to capture your words.

8. If you are still blocked, put the project aside and work on something else. Your mind is perfectly capable of working on the back burner to solve a problem while working on another project at a conscious level. Ideas for the blocked project will come as it simmers on the back burner of your mind. Keep a tape recorder or a notepad handy, as ideas may come to you as you are driving or watching TV. If you don't capture them, they may well disappear.

If you try these strategies, you will be pleasantly surprised by how much you have to say—and by how little time (comparatively speaking) it takes to get it down.

Getting words on paper or screen will help you feel a sense of accomplishment, which in turn will motivate you to keep working on the document. Seeing words allows you to use your visual intelligence to organize what you have to say and to fine-tune your writing for your purpose and audience. Getting words down, even if the ideas are poorly organized, can help you think in ways that are just not possible when the ideas are simply milling about inside your head.

Drafting—facing that intimidating blank page or screen—may not immediately become easy, but the strategies suggested above should help it become *easier.*

The Rewriting Stage

Once you have drafted your text, you are ready to begin rewriting for effectiveness. Two separate activities go on during rewriting:

REVISING: rewriting for large concerns like appropriateness to your audience, clarity of purpose, and overall organization

EDITING: rewriting to make your sentences clear and your word choice correct and effective

Much of the rest of this book is concerned with **editing**—getting your sentences correct, your words appropriate, your style strong. We could jump immediately to these sentence and word-level concerns, as many writing books do. But we feel it is appropriate to think about those concerns in terms of your larger goal of producing whole, effective documents.

So, in rewriting, you will want to first consider how well your document fits with your overall goals:

- Is your purpose clear?
- Is the tone right for your intended audience?
- Have you included the right amount of detail for the level of understanding you want your audience to have?
- Is the overall document organized logically?
- Does the text flow smoothly from section to section?
- Is the text visually appealing? Is it inviting, or does it look forbidding?
- Do you make good use of figures and tables to support your main points?

These questions are the domain of **revising.** It is a mental challenge to look at the whole document and to make large-level decisions about whether it works. But you need to see the big picture before you start the nitty-gritty work of editing—or you will end up with well-constructed sentences and paragraphs that don't add up to anything for your audience.

One critical piece of advice in rewriting is to *sweat the small stuff last.* By *small stuff,* we mean spelling, punctuation, grammar, and phrasing—all those things that immediately jump out from the page at you when you reread something you have written. Sweating the small stuff last means that you should revise before you edit. Why is that good advice, when it seems easier to edit the small stuff first? Well, for the same reason that we encouraged you to draft the whole document or section completely before you start rewriting any particular section: otherwise, you may later find yourself deleting a highly edited, brilliantly written paragraph because it doesn't fit the tone of rest of the document. And that's a waste of your writing time.

Of course, separating revising from editing means that you have to make multiple "passes" through a document when you're rewriting. And that makes sense, because it's difficult to read for both revising and editing concerns at the same time. It takes a lot of concentration to evaluate the logic and organization of a document, so you need to keep reminding yourself of your focus of concern. It's easy to get distracted by details.

Two Styles of Writing Process

Our discussion of the writing process would be complete at this point if all good writers followed the process the same way. But they don't. So we will conclude with a discussion of two different styles of writing process, each with its own strengths and corresponding weaknesses. It's important for you to know about this difference, not only in validating your *own* process of writing but also in understanding those writers around you who have a *different* process.

When researchers first began to study the processes of writers on the job, they expected to find that all good writers follow the same process, devoting the same proportion of time to the same stage of the process. The researchers expected to find that good writers spend about 50 percent of their writing time planning, about 20 percent drafting, and the remaining 30 percent rewriting.

But when these researchers studied the process of actual writers on the job, they found that writers tend to fall into one of two groups: In the first group are writers who spend a great deal of time planning— even to the point of drafting individual sentences in their minds before they begin to write—and then pour out their text in almost final form. These writers—whom we will call **planner-drafters**—do very little rewriting, because they have already done a good deal of it mentally.

The other group are writers who begin to write almost immediately upon receiving an assignment. These writers spend almost no time planning but instead do a lot of their planning work in the process of refining their message through numerous drafts. We will call these writers **drafter-rewriters.**

In the following sections, we look at the strengths and weaknesses of each type. In some ways, the strengths and weaknesses of the two types are complementary: the strengths of the planner-drafter turn out to be the weaknesses of the drafter-rewriter, and vice versa.

Planner-Drafter

The planner-drafter's strategy works especially well when he or she is in a hurry, or when the time and patience of information sources are limited. The planner-drafter appreciates the way that advance planning can save time. By doing the planning all at once up front—rather than piecemeal in the drafting and rewriting stages—the planner-drafter is saved from the need to produce an infinite number of rewrites of a document.

However, the planner-drafter has little appreciation for the way that putting ideas into words can change the shape of ideas and may look at the drafting stage as a merely mechanical process of "pouring out" the contents of the document onto a page or screen. You're likely to have heard planner-drafters say things like, "I've almost finished that report; all I have to do now is write it." But the planner-drafter may get blocked in drafting when what he or she planned to say just doesn't turn out as expected.

So a good corrective balance for the planner-drafter is to consciously allot some time at the end of the process to let the draft sit, then to come back to it with a fresh perspective and ideas on how to improve it by rewriting. Usually that means setting an artificially early deadline because the planner-drafter often doesn't finish a first draft until the document deadline.

Drafter-Rewriter

The drafter-rewriter, on the other hand, appreciates the way that numerous rewrites can shape and prune a draft. He or she is familiar (and comfortable) with the experience of words not matching ideas, so it is no problem for this writer to put half-formed thoughts and disorganized ideas on paper. The drafter-rewriter also knows that quick drafting is a wonderful tool for discovering new connections and dimensions of ideas as they are put into words.

In contrast to the planner-drafter, the drafter-rewriter has too little appreciation for the way that planning up front can save time and aggravation. The simple truth is that work situations often do not allow a writer the luxury of more than one or two rewrites, so a draft-rewrite strategy with its insistence on multiple rewrites may cause consternation at work.

The corrective balance for the drafter-rewriter is to carve out some planning time up front, forcing himself or herself to answer some questions about scope, purpose, and organization and to gather all the necessary information *before* beginning to write. Doing so will save time by eliminating several of the rewrites spent developing a scope and purpose.

Writing Styles in a Group Situation

In the preceding portraits, you may recognize not only yourself but also supervisors, colleagues, and other employees. You may be a planner-drafter supervising a team of drafter-rewriters. When you see hard copy coming off the printer, you think they're close to completion when in fact they have only begun. And so you begin criticizing details that are really rewriting concerns, not drafting concerns.

Conversely, you may be a drafter-rewriter leading a team of writers who are all planner-drafters. You are understandably nervous when, three weeks into a six-week project, your team assures you that they are making progress although they haven't yet produced a first draft—coherent or otherwise.

In such situations, recognizing the different writing processes and the strengths of each will allow you to temper your response with understanding and to use that understanding of the two styles of writing process to help finish the project efficiently.

Good writing—following *either* style of writing process—is always hard work, but with practice you can learn to control your writing process and to balance your preferred style with the strengths of the other process style. Knowing how you work best and experimenting with new approaches can give you a sense of control over your work. This control, in turn, can make writing seem like less of a huge, unmanageable chore and more like what it should be—a productive, rewarding part of your career.

chapter 3

Real Rules, Nonrules, and House Rules

In This Chapter

This chapter tackles a subject that is uncomfortable for most writers—the **rules** of English. There is a standard response familiar to all English teachers whenever they reveal their profession: "Oh, oh...I'm not too good at grammar. I better watch myself!" Most people were made to feel in school that they are not totally in control of the rules of English. They feel a little guilty, at least when reminded by the intimidating presence of an English teacher, that they didn't learn their grammar in school properly.

That's unfortunate, because English is a fascinating language to study in its own right (and it could be taught in ways to make that fascinating quality more apparent). But more to the point, many of the "rules" you learned in school weren't really rules about English at all: they were *preferences* about the way English was *supposed* to be written—dearly held preferences of generations of schoolteachers, to be sure, but preferences often based on misconceptions about trying to force English grammar into the mold of Latin.

In this chapter, therefore, we will draw a distinction between the **real rules** of English that dictate how correct English *must* be written and the pseudo-rules—we call them **nonrules**—that are really individual preferences about how English *ought* to be written.

A third category of rules—**house rules**—acknowledges that individual organizations evolve their own rules to encourage consistency in things like punctuation and capitalization. Though we will discuss the category of house rules below, we obviously can't teach you the rules of your house. You need to use the style guides that have been adopted by your company or organization and be alert to those documents that serve as models of good writing within it.

Preferences versus Rules

You were probably told to not split **infinitives**—that is, not to put any modifying words in the middle of the *to* form of a **verb.** Thousands of English teachers must wince at the opening prologue of the television show *Star Trek,* which contains the following phrase:

...to boldly go where no man has gone before...

Presumably those teachers would have you write *boldly to go*...or *to go boldly*....But for most of us, *to boldly go* works just fine. In fact, the prescription against splitting infinitives comes from a misguided attempt to make English like Latin. In Latin (and other Romance languages), the infinitive form of the verb is one word (English "to go" is *ire* in Latin, *aller* in French) so the infinitive *can't* be split there.

You can probably make your own additions from your English class experiences to the following list of nonrules, which are really more like preferences:

- Don't end a sentence with a **preposition.**
- Don't use **contractions** in business writing.
- Don't begin a sentence with *and* or *but.*
- Avoid the use of *you.*
- Vary your word choice and sentence structure.

The unfortunate result of concentrating on so-called rules like the above is to make people feel that English grammar is concerned with fussy little distinctions that don't have much to do with the way normal people talk and write. Another unfortunate consequence is that many students throw up their hands at some point and simply give up. There just seem to be too many picky little rules—hundreds of them—waiting to trap unwary writers. Instead of figuring out those rules that really are important to learn, many feel overwhelmed.

This is unfortunate because these learners often miss the point: there *are* important grammar rules to follow, a set of practices reflected in the writing of educated professionals. If you don't observe those rules, others will judge not only your handling of English grammar (*how* you say what you say) but your handling of your topic as well (*what* you say).

Real Rules

What are the real rules of English and how do you learn them? Fortunately, you already know most of them; in fact, you knew the real rules by the time you were five or six years old. The interesting thing about the real rules of English is that you're generally not conscious of them. For example, no one congratulates you on putting **adjectives** in the right order before a **noun,** as in the following:

six important principles

Yet there *is* a real rule for the order of **modifiers** preceding a noun: Adjectives of quantity (*six,* in the above example) go before adjectives of quality (*important,* in the above phrase). Try breaking the real rule about their order, and people will think you're either being funny or you're not a native speaker of English. Go ahead and reverse *six* and *important:*

important six principles

Notice that nobody had to teach you this rule about the correct order of modifiers. You learned it like you learned many of the real rules of English—simply by growing up in a community of people speaking the language every day. However, even though you follow most of the real rules of English (often more out of habit than conscious choice), there are still a few sticky spots in writing where you need to apply conscious effort to follow the rules. We will deal with such rough spots in the following chapters; for now, we will just mention a few of the real rules that give writers problems.

Several real rules have to do with **agreement,** the ties between various parts of a sentence. For example, verbs agree with their **subjects;** that is, in their ending, verbs reflect a tie to the subject with which they're connected. (For more discussion on this topic, see Chapter 6, "Common Problems with Verbs.") Compare the following two sentences:

Jane *has* the reports.

We *have* the reports.

The *-s* ending on the verb *has* shows that it is tied to a third-person singular subject. Violating this agreement rule (*Jane have the reports*) will identify you as a nonnative user of English.

Another type of agreement, similar to that between subject and verb, is **pronoun-antecedent agreement.** (See Chapter 8, "Pronoun Problems.") It is a real rule of English that third-person pronouns are tied to the noun they refer to according to **gender** (masculine, feminine, or neuter). For example:

My *brother* is taking *his* vacation early this year, while my *sister* is taking *her* vacation in August with the rest of the family.

People would think you were either being funny or lacked fluency in English if you said:

> My *brother* is taking *her* vacation early this year, while my *sister* is taking *his* vacation in August with the rest of the family.

Other real rules involve the following:

- the presence of negative elements in a clause—either the subject or predicate elements may be negative, but not both:

  WRONG: *None* of the racers *didn't* finish.

- the use of indefinite and definite articles in a sequence—use *a* when something is introduced; use *the* when it is referred to thereafter:

  CORRECT: *A* rule change was introduced to prevent doping. *The* rule says that all participants are subject to random testing.

- the order of modifiers before a noun—the more a modifier "belongs to" the noun it modifies, the closer it goes to that noun:

  WRONG: A *German young tall* sprinter captured first place in the 100-meter dash.

- the need for both a subject *and* a predicate in a complete clause:

  WRONG: Provided a remarkably strong finish.

- the use of an apostrophe with pronouns to indicate contractions, not possession:

  WRONG: *Its* important for a committee to define *it's* own agenda.

(The correct use of apostrophes dictates *It's* and *its,* since the first is a contraction and the second is not.)

- the need to choose correct word forms:

  WRONG: *To* many writers are unsure about *alot* of punctuation rules.

(This sentence requires *Too* and *a lot* to be written correctly.)

It takes some learning to understand some of the terms used here: subject, predicate, article, modifier. Subsequent chapters define these terms and offer practice exercises so you can be certain of the real rules and can explain the grammatical choices you make.

It's almost impossible to list all of the real rules or to list them in order of importance. What's important about these rules—real rules that all careful writers observe—is that readers notice them only when they are *not* observed.

EXERCISE 3-1

Correct the following sentences. As you do, try to state what real rule of English is being violated in each.

1. If someone is interested in the issue, they should attend the meetings where they can make their opinion heard.

2. He don't know where the new manufacturing site is going to be.

3. The dilapidated, green old garage on the corner is for sale as a "business valuable property."

4. For a person to succeed in his career, you must stay on top of your correspondence.

5. Is responsible the manager for communication, effective, two-way.

6. Our company is instituting the new policy on transportation. Under a program, employees who carpool regularly to work will receive the bonus of $50 a month.

7. Their econometric model is more better than the ones based on previous research.

Compare this sentence with:

Their econometric model is more precise than the ones based on previous research.

8. I need twenty woods to build this geometric solid.

Compare this sentence with:

I need twenty boards to build this geometric solid.

Nonrules

How about nonrules? Where do they come from? We said previously that many nonrules are based on an attempt to force English grammar into the mold of Latin. The "rule" about not splitting an infinitive is one of these; so is the "rule" about not ending a sentence with a preposition, which many still pay attention to.

The body of real rules doesn't change from generation to generation, but what is considered to be good style changes like fashion. Certain fiction writers today are considered to be good stylists, but their style may seem over-elaborated or artificially spare to a later generation of writers. The stylistic preferences of earlier generations are the source of many of today's nonrules. For example, *data* is actually the plural form of the Latin *datum* ("given") and entered English as a plural word. Over time, it has come to be treated as a singular, collective noun (similar to *committee*) in sentences like the following. (Notice the third-person singular *-s* ending on *shows*.)

The data shows a marked increase in productivity in the past six months.

Yet many conservative users of English insist on using *data* as a plural noun in sentences like the preceding example. Thus these users would prefer the following version of the example sentence:

The data *show* a marked increase in productivity in the past six months.

Such users also typically insist on speaking of an individual *datum,* where other users would speak of (or write about) *a piece of data* or *a data point.*

Who is correct? The conservative users typically insist that *they* are, since they are using the words according to the way that those words entered English. Yet once a word enters a language from another language, the speakers of the language are free to use it or pronounce it according to the rules of the new language. The majority of educated speakers and writers of English use *data* as a singular, collective noun, so that is what is now considered correct. The preference for observing the distinction between *data* and *datum* is just that—a preference (and one that may mark the user as overly fastidious). A preference is not a rule.

Another source of nonrules is the application of language practices from one dialect area to another. British English and American English are different in certain respects. But because of the prestige accorded to British English, conservative writers often try to force American English to observe what are essentially British distinctions. Few Americans control the distinctions between *shall* and *will* in the way that cultivated Britishers do. In cultivated British English, the simple future is expressed by *shall* for first-person forms but *will* for all other forms. Hence the sentence:

We shall be at the party on Saturday and so will the Bakers.

That doesn't mean, though, that American writers are less cultivated or that American English is inferior to British English. It is simply *different than* British English. (*Different from* versus *different than* is another British/American distinction. A handbook will identify usage preferences for these structures, but don't be surprised if the advice in one handbook is different from the advice of another.)

The point is that language (and especially vocabulary) changes over time and locale. New words come into the language constantly, while unused words fade into archaisms. Some words or distinctions gain currency in one region but are not observed in another. While writing is necessarily more conservative than speech, any attempt to freeze the written language at a particular stage of development in time and space (often an earlier time and a foreign place) invariably fails.

As a writer of business and technical prose, you don't want to be at the vanguard of language change, but you don't want to be at the rear guard either! Often that means striking a balance between an overly casual tone and an overly formal one. For example, you probably want to avoid most contractions in your writing (too many will make your writing sound "slangy"), but you want to use *I* when speaking of yourself and *you* when addressing the reader (instead of using *the present writer* and *the reader*).

What you generally want to write is prose that is clear and that doesn't call attention to itself. And that is an interesting way that nonrules differ from real rules. Real rules are noticed only when they're broken (remember Exercise 3-1?); nonrules are often noticed only when they are *followed*. Writers constantly break nonrules with no effect on the reader. But a slavish attention to nonrules usually results in a fussy prose that sounds like it was written by a writer wearing white kid gloves.

It is natural to have personal preferences about certain words that you don't like and would not use or about other words that you don't use because you know they bother your readers. But you should guard against elevating those personal *preferences* to the status of real *rules*.

So how do you distinguish real rules from nonrules? One way is to use your ear. Does following the rule produce a sentence that sounds funny to you? If it does, chances are you have followed a nonrule, and you need to rewrite the sentence in a more natural-sounding way. Sometimes, you need to do an "end run" around a real rule if following it also produces an awkward-sounding construction.

But sometimes your ear won't help you and you need to consult a writing handbook. A rule of thumb for separating real rules from nonrules is that most of the highlighted statements beginning with "Do..." or "Always..." or "Make sure to..." are probably real rules; statements beginning with "Never..." or "Do not..." are probably nonrules. Of course, to be really sure, you need to consult the designated writing handbook approved or produced by your company or organization. That will help you observe the house rules that promote consistency in written documents.

EXERCISE 3-2

Each of the sentences below is "correct" according to certain nonrules. Identify the ones that sound "funny" to you and change them to sound more acceptable.[1]

1. Management at Instrutech prefer personal computers to mainframes.

2. "Who will edit this report?" "I shall."

3. Twenty-five cents are a lot to pay for a first-class stamp.

4. We have gathered a number of data.

5. A total of 157 people has completed registration.

6. Everybody has his own point of view.

7. The stress function may also be written in equation form.

8. Conditions were changed to represent approximately the wear from constant friction.

9. The solution of Anderson has proven to be the best one.

10. How do you write a mathematical formula to represent a structure the shape of which is conical?

---

[1]Adapted from Don Bush, "Correctness vs. Communication," *Technical Communication,* Third Quarter, 1986 and "'Super-correctness' in Technical Writing," *Technical Communication,* First Quarter, 1987.

House Rules

Good writing handbooks tend to agree on the basics of correct grammar, but it is easy to find disagreement among various handbooks on particular points of punctuation. For example, in one handbook you might read that the correct way to punctuate three items in a series is as follows:

a, b, and c

Another handbook might prescribe the following:

a, b and c (note the absence of a final comma)

Which is correct? Each form is used by educated writers, so you might say that *both* forms are correct. But that's not much help when you're trying to decide which form to use.

Another area where reputable handbooks differ is in advice about the use of spelled-out versus numerical forms of numbers. Some handbooks dictate that numbers of quantity from one to one hundred be spelled out, while most numbers over one hundred be indicated with numerals. Thus, you read:

three textbooks

but

221 notebooks

Other handbooks dictate that only numbers from one to ten be spelled out, while numbers from eleven to ninety-nine be indicated with numerals.

To achieve internal consistency, many companies and organizations select one handbook to use as an arbiter in cases like the preceding one. This handbook becomes the basis of the house rules used by that organization. House rules usually cover punctuation, spelling, and capitalization irregularities. In addition, companies may produce internal guidelines that "piggy back" off the handbook, supplementing the handbook rules or replacing individual rules with practices peculiar to the company.

It is important to know what the house rules are for your organization. If you don't know what the standard writing handbook is where you work, find out. Learning and following those house rules will save you the trouble of learning variant practices, and may save you a fruitless argument or two about correct style.

In Summary

What is the status of the six principles of good writing set out at the end of Chapter 1—are they real rules, nonrules, or house rules? Some of them (the principles about correct grammar and punctuation) have the status of real rules, but we think of our principles mainly as *guidelines* rather than rules. Guidelines are meant to be applied flexibly and intelligently, rather than slavishly. Guidelines sometimes have to be adjusted or bent in order to follow other guidelines. And not following guidelines does not yield errors in the way that not following real rules does.

So you won't be *wrong* if you don't follow our six principles for good writing. However, following them will make your prose more effective, make it have more clarity and impact. And chances are, that's what you were looking for when you picked up this book.

Putting It All Together

Read the following letter that appeared inside the cover of a catalog for computer products. Do you find the problems in the letter with "the grammar, a few errors in punctuation and spelling," as the author claims? (You might point out awkward sentence constructions but are they ungrammatical?)

What does the function seem to be of the author's disclaimer about his grammar? How much is it an apology? How much is it a sales technique?

What is *your* attitude when you see errors in grammar, punctuation, or spelling in a document? Does your reaction depend on the type of document?

Dear Reader,

English was never my favorite subject. In fact, if you read many of my articles here you'll probably discover some uses of the English language that you never knew existed.

If you'll just overlook the grammar, a few errors in punctuation and spelling and read what I'm saying, not how badly I'm saying it, I promise that you'll enjoy what you read. Here's why.

Every product I present I have personally used and continue to use. And then instead of letting some professional high-priced copywriter tell you in slick clichés and fancy buzz words, I have written all the copy myself. It may not be the most correct English but it's my way of sharing with you both my enthusiasm, knowledge and corporate philosophy.

I want to supply you with products you can tell your friends about. I want to present them honestly and offer fair prices and have you become a repeat customer for many years to come. And if you do buy anything from us and are not satisfied, for any reason, please return your purchase to me personally for a prompt and courteous refund.

I hope you enjoy the articles in this issue and I hope you join with me as one of our valued customers.

EXERCISE ANSWERS

Exercise 3-1 Answers

Problems in the original sentences are *italicized*. Corrected versions appear after the discussion.

1. If *someone* is interested in the issue, *they* should attend the meetings where *they* can make *their* opinion heard.

*The issue here is agreement of **number** (singular vs. plural) between nouns and the pronouns standing for them. Someone is technically singular, while they and their are plural. (Perhaps gender is also an issue, since the singular someone is gender neutral, as is the plural pronoun they.) Correct forms would be either:*

If someone is interested in the issue, *he or she* should attend the meetings to make his or her opinion heard.

or

If people are interested in the issue, they should attend the meetings where they can make their opinion heard.

2. *He don't* know where the new manufacturing site is going to be.

The issue here is **subject-verb agreement:** *A singular subject* (he) *has to have a singular verb* (doesn't). *Thus:*

He doesn't know where the new manufacturing site is going to be.

3. The *dilapidated, green old* garage on the corner is for sale as a "*business valuable* property."

There is a real rule of **word order** *for adjectives in English that requires the more inherent qualities of a thing (such as color) to be placed nearer the head noun, while the less inherent qualities (such as age and quantity) are placed further away. So, in the above example,* old, dilapidated, green garage *sounds like a more natural word order than the one given. Similarly,* valuable business property *sounds better than* business valuable property. *Hence:*

The old, dilapidated, green garage on the corner is for sale as a "valuable business property."

4. For *a person* to succeed in *his* career, *you* must stay on top of *your* correspondence.

Consistency of **person** *is the problem here: Generic statements that begin with the third-person* a person *should maintain that person all the way through, not switch to second-person* you *and* your, *as the example here does. (Another problem might be the* **sexism** *of the third-person singular, masculine pronoun* his *to refer to a gender-neutral person.) Thus, there are three possible revisions:*

For a person to succeed in his career, he must stay on top of his correspondence.

or

For a person to succeed in his or her career, he or she must stay on top of his or her correspondence.

But this one, while correct, may sound awkward, so we would recommend an "end run" around it to make the whole statement second-person:

For you to succeed in your career, you must stay on top of your correspondence.

5. Is responsible the manager for communication, effective, two-way.

Word order is the problem here; subjects precede predicates in statements. There is also a problem of word order in the modifiers of communication. The correct form would be:

The manager is responsible for effective, two-way communication.

6. Our company is instituting *the* new policy on transportation. Under a program, employees who carpool regularly to work will receive the bonus of $50 a month.

*The problem here is one that is sometimes called **discourse reference.** This means that the first time a topic is mentioned in a discourse, it is introduced with the indefinite article a or an; thereafter, it can be referred to with the definite article the, since it has already been introduced. In this example that guideline is reversed, with a rather odd sound. Also, to be clear, we would repeat the word policy to show reference back to the first sentence. The corrected sentence would read:*

Our company is instituting a new policy on transportation. Under the policy, employees who carpool regularly to work will receive a bonus of $50 a month.

7. Their econometric model is *more better* than the ones based on previous research.

Compare this sentence with:

Their econometric model is *more precise* than the ones based on previous research.

*This example shows the different ways that adjectives **inflect** (or change form) for comparisons. Typically, one-syllable adjectives (good) inflect by adding -er and -est (hence better and best, even though the root form also changes), while most two-syllable adjectives (precise)—and all others of more than two syllables—inflect by adding more and most. (Try it with some other adjectives.) Writers rarely make the mistake of doubly inflecting adjectives as demonstrated in this example, but it does sometimes happen in the heat of conversation when a speaker is being extra emphatic. Obviously, the correct version is:*

Their econometric model is better than the ones based on previous research.

8. I need twenty *woods* to build this geometric solid.

Compare this sentence with:

I need twenty *boards* to build this geometric solid.

*Unless the speaker means that he or she needs twenty different types of wood (which does not seem to be the case here), the problem here is of count nouns vs. mass nouns. **Count nouns** (like board) are ones that can be counted without using an additional noun to count them; hence one board, two boards, three boards, and so on. **Mass nouns** (like wood) require an extra (count) noun in front of them in order to count; hence one piece of wood, two pieces of wood, and so on. Thus:*

I need twenty pieces of wood to build this geometric solid.

Exercise 3-2 Answers

Each of the sentences below is "correct" according to certain nonrules. The "funny" parts have been *italicized*.

1. *Management at Instrutech prefer personal computers to mainframes.*

Is management singular or plural? If singular, the verb will have to change to prefers. Thus:

Management at Instrutech prefers personal computers to mainframes.

2. "Who *will* edit this report?" "I *shall.*"

You probably don't observe this distinction (it's more observed in formal British English) between will and shall with respect to grammatical **person:** *Shall is used to indicate intention with first person pronouns I and we, while will is used to indicate intention for second and third person pronouns. (For indicating obligation, the forms are reversed: will is used for first person pronouns, while shall is used for second and third.) The more common American usage would be:*

"Who will edit this report?" "I will."

3. *Twenty-five cents are a lot to pay for a first-class stamp.*

Is twenty-five cents a plural collection of coins or a singular amount? If the latter, we would have to say:

Twenty-five cents is a lot to pay for a first-class stamp.

4. We have gathered a number of *data.*

Is data a count noun or a mass noun? If it is a mass noun, we need to have a count noun like pieces in front of it in this example:

We have gathered a number of pieces of data.

5. A total of 157 people *has* completed registration.

Has may sound funny here following the plural people, but actually total is the head noun (and it is singular). To avoid the funny sound of this grammatically correct sentence, we might rewrite it as:

One hundred fifty-seven people have completed registration.

6. *Everybody has his own point of view.*

Though clearly singular (as shown by the singular verb has), everybody is not so clearly masculine. To make up for the lack of a gender-neutral singular pronoun in English, most speakers would use their in place of his in this example. Careful writers, though, would probably use "his or her," or would recast the sentence with a plural subject in order to justify using their:

Everybody has his or her own point of view.

or

All people have their own points of view.

7. The stress function *may* also be written in equation form.

To avoid the possible reading of may *as "granting permission," many writers would use* can *here to mean "possibly":*

The stress function can also be written in equation form.

8. Conditions were changed *to represent approximately* wear from constant friction.

The placement of approximately *in order to avoid splitting the infinitive* to represent *is quite awkward. Revisions of this sentence might read:*

Conditions were changed to approximately represent wear from constant friction.

or might delete approximately *altogether:*

Conditions were changed to represent wear from constant friction.

9. The solution *of Anderson* has proven to be the best one.

Some writers might be tempted to write of Anderson's *though that's technically a double* **possessive** *form (of already indicates* **possession***). The better solution might be to write:*

Anderson's solution has proven to be the best one.

10. How do you write a mathematical formula to represent a structure *the shape of which* is conical?

The shape of which is an awkward way to avoid using the possessive pronoun whose *to refer to the inanimate noun* structure. *Most speakers—and writers—would not be bothered by:*

How do you write a mathematical formula to represent a structure whose shape is conical?

"Professional writing is grammatically *correct*."

Professional writing must be correct. You want readers to notice *what* you say, not *how* you say it. Grammatical errors and inconsistencies jump off the page at most readers, announcing, "This writer's grammar is unprofessional." And if your grammar suggests incompetence, it will color others' judgments about the quality of your work. You may think this unfair; you may wish people would pay attention to your message, not your grammar. But the fact is that most readers will tolerate only two or three errors before questioning the accuracy of the text and the ability of the writer.

This unit focuses on avoiding those errors that call attention to themselves—sentence fragments and run-ons (Chapter 5), problems with verbs (Chapter 6), misplaced or dangling modifiers (Chapter 7), and problems with pronouns (Chapter 8)—so that your readers can focus on your message instead. Many of those errors relate to basic sentence structure, so the unit begins with a "refresher" on parts of sentences and parts of speech (Chapter 4).

As discussed in Chapter 3, "Real Rules, Nonrules, and House Rules," many so-called errors really *aren't* errors so much as stylistic preferences: most educated readers don't even notice if you fail to observe some of the fussy little details of correctness enshrined in many handbooks. Many of the errors discussed in this unit, however, are violations of *real rules* in English—they are highly visible and usually noticed. You must recognize and control these kinds of errors or risk being labeled in ways you would rather not.

chapter 4

Parts of Sentences
and
Parts of Speech

This chapter reviews basic sentence structure. To take control of your writing style, you need a few tools of analysis. If you hired a carpenter, you would expect that person to have command of the language and tools of carpentry. A carpenter wouldn't get much respect if he or she pounded screws with a hammer or constantly asked for "that thingamajig with the doohickie on it." If you had a friend who asked for a "plus or minus" screwdriver, though he or she might get the job done, you probably wouldn't hire that friend to build a deck.

Similarly, you need certain language and tools to be a writer. You need to know:

- How to differentiate among clauses, phrases, and sentences
- How to identify subjects and predicates within clauses
- How to recognize different patterns of clause constructions
- How to distinguish independent from dependent clauses
- How to identify simple, compound, and complex sentences

Throughout this book, you will need to use the terms and structures exemplified in this chapter. Think of this chapter as a review of fundamentals that will be reinforced in every chapter. If you don't feel comfortable now with the objectives stated above, be patient. You will have plenty of opportunities to reinforce what you know, and you can always come back to this chapter for a quick second reading. To understand style, and to take control of your own style, you need the basic "tool kit" presented here.

The Building Blocks of Sentences

The sentence is the basic unit of writing and the focus of this book. You can learn to control your sentence structures so that your sentences perform efficiently, with clarity and emphasis.

Sentence structure can be analyzed at various levels, but the basic unit of analysis we will use here is the **clause. Sentences** are made of one or more clauses; clauses are made of one or more **phrases;** and phrases are made of one or more **words.** It might help to define each term briefly:

WORD: any individual member of one of the parts of speech (nouns, verbs, adjectives, adverbs, pronouns, prepositions, conjunctions, and expletives)

PHRASE: a group of words built around a main word

CLAUSE: a group of words or phrases, with at least one word or phrase acting as the subject and one word or phrase acting as the predicate

SENTENCE: one or more clauses that can stand alone—or everything between a capital letter and a mark of final punctuation (period, question mark, or exclamation mark)

We will use an approach to sentences that first describes clauses, then shows how clauses are made up of phrases, and finally shows how clauses form different kinds of sentences.

Basic Clause Structure

A clause is a group of words containing a subject and a predicate. The **subject** is who or what you are talking about. The **predicate** says something about the subject. Clauses also typically contain modifiers, words or phrases added to the clause that describe the subject or predicate.

Subjects

Subjects establish your focus, the beginning point within a clause. The grammatical term **complete subject** refers to the whole **subject phrase,** including the main word (most often, a noun) and any other words that make up its phrase. The **simple subject,** in contrast, refers to the single main word of the subject phrase. Any of the following words or phrases could be a subject for a clause:

Johnson...

The editorial assistant...

The oil-pressure gauge...

The figures in the third-quarter report...

Each of these possible subject constructions announces a topic about which you have something to say. If you walked up to a coworker in the hall and said, "The editorial assistant...," your coworker would stand there waiting for you to finish your sentence. You would have announced a topic but not said anything about it. You would have stated your subject.

Every time you state the subject of a sentence, you have the opportunity to focus your reader's attention. The subject is an important slot in a clause because it gives you a chance to make an announcement to the reader, an announcement that prepares the reader for what is to come.

Predicates

The part of the clause that says something about the subject is the predicate. The predicate includes the verb phrase plus any words and phrases that go along with it. Each of the following examples now includes a predicate along with the subject constructions:

Johnson recommended a change.

The editorial assistant introduced errors.

The oil-pressure gauge revealed a loss.

The figures in the third-quarter report support Sam's theories.

EXERCISE 4-1

Draw a vertical line between the subject construction and predicate in each sentence below. Recognizing the division between subject and predicate is critical to achieving control over your style.

1. Johnson recommended a change.

2. The editorial assistant introduced errors.

3. The oil-pressure gauge revealed a loss.

4. The figures in the third-quarter report support Sam's theories.

Predicates are important because they focus on the action of the clause. Predicates contain the important, new information about your announced subject. Within the predicate, you advance your arguments, offer your evidence, or direct the actions of your reader.

Each group of words in Exercise 4-1 is a clause because each contains both a subject and a predicate tied to the subject. As you may recognize, each of these examples is also a sentence, since each group is a clause that is grammatically complete and punctuated to stand alone.

Modifiers

Typically, subject and predicate constructions are not single words but carry **modifiers** with them—words that describe. **Adjectives** are modifiers that describe nouns; adjectives characterize properties of things (quantity, color, size, age, nationality):

> the dusty, crowded, hot storeroom
>
> one incredible, surprising, final effort

Adverbs are modifiers that describe verbs or other modifiers; they characterize actions, telling *when* or *how* or *in what manner.*

> He complained *loudly, frequently,* and *obnoxiously.*
>
> She *timidly* asked her question.

Sometimes modifiers are single-word adjectives or adverbs, as in the above examples. Often, whole phrases, especially **prepositional phrases,** work as modifiers:

> the switch *on the back of the rear panel*
>
> asked *without fear of retribution from her superiors*

Prepositional phrases always begin with a relational word (the **preposition**) showing position, time, location, or manner. They typically end with a noun (called the **object of the preposition**).

Sometimes whole clauses function as modifiers, as discussed below. *Modifier* is a useful general term for the function of those words, phrases, and clauses that are added to sentences for descriptive purposes.

Parts of Sentences versus Parts of Speech

Thus far, we have been using grammatical terms *subject, predicate, noun, verb,* and *modifier* as if all of them were members of one set of terms. In fact, they are members of two different sets: parts of sentences and parts of speech. **Parts of sentences** are the units that make up sentences: the clauses of various types that make up sentences and the subjects, predicates, and modifiers that make up clauses. We have defined these units on the basis of their *function,* that is, what they do in the larger unit they make up. ("Subjects announce your topic"; "Predicates center on the action of the clause"; and "Modifiers add information to subjects and predicates.")

Parts of speech, on the other hand, are the individual words that combine to make up phrases. The distinction between parts of sentences and parts of speech is an important one, because the same part of speech can function as different parts of a sentence. For example, a noun can function as a subject or, as you will read in the next section, as an object (part of the predicate).

The one place where we are inconsistent in maintaining the distinction between parts of sentences and parts of speech is in using the term *verb* both as part of the predicate *and* as a part of speech. We have chosen to use the term in both places because of its common usage in both senses.

Clause Patterns

Sentences take many shapes; indeed, their variety is infinite since there is no limit to the ways that words can be combined. Within this variation, however, several clause structures can be described as typical patterns. While the typical patterns of clauses that are described below cannot account for all clause structures, they do characterize the most commonly occurring ones and offer a useful basis for talking about grammar and style.

Subject-Verb-Object

The patterns represented in the above examples are basic to English sentences and, indeed, to the subject/predicate structures of most languages. You announce what you are talking about in the subject; then you say something about it in the predicate. (You can find in your dictionary a definition of *predicate* as a verb: "to affirm or declare.")

Subjects and predicates can each consist of single words ("I declare!" or "Sally cooperated.") or even no words (as in "Scram!" where the subject *you* is understood). More typically, subject constructions and predicates are composed of phrases—groups of words built around a main word, often with modifying phrases attached here or there. There is no limit to the number of modifiers you can attach to subjects and predicates, and modifiers often can be moved somewhat freely around the sentence.

Subject constructions are typically single-word nouns or noun phrases:

Johnson . . .

The editorial assistant . . .

The oil-pressure gauge . . .

The figures in the third-quarter report . . .

You can easily spot the simple subject *Johnson*. It is not much more difficult to find the main words in the other subject constructions: *assistant, gauge,* and *figures.*

Sometimes a **pronoun** fills in for a noun. In the above examples, *he* or *she* could stand in for *Johnson* or *the editorial assistant.* The pronoun *it* could replace *the oil-pressure gauge* and the pronoun *they* could replace *the figures in the third-quarter report.*

Remember that the grammatical term *complete subject* refers to the whole subject phrase, including the main word and its modifiers. The simple subject, in contrast, refers to the single main word of the subject phrase. You should be able to look at the whole phrase that constitutes the complete subject and pick out the single word—the head noun—that is the simple subject.

Within the predicate, you always find a main verb, and you often find an **object,** the receiver of the action. The verbs and objects frequently have various modifiers as part of their phrases. Stripping away the modifying words from the previous examples reveals the underlying, simple clause structures:

    s   **v**   **o**
Johnson recommended a change.

      s   **v**   **o**
The assistant introduced errors.

     s   **v**   **o**
The gauge revealed a loss.

     s   **v**   **o**
The figures support Sam's theories.

In each example, you see a very basic pattern of English sentences: **subject-verb-object (S-V-O).** In each sentence, the subject tells who or what is doing something, and the predicate tells what was done. Within the predicate, the object receives the action of the verb—the object is what is acted upon. (For example, *errors* were introduced and *theories* were supported. Both objects receive the action of the verb.)

The S-V-O pattern can also characterize the structures of sentences with **compound** constructions. Each of the following examples includes a compound construction:

The design engineers and the quality-assurance team recommended changes in the mounting hardware. (compound subject)

The editorial assistant identified errors in the documentation but also introduced some new ones. (compound predicate)

The gauge underneath the front panel revealed a loss of pressure and a rise in temperature. (compound object)

The collection agency broke the agreement and refused our request for additional assistance. (compound verb/object constructions)

The metals shop fabricated new panels and fasteners. (compound object)

The private auditors and the IRS agents found errors in the books. (compound subject)

EXERCISE 4-2

Rewrite each of the following sentences, keeping only the essential information (the main words plus whatever minor words you need so that the sentence still makes grammatical sense). Cross out nonessential words. Label the main words as S, V, or O. The first one is done for you.

1. The ~~design~~ engineers and the ~~quality assurance~~ team recommended changes ~~in the mounting hardware~~.

2. The editorial assistant identified errors in the documentation but also introduced some new ones.

3. The gauge underneath the front panel revealed a loss of pressure and a rise in temperature.

4. The collection agency broke the agreement and refused our request for additional assistance.

5. The metals shop fabricated new panels and fasteners.

6. The private auditors and the IRS agents found errors in the books.

In Exercise 4-2, you are deleting modifiers, those words that describe the simple subjects or that tell us something about the action in the predicate. Modifiers add details to the sentence, but they can be removed, and the sentence will still be grammatically complete.

To create powerful sentences, sentences that really show who is doing what to whom, you need to be able to recognize S-V-O patterning. To find the S-V-O pattern, you can strip sentences down to their bare-bones structures, as in the exercise. All you did was to remove the modifiers—the adjectives and adverbs (words or phrases)—that describe the subjects, verbs, and objects in the sentences.

Modification is something extra in these sentences. It is meaningful, but you can strip it away and still have a full sentence. You *can't* strip away the subject or the predicate and still have a full sentence. Stripping away the modification allows you to see the foundation upon which your sentences are built.

Clauses without Objects

The S-V-O pattern characterizes many of the strongest sentences; psychologically, readers expect this pattern. But not all verbs take objects. Recall the sentence used above: *Sally cooperated.* This is a complete sentence, consisting of a one-word subject and a one-word predicate, with no object. It's also a bit artificial. Readers expect more from a sentence, some modification or some indication of attitude, as in *Sally cooperated willingly.* It is as though readers *expect* something in the object slot.

Other sentences in this pattern include:

John left.

Joanne complained to her supervisor in no uncertain terms about the difficulty with the new logging system.

The engine runs smoothly.

He cannot work past five o'clock for the next two weeks.

Linking-Verb Clauses

The most important example sentences presented so far share an underlying S-V-O pattern, a structure you should recognize and control. Exemplified above is a second sort of sentence, one with no object. English also has a third sort of sentence structure that you will frequently see:

Gerry Jacobs will be the new manager of the technical-support group.

She is from Dayton, where she was a key member of the documentation department.

Her work is highly regarded, and she is experienced with our advanced platform.

Can you spot the verbs in these examples? If you start looking for actions, you won't find any. Each verb is actually some form of *to be,* a verb that doesn't express an action but simply a state of being or existence. Such sentences are called **linking** constructions because they are built around verbs that link the subject to what follows the verb. What follows the verb is a **subject complement,** the part of the sentence that identifies or describes the subject. Sometimes the subject complement is a noun identifying the subject: *Gerry will be **manager.*** Sometimes the subject complement is an adjective describing the subject: *Her work is **highly regarded.***

Only a few verbs in English form linking sentences. The verb *to be* is the main one; its forms include:

be
being
been
am
is
are
was
were

Other verbs that can form linking sentences include:

seem
appear
look
become
feel
remain

These verbs often relate to people's perceptions or senses. The paired examples below show how linking sentences are built around these verbs:

The test results *look* positive.

The test results *are* positive.

Sue *became* pale as she stood before her audience.

Sue *was* pale as she stood before her audience.

Because linking-verb sentences have no center of action in a verb, they are inherently weaker than sentences organized around an S-V-O pattern. Unfortunately, many writers use too many linking-verb sentences. Recognizing the linking-verb pattern can help you decide when linking-verb sentences are effective and when you might write stronger sentences around the S-V-O pattern.

Clauses and Sentences

Each of the sample sentences discussed previously contains a single clause built around a subject and a predicate. Such sentences are called **simple sentences.** However, things can get more complicated: Each of the sentences in the following exercise contains more than one subject/predicate group, so each has more than one clause.

EXERCISE 4-3

Each of the example sentences below has at least two subject/predicate constructions. Take apart the sentences in the following ways:

- **Put parentheses around each clause.**
- **Draw a vertical line between the subject and predicate of each clause.**
- **Draw a single underline under each complete subject.**
- **Bracket the clauses that could stand alone as full sentences.**

1. Johnson recommended a slight design change in the motor mount, but the staff engineers pointed out a torque problem.

2. Because he was under pressure to get the documentation out by June 25, the editorial assistant unintentionally introduced several errors into the final copy.

3. The oil-pressure gauge revealed an unacceptable pressure loss that must be corrected before the next test.

4. The figures in the third-quarter report corroborate Sam's hunch: we have increased our sales in Japanese markets.

One sort of sentence structure in Exercise 4-3 is compound. **Compound sentences** contain two or more **independent clauses,** clauses that can be punctuated to stand alone as full sentences. Examples 1 and

4 in the previous exercise each contain two independent clauses. Either sentence could be punctuated as two sentences:

> Johnson recommended a slight design change in the motor mount. But the staff engineers pointed out a torque problem.
>
> The figures in the third-quarter report corroborate Sam's hunch. We have increased our sales in Japanese markets.

In both of these examples, the two independent clauses are so closely related that you would probably prefer to keep them together as one punctuated, compound sentence. You can do so with a **colon** or a **semicolon** between the clauses or with a **conjunction,** a word that joins related phrases or clauses (as the word *but* does in the example).

Just as sentences can be compound, with two independent clauses joined with a conjunction, so other parts of clauses can be compound. A subject phrase might be compound:

> *The parts orders* and *the billing receipts* were filed in the requisition department.

Predicates can be compound, too:

> The new employee *received a handbook* and *was assigned a cubicle.*

However, neither of these examples constitutes a compound sentence, since neither has two subject/predicate pairings. Each has some part of its single clause compounded—the subject in the first example and the predicate in the second.

You will notice that not every clause can stand alone—not every clause is an independent, or main clause. The following example is not an independent clause but a **dependent clause** (of a type called a **subordinate clause**):

> Because he was under pressure to get the documentation out by June 25,

A dependent clause can't stand alone; it has to be attached to another, independent clause:

> Because he was under pressure to get the documentation out by June 25, the editorial assistant unintentionally introduced several errors into the final copy.

The dependent clause actually works as a modifier of the independent clause, telling us *why* the assistant introduced errors.

Another example of a dependent clause is the following:

that must be corrected before the next test.

This dependent clause (a particular type called a **relative clause**) modifies *pressure loss* in the example sentence, and must be attached to the independent clause:

The oil-pressure indicator gauge revealed an unacceptable pressure loss that must be corrected before the next test.

Thus, dependent clauses can modify either whole clauses (as subordinate clauses do) or phrases or single words (as relative clauses do), and this is one way to distinguish the two types of dependent clauses—by what they modify. In addition, you can also distinguish the two different types of dependent clauses by the way they begin: Subordinate clauses begin with a **subordinating conjunction** (like *although* or *because*), and this subordinating conjunction is not an actual part of the S-V-O clause structure. In contrast, the **relative pronoun** (like *that* or *which*) that begins a relative clause *is* part of the S-V-O clause structure. You will read more about the different functions of subordinate versus relative clauses in Chapter 9, "Commas."

Sentences that contain at least one dependent clause along with the independent clause are termed **complex sentences.** Knowing the differences between simple, compound, and complex sentences can help you avoid monotony by varying your sentence structures. Recognizing these structures can help you punctuate your sentences based on clause structure rather than simply depending on your ear. Controlling the structures can help you match the structure of your sentences to the ways you want to present information.

In Summary

We have presented a set of terms in this chapter that we will use throughout the book to describe effective sentences. The set (presented in Figure 4.1) is really quite small. Knowing the meaning of these terms will offer tools for understanding both correct grammar and effective style.

If you feel a bit dizzy, one way to simplify all this information is to remember that there are basically only *two* kinds of grammatical relationships: equal-to-equal and higher-to-lower. In most phrases, words are joined as higher-to-lower, with the main word of the phrase (the head) being higher and the modifiers being lower in importance. (The

Figure 4.1 *Levels of Grammatical Analysis*

LEVEL OF ANALYSIS	TYPE OF CONSTRUCTION
WORD	**TYPES OF WORDS (PARTS OF SPEECH)**
	noun
	pronoun
	verb
	action verb
	linking verb
	adjective
	adverb
	preposition
	conjunction
PHRASE	**TYPES OF PHRASES**
	noun phrase
	pronoun phrase
	verb phrase
	adjective phrase
	adverb phrase
	prepositional phrase
	conjunction phrase
CLAUSE	**TYPES OF CLAUSES**
(Parts of a Clause)	dependent
subject	subordinate
predicate	relative
main verb	independent (main)
object/subject complement	
modifier	
SENTENCE	**TYPES OF SENTENCES**
	simple
	compound
	complex

exception is for compound phrases, where the two [or more] heads have an equal-to-equal relationship.)

At the clause level, subjects and predicates are joined as equal-to-equal; modifiers are added as lower elements. At the sentence level, compound sentences are joined as equal-to-equal independent clauses; in complex sentences, independent clauses are joined to dependent clauses in a higher-to-lower relationship.

EXERCISE ANSWERS

Exercise 4-1 Answers

The vertical lines divide subject and predicate:

1. Johnson | recommended a change.

2. The editorial assistant | introduced errors.

3. The oil-pressure gauge | revealed a loss.

4. The figures in the third-quarter report | support Sam's theories.

Exercise 4-2 Answers

In the following answers to the exercise, the modifiers have been stripped away and the main words that form the S-V-O pattern labeled.

1. The ~~design~~ engineers and the ~~quality-assurance~~ team recommended changes ~~in the mounting hardware~~.

       s   s   v   o

The engineers and the team recommended changes.

2. The ~~editorial~~ assistant identified errors ~~in the documentation~~ but ~~also~~ introduced ~~some~~ new ones.

       s   v   o   v   o

The assistant identified errors but introduced new ones.

3. The gauge ~~underneath the front panel~~ revealed a loss ~~of pressure~~ and a rise ~~in temperature~~.

       s   v   o   o

The gauge revealed a loss and a rise.

4. The ~~collection~~ agency broke the agreement and refused our request ~~for additional assistance~~.

       s   v   o   v   o

The agency broke the agreement and refused our request.

5. The ~~metals~~ shop fabricated ~~new~~ panels and fasteners.

       s   v   o   o

The shop fabricated panels and fasteners.

6. The ~~private~~ auditors and the ~~IRS~~ agents found errors ~~in the books~~.

       s   **s**   **v**   **o**

The auditors and the agents found errors.

Exercise 4-3 Answers

The following exercise sentences have been marked up to show their structures. Parentheses surround each clause. A vertical line divides the subject and predicate of each clause. A single underline identifies each complete subject. Brackets identify the clauses that could stand alone as full sentences.

1. [(<u>Johnson</u> | recommended a slight design change in the motor mount)], [(but <u>the staff engineers</u> | pointed out a torque problem)].

2. (Because <u>he</u> | was under pressure to get the documentation out by June 25th), [(<u>the editorial assistant</u> | unintentionally introduced several errors into the final copy)].

3. [(<u>The oil-pressure gauge</u> | revealed an unacceptable pressure loss)] (<u>that</u> | must be corrected before the next test).

Or you may choose to analyze the second clause as part of the first one and therefore put the entire sentence in brackets. Since the second clause modifies the object pressure loss *in the independent clause, you could analyze it as part of that clause:*

[(<u>The oil-pressure gauge</u> | revealed an unacceptable pressure loss) (<u>that</u> | must be corrected before the next test)].

4. [(<u>The figures in the third-quarter report</u> | corroborate Sam's hunch)]: [(<u>we</u> | have increased our sales in Japanese markets)].

chapter 5

Sentence Completeness

This chapter reviews two major errors associated with writing complete sentences: sentence fragments and run-on sentences. Our assumption is that in most professional writing, complete sentences are called for. Readers have little tolerance for "creativity" when it comes to where the periods are placed. In this chapter, you will learn:

- How to recognize and correct sentence fragments
- When sentence fragments are useful
- How to recognize and correct run-on sentences and comma splices

Fragments

Fragments are simply groups of words that do not form a sentence although they are punctuated as sentences. If you unintentionally treat a phrase as a sentence, giving it a capital letter and a period, you violate a "real rule" in formal writing.

You already have a well-developed sentence sense—you speak and write in full sentences simply because you have been using the language all your life (assuming you are a native speaker of English). If you write a fragment, it isn't because you don't know how to write a sentence. Typically, the fragment fits in well with the surrounding language context. Consider the following example, which contains both a full sentence and an accompanying fragment:

> We did not quite reach our goals for the third quarter. Because we had adverse market conditions, a falling dollar, and generally unstable commodity prices.

The problem is not that the passage can't be understood—to the writer, at least, it is perfectly clear. A reader, on the other hand, may have trouble, especially after being brought up short by the period after *quarter*. The reader may begin reading the second group of words (*Because . . .*) and expect more to follow: an independent clause. When it doesn't, the reader would then have to backtrack to figure out what was going on.

Notice, too, that the problem isn't one of inadequate length—the fragment (the second group of words) is actually longer than the full sentence. The problem is a grammatical fault—in this case, punctuating a *because* clause as though it were a sentence. The word *because* makes the clause dependent: the clause has to be attached to an independent clause. But it fits logically with the preceding sentence, and the writer might not even notice the problem.

Try reading the passage with the writer's intended meaning. Notice you can use your voice to make the dependent clause join the independent clause. If the writer spoke this passage, no one would hear the fragment. It is only when written that the fragment causes a problem.

EXERCISE 5-1

Identify the fragments in each of the following examples; then correct them. Notice in each case that the fragments make sense—they fit with the surrounding sentences.

1. Two of the standing orders were left unfilled at the end of the month. The order for the Pine Brothers and the order for the Randolph Company.

2. We don't need to get too worried about the February order for the Pine Brothers. Since February is a short month.

3. Why did we fail, though, to get the order out to Randolph? Perhaps a breakdown in our billing procedures, an unnoticed glitch in production, or a lag in delivery from our supplier.

Each of the second group of words in Exercise 5-1 is a phrase that is punctuated as a sentence. In Example 1, the compound noun phrase has no predicate. In Example 2, the clause beginning with *since* is a dependent clause, not an independent clause. In Example 3, we have a series of noun phrases in answer to a question; this construction is common in conversation but inappropriate in written English.

Fragments abound in many language situations. Spoken conversation uses many fragments, as does advertising. An actual ad drawn from the newspaper is loaded with fragments:

> Wonderful Rowe chairs accent rooms from formal to casual. Rich velvets and tailored textures... from peach to plum and back again. Academy Furniture Mart's professionals can assist you in selecting just the right fabric and color for your new chair. Quality, comfort, style, and savings. Special price offer in effect for one week only. Shop Sunday 9 A.M. until 6 P.M.

Can you spot the fragments in this passage? (There are three sentences and three fragments.) Readers expect to see fragments in such writing—advertising is known for its freewheeling use of the language. Most business writing, however, is much more conventional, shaped by the conservative standards of acceptable, formal, written English.

This is not to say that fragments don't have their uses, even in formal reports. Consider the following example:

> My current proposed tolerances are as follows:

Boresight:	Within $\pm$ 4 arc minutes of LOS determined by 3 rest buttons on UUT mounting bracket.
Laser Target Spot:	Diffuse backlighted disc with a radius, R, 6 arc minutes > R > 2 arc minutes.
Laser Target Focus:	Target surface located at infinity focus with lambda/2 wavefront error.

In this example, each of the proposed tolerances is stated as a fragment—it is simply a value, not a clause construction with subject and predicate. Other fragments appear as labels under diagrams, as headings in documents, and as bulleted entries in lists. All of these uses are perfectly acceptable. What is important is to recognize and control fragments, knowing when they can be used appropriately and when they should be avoided.

Fixing Fragments

If you can recognize fragments, you can fix them. A fragment can either be made into a full independent clause, or it can be joined to an existing sentence. Let's reconsider the following passage, which contains several fragments:

1. Wonderful Rowe chairs accent rooms from formal to casual. 2. Rich velvets and tailored textures...from peach to plum and back again. 3. Academy Furniture Mart's professionals can assist you in selecting just the right fabric and color for your new chair. 4. Quality, comfort, style, and savings. 5. Special price offer in effect for one week only. 6. Shop Sunday 9 A.M. until 6 P.M.

Sentences 1, 3, and 6 are complete clauses and can stand alone. But the groups of words contained in 2, 4, and 5 are fragments. There are several ways to make these fragments into full clauses:

2. We offer a variety of fabrics, including rich velvets and tailored textures...from peach to plum and back again. (introducing a subject/verb/object construction, to which the original words are attached as modifiers)

2. and 3. Academy Furniture Mart's professionals can assist you in selecting just the right fabric and color for your new chair: rich velvet or tailored textures, from peach to plum and back again. (using punctuation to join the fragment to a full clause)

4. Quality, comfort, style, and savings can all be found at Academy Furniture Mart. (making the string of nouns the compound subject of a full clause)

4. We offer quality, comfort, style, and savings. (making the nouns the object of a new subject/verb construction)

5. Special prices will be in effect for one week only. (introducing a finite verb)

As with many of the grammatical constructions we discuss in this book, so with fragments you have choices about whether to keep or change them. You can choose to use them in some situations or maintain a formal pattern of full clauses. If you recognize fragments, you have choices, too, concerning how you choose to fix them. More practice in recognizing and fixing fragments will follow in this chapter.

Run-On Sentences and Comma Splices

Run-on sentences and comma splices are in some ways the opposite of sentence fragments: instead of being a group of words that do not form a complete sentence, a run-on sentence or a comma splice is actually *more* than one complete grammatical sentence punctuated as if it were a single sentence. Unlike fragments, which frequently have legitimate uses in professional writing, run-on sentences and comma splices are almost always marks of bad writing.

If two independent clauses are simply jammed together with no punctuation, the result is a **run-on sentence.** If two independent clauses are joined with only a comma, the result is a **comma splice.** Each represents a major sentence error, one that many people notice and that you should take pains to avoid. For simplicity sake, we will simply use the term *run-on* for any sentence that inappropriately jams together more than one independent clause.

Notice that the following example has two independent clauses punctuated as one complete sentence:

> Marketing recently announced a new entry into the low end of the personal computer market, the PC-Pro takes its place alongside other, more powerful machines.

These two independent clauses make sense, just as the fragments did. There's not much problem reading them aloud, either. So unless you recognize that what you have is two independent clauses spliced together with only a comma, you won't recognize the grammatical problem. Even if *you* don't recognize the problem, however, *others* will, and they may form judgments about you on the basis of your writing.

Some handbooks will let you get away with a run-on if the clauses are quite short. The classic example is frequently parodied:

> I came, I saw, I conquered.

Replacing the commas in such an example with semicolons would almost be overkill, and inserting an *and* before the final short clause would destroy the rhythm. You probably agree that such sentences are fairly rare and that you would have to work hard to find a writing situation in which you could comfortably use such a construction. If you understand the rule and can write sentences correctly, however, you are entitled to break the rule for some special effect.

Fixing Run-Ons and Comma Splices

There are several ways to fix a comma splice. First, you can insert a period and form two separate sentences:

> Marketing recently announced a new entry into the low end of the personal computer market. The PC-Pro takes its place alongside other, more powerful machines.

But you may decide the two independent clauses are closely related and really should be kept together. In that case, you can balance the two independent clauses on either side of a semicolon:

> Marketing recently announced a new entry into the low end of the personal computer market; the PC-Pro takes its place alongside other, more powerful machines.

If you decide the two clauses are equal in weight and importance, you can insert a comma followed by a **coordinating conjunction** *(and, or, nor, but, yet, for, so)*. Like a semicolon, a coordinating conjunction balances the two independent clauses:

> Marketing recently announced a new entry into the low end of the personal computer market, and the PC-Pro takes its place alongside other, more powerful machines.

You can also subordinate the first independent clause, thereby making it dependent on the second clause. Notice that the first clause, beginning with *when,* can no longer stand by itself. This strategy effectively shows the relation between the two clauses:

> When marketing recently announced a new entry into the low end of the personal computer market, the PC-Pro took its place alongside other, more powerful machines.

Certain trouble spots exist that cause even careful writers to write run-on sentences. You need red flags in your brain that fly up whenever you use certain expressions. The problem is often caused by words that feel like conjunctions but are actually modifiers, words like *then* and *however.* (See the section on semicolons in Chapter 10, "Semicolons and Colons," for more information on these **conjunctive adverbs.**)

One order was received approximately three days after shipment, then a second order arrived a week later.

Inland wetlands provide essential water-holding capacities during rainy seasons, however, wetlands alone cannot always absorb all the runoff from major storms.

Both examples represent run-on sentences of the sort that sometimes escape the notice of even very careful writers. Both can be fixed in one of several ways: by breaking the run-on into two sentences, by balancing both independent clauses around a semicolon, or by subordinating one of the clauses. (You may need to adjust the wording, too.)

EXERCISE 5-2

The following exercise will give you some practice with fragments and run-ons in the context of full paragraphs. Identify and correct the fragments and run-ons. Then check your work against the suggested corrections at the end of the chapter.

Interest rates on new one-year, adjustable-rate mortgages surged to the highest level in nine months. While fixed-rate mortgages jumped almost to the high point for the year. Adjustable-rate mortgages averaged 8 percent last week, up from 7.9 percent the week before. It was the highest since last November 6, then the rates averaged 8.11 percent.

Thirty-year, fixed-rate mortgages jumped to 10.57 percent from 10.44 percent the previous week. A figure slightly below the high for the year so far—10.58 percent.

The jump in rates followed a move by the Federal Reserve Board last Tuesday, it decided to push rates up by raising the key bank lending rate to slow the economy and fight inflation. Major U.S. banks then boosted their prime lending rate half a percentage point.

Fixed-rate mortgages hit a peak of 11.58 percent just before the October stock-market crash. But as the Fed pumped money into the economy to avoid a recession, the average dropped to 9.84 percent by early February.

Fixed-rate mortgages likely will rise another three-quarters of a percentage point by the end of the year, however, these mortgages have fluctuated widely over the past several years, and it is difficult to accurately predict the influence on the rates of the financial market assessment of inflation dangers.

EXERCISE 5-3

What follows is the actual text of an advertisement for the Franklin Mint composed almost entirely of fragments. Rewrite the ad copy in complete sentences, grouping the fragments and adding subject/ predicate constructions as necessary.

An original sculpture by an artist who has created works for world leaders. AMERICAN MAJESTY.

An exhilarating tribute to our heritage and liberty. An American masterpiece by Ronald Van Ruyckevelt, whose works have been presented to such world leaders as President Kennedy, Queen Elizabeth II, and the Emperor of Japan.

Experience his genius. In sculpture as powerful as the American eagle. An original work of art—*individually handcrafted and hand-painted*—in imported porcelain of exceptional quality.

American Majesty by Ronald Van Ruyckevelt. A sculpture destined for glory. Available exclusively through The Franklin Mint.

In Summary

This chapter has described two major sorts of sentence errors: fragments and run-ons. Fragments are incomplete sentences punctuated like complete sentences; run-ons string together too many independent clauses without appropriate punctuation.

Fragments have good uses in professional writing, but only when used carefully and intentionally. Run-ons, on the other hand, are never useful.

You might check a recent piece of writing of yours for fragments and run-ons. Identifying subjects and predicates for each clause will help you spot sentence fragments. Reading the sentences aloud will help you spot run-on problems.

Do you intentionally use any fragments or lists of phrases? Can you find an example in your writing in which you purposefully chose to use sentence fragments? Are there writing situations that call for fragments that were not mentioned in this chapter?

EXERCISE ANSWERS

Exercise 5-1 Answers

The fragments are *italicized*. Possible corrections appear below.

1. Two of the standing orders were left unfilled at the end of the month. *The order for the Pine Brothers and the order for the Randolph Company.*

Two of the standing orders were left unfilled at the end of the month: the order for the Pine Brothers and the order for the Randolph Company.

2. We don't need to get too worried about the February order for the Pine Brothers. *Since February is a short month.*

We don't need to get too worried about the February order for the Pine Brothers since February is a short month.

3. Why did we fail, though, to get the order out to Randolph? *Perhaps a breakdown in our billing procedures, an unnoticed glitch in production, or a lag in delivery from our supplier.*

Why did we fail, though, to get the order out to Randolph? Perhaps it was because of a breakdown in our billing procedures, an unnoticed glitch in production, or a lag in delivery from our supplier.

Exercise 5-2 Answers

The correction marks show possible strategies for fixing the fragments and run-ons:

Interest rates on new one-year, adjustable-rate mortgages surged to the highest level in nine months,~~W~~while fixed-rate mortgages jumped almost to the high point for the year. Adjustable-rate mortgages averaged 8 percent last week, up from 7.9 percent the week before. It was the highest since last November 6~~.~~. ~~T~~then the rates averaged 8.11 percent.

Thirty-year, fixed-rate mortgages jumped to 10.57 percent from 10.44 percent the previous week, a~~.~~ ~~A~~ figure slightly below the high for the year so far—10.58 percent.

The jump in rates followed a move by the Federal Reserve Board last Tuesday, when it decided to push rates up by raising the key bank lending rate to slow the economy and fight inflation. Major U.S. banks then boosted their prime lending rate half a percentage point.

Fixed-rate mortgages hit a peak of 11.58 percent just before the October stock market crash. But as the Fed pumped money into the economy to avoid a recession, the average dropped to 9.84 percent by early February.

Fixed-rate mortgages likely will rise another three-quarters of a percentage point by the end of the year. ~~,~~ ~~h~~However, these mortgages have fluctuated widely over the past several years, and it is difficult to accurately predict the influence on the rates of the financial market assessment of inflation dangers.

Exercise 5-3 Answers

What follows is one possible revision to eliminate fragments:

AMERICAN MAJESTY is~~A~~an original sculpture by an artist who has created works for world leaders.

American Majesty is ~~A~~an exhilarating tribute to our heritage and liberty~~.~~ ~~An American masterpiece~~ by Ronald Van Ruyckevelt, whose works have been presented to such world leaders as President Kennedy, Queen Elizabeth II, and the Emperor of Japan.

You can ~~E~~experience his genius~~.~~ ~~I~~in sculpture as powerful as the American eagle. ~~An~~ This original work of art—individually handcrafted and hand-painted—is produced in imported porcelain of exceptional quality.

American Majesty by Ronald Van Ruyckevelt is a~~.~~ ~~A~~ sculpture destined for glory. It is ~~A~~available exclusively through the Franklin Mint.

chapter 6

Common Problems with Verbs

Verbs are the "nucleus" of clauses, the core around which subjects and objects revolve. As the nucleus, verbs contain a lot of information and this information is reflected in the changes (**inflections**) in the form of the verb. If you have ever studied a foreign language, you may remember lots of charts with inflectional changes of verbs. Here, we're going to limit our discussion to those inflections in English that commonly cause problems for writers.

The overall goal of this chapter is to help you choose verb forms that accurately reflect your intended meaning. In this chapter, you will learn:

- How to recognize different forms of the verb
- How to avoid common problems with verbs—problems of agreement between subject and verb in person and number; unmotivated shifts in tense, aspect, and mood
- How to use shifts of tense, aspect, and mood to more accurately reflect your meaning and to vary your sentence style

Basic Form of the Verb

The basic form of the verb is the **infinitive**—the *to* form of the verb, as in *to go, to have, to be.* The infinitive form is the base to which are added all the various inflections that reflect information about time, degree of certainty, subject of the action, and so on.

When the infinitive is used in its unchanged form in a clause—that is, with the marker *to*—it fills a role normally played by nouns. Thus, the infinitive can act like a subject:

    S   **S**   **S** **V**   **S Comp** (for subject complement)
To *be* or not to *be,* that is the question.

The infinitive can also act like an object:

```
S   V    O
```
I want *to go.*

Or it can act like a subject complement:

```
   S  linking V        S Comp
```
The answer is simply *to say nothing.*

However, the infinitive verb cannot stand alone as the main verb in a clause. The main verb must be inflected as a finite verb form—that is, it must have tense.

Tensed Forms of the Verb

Tense is the grammatical category most closely associated with *time.* To be in time is to be finite; hence the name **finite** verb (just as the nontensed verb is called the nonfinite or infinitive). There are really only three tenses in English: **past, present,** and **future.** (Other verb forms are created by adding mood and aspect to these "tensed" forms.) Past and present tenses are expressed by changing (or inflecting) the form of the infinitive; the future tense is formed by adding the helping verb *will* to the infinitive form of the verb.

What changes occur to the infinitive verb to create present and past tense forms? Except for the third-person singular form, the present tense is often the same as the infinitive verb (though without the *to*). The third-person singular form has an *-s* (sometimes an *-es*) ending, which is a vestige of the time in English when *all* present-tense verbs had inflectional endings. Why is this important? Because third-person singular verb forms sometimes cause problems in subject-verb agreement, as we will see in the next section.

Past tense verbs are also created by inflecting the form of the infinitive. Some infinitive verbs are **regular**—that is, they form the past tense by adding *-ed* to the root of the verb. Other infinitive verbs are **irregular,** which means that they form the past tense by inflecting the root, infinitive form (often through a word-internal vowel change, as when the verb *wind* becomes *wound* in past tense, or when *swim* becomes *swam*). Many irregular verbs are very common: *be, go, have, come,* and *see* all have irregular past tenses. They tend to be the oldest verbs in the language; when new verbs were borrowed from other languages, they took the regular pattern. Figure 6.1 shows the tensed forms of some common regular and irregular infinitive verbs.

Figure 6.1 *Tensed Forms of Common Regular and Irregular Infinitives*

INFINITIVE		PRESENT		PAST	FUTURE
		ALL OTHERS	3RD-PER. SING.		
REGULAR VERBS	walk	walk	walks	walked	will walk
	listen	listen	listens	listened	will listen
	look	look	looks	looked	will look
	stop	stop	stops	stopped	will stop
IRREGULAR VERBS	be	am/are	is	was/were	will be
	do	do	does	did	will do
	have	have	has	had	will have
	go	go	goes	went	will go
	come	come	comes	came	will come
	see	see	sees	saw	will see
	drive	drive	drives	drove	will drive

As was mentioned above, no inflections occur to form the future tense. It is created simply by adding the word *will* as a helping verb before the infinitive. (Some more conservative dialects use the helping verb *shall* for forms with *I*.)

Subject-Verb Agreement

English verbs agree with their subjects in person and number. **Person** is the grammatical category that indicates who is speaking; in English there are three persons:

FIRST PERSON: the one or ones speaking

SECOND PERSON: the one or ones spoken to

THIRD PERSON: the one or ones spoken about

Number is the grammatical category that indicates how many people or things we're talking about: one (**singular**) or more than one (**plural**).

At one time, English verbs had a whole system of inflections indicating person and number to show what verb went with what subject. (The technical name for this grammatical relationship is **agreement.**) While we still say that English verbs "agree with" their subjects, that agreement is only apparent in third-person, present-tense, singular forms and in forms involving the verb *to be*. Figure 6.2 shows the present tense forms

Figure 6.2 *Present-Tense Forms of* To Go

	NUMBER	
	SINGULAR	PLURAL
PERSON		
FIRST PERSON	I go	we go
SECOND PERSON	you go	you go
THIRD PERSON	he/she/it goes	they go

Figure 6.3 *Present- and Past-Tense Forms of* To Be

	NUMBER	
	SINGULAR	PLURAL
PRESENT TENSE		
FIRST PERSON	I am	we are
SECOND PERSON	you are	you are
THIRD PERSON	he/she/it is	they are
PAST TENSE		
FIRST PERSON	I was	we were
SECOND PERSON	you were	you were
THIRD PERSON	he/she/it was	they were

for the verb *to go;* notice how the third-person singular form stands out from the others. (The pronouns are added for the sake of illustration; they are not part of the verb form.) Subject-verb agreement also surfaces with present- and past-tense forms of the verb *to be* (see Figure 6.3).

Problems with Subject-Verb Agreement

We said in the preceding section that verbs in English agree with their subjects in person and number (they don't in all languages). Where that agreement shows up most dramatically is between verbs and third-person, singular subjects. When one of these subjects is paired with a present-tense verb, the verb must end in *-s* or *-es*. Why do writers err in terms of subject-verb agreement? Typically, it's not because they don't *know* that verbs have to agree with their subjects. Rather, it's because certain constructions make choosing correct subject-verb forms difficult or confusing. These constructions include:

- Long modifiers separating the simple subject from the verb
- Collective nouns as subjects
- Coordinate subjects joined by correlative conjunctions (e.g., *either...or*)
- Inverted sentence order and "dummy" subjects

Modifiers Separating Subject from Verb

One source of confusion about subject-verb agreement arises when modifiers (often long ones) separate the main subject from its agreeing verb. Consider the following examples of faulty agreement:

WRONG: *Each* of the students *are* eligible to participate in the company education program.

WRONG: However, only *courses* taken at an accredited school, college, or certified institute *is* subject to reimbursement.

In the first example, the subject *each* is singular, but the verb *are* is plural. In the second example, the situation is reversed: the subject *courses* is plural, but the verb *is* is singular. Why would a writer make these mistakes? Because in each example there is at least one intervening noun of the opposite number (singular or plural) between the main subject word and its verb. Changing the verbs to agree with the main subject word, regardless of the intervening nouns, makes the examples read as follows:

Each of the students *is* eligible to participate in the company education program.

However, only *courses* taken at an accredited school, college, or certified institute *are* subject to reimbursement.

Your ear may tell you that these sentences still sound awkward. If they do, you may need to rewrite the sentences to make *all* of the nouns in the subject construction (the simple subject and its modifiers) agree in number with the main verb:

All of the *students are* eligible to participate in the company education program.

However, only course *work* taken at an accredited *school, college,* or certified *institute is* subject to reimbursement.

Collective Nouns as Subjects

Another source of subject-verb agreement problems is the use of **collective nouns** (like *committee, company, army*) as subjects. Although collective nouns refer to a plurality of individuals, they frequently take singular verbs and pronouns—especially when that plurality acts as a single entity, as in the following example:

> The *committee wants* to gather more information before making *its* decision.

However, when the collective entity acts as a divided entity, correct usage calls for a plural verb and pronoun:

> The *committee are* divided in their thinking and *are* requesting more time to consider *their positions.*

The use of a plural verb may strike many readers' ears as sounding "funny," more like British than American English. The solution is to add a plural noun as the new simple subject and to make the collective noun a modifier, as shown below:

> The *members of the committee are* divided in their thinking and *are* requesting more time to consider *their positions.*

Subjects with Correlative Conjunctions

Yet another common source of subject-verb agreement problems is the use of **correlative conjunctions** (*either...or, neither...nor*) to join coordinate subjects. Consider the following example:

> Neither the *boss* nor the *employees*...

The first subject is singular, the second one, plural. Shall we pick a singular verb or a plural verb to agree? The answer depends on which subject is closer to the verb. In the preceding example, *employees* is closer, so the verb should be plural:

> Neither the *boss* nor the *employees accept* responsibility for the problem.

If the subjects were reversed, with *boss* being closer, the verb would need to be singular:

> Neither the *employees* nor the *boss accepts* responsibility for the problem.

It is important to notice that this rule only works with correlative conjunctions that *exclude* alternatives (*either...or, neither...nor*). Correlative conjunctions that *include* both alternatives (*both...and, not only...but also*) create plural subjects, as in the following example:

Both the *boss* and the *supervisor accept* responsibility for the problem.

You can think of some correlative conjunctions as joining, and the joining creates plurals: one plus one is two.

Inverted Sentences and "Dummy" Subjects

A final source of errors in subject-verb agreement derives from certain unusual sentence constructions. Sometimes, normal phrase order is inverted and subjects are out of place, as with the italicized subjects below:

Described here are certain *exceptions* to the procedures used to qualify bidders.

Eliminated from the competition was the late *bid* from W. W. Jones & Co.

In these cases, you need to look past the verb to the inverted subject to find that the subject in the first example is plural and the subject in the second is singular.

A similar structure demands careful attention to number: linking verb sentences that begin with *There is* or *There are*. The word *there* won't tell you whether the linking verb should be singular (*is*) or plural (*are*). The word *there* is actually just a placeholder; the real subject follows the linking verb. Look beyond the linking verb to determine the proper verb form:

There are several new *products* in the new fall catalog.

There is a fine *line* between just-in-time and out-of-stock.

In the first example, the postponed subject *products* is plural, so the form of the linking verb should also be plural (*are*). In the second example, *line* is singular and properly takes the singular verb (*is*). Again, you need to look past the verb to the displaced subject to recognize the subject as plural or singular. Your ear probably won't help you much in these constructions.

EXERCISE 6-1

Correct any problems with subject-verb agreement in the following sentences. You might wish to underline the simple subjects and bracket the verbs to help identify the problems. Some sentences may not need correction.

1. An overview of all the approaches that have been analyzed to date were presented by test engineering.

2. The functional requirements for data communications services, audio communications services, and video communications services to accomplish the planning for, and execution of, a mission operation are described herein.

3. The list of requirements are divided into two classes.

4. There is during December certain discounts promoted by retailers.

5. Each of the five options is unacceptable.

6. I feel that fresh approaches to the solution of this difficult engineering problem is essential.

7. Despondent over the losses, but determined to recoup their investments, the Mullins and Howe lawyers in the swank 5th Avenue office gambled everything on a single desperate play.

8. Left without any cash reserves was three of their best clients.

9. Facilities has been notified about the sink.

Other Verb Inflections

The section above treats some fairly straightforward problems of subject/verb agreement. Errors of subject/verb agreement are often quite logically explained: the subject and verb are separated by intervening phrases, inverted constructions, or conjoined phrases that make the choice tricky; or collective nouns as subjects are sometimes singular and sometimes plural. Choosing the appropriate verb form is a matter of being alert to these tricky constructions, especially when editing a piece of writing.

The rest of the chapter discusses somewhat more difficult distinctions. There is no escaping the complexity of the English verb system and the careful distinctions it allows. Verbs tend to cause writers not only the most obvious problems but also some of the most subtle problems of controlling shades of meaning.

Aspect

Aspect is the verb inflection that shows the degree of completeness of an action. There are three degrees of aspect for English verbs: **simple** (treating the action as a single point in time), **progressive** (ongoing action), and **perfective** (completed action). The progressive and perfective forms are called **participles** and correspond to the *-ing* and *-en* (or sometimes *-ed*) verb forms, respectively. Figure 6.4 shows the progressive and perfective participles for the verbs listed above in Figure 6.1.

When used alone in a clause, participles may act (similar to infinitives) as parts of the clause typically filled by nouns. (The technical term for a participle used as a noun is a **gerund.**) Participles may act as subjects:

    s   **v**   **S Comp**
Walking is good exercise for you.

They may also act as objects:

               s   **v**   **o**
However, my favorite exercise involves *sitting*.

Participles may also function as subject complements:

         s   **v** **S Comp**
My favorite exercise is *rowing*.

Figure 6.4 *Participles of Common Regular and Irregular Infinitives*

INFINITIVE		PROGRESSIVE	PERFECTIVE
REGULAR VERBS	walk	walking	walked
	listen	listening	listened
	look	looking	looked
	stop	stopping	stopped
IRREGULAR VERBS	be	being	been
	do	doing	done
	have	having	had
	go	going	gone
	come	coming	come
	see	seeing	seen
	drive	driving	driven

They may also act as modifiers in a clause:

Walking along the seashore, they spotted a storm on the horizon.

Darkened by the storm, the horizon appeared prematurely black.

When participles are used as the main verb in a clause, they must be combined with helping verbs to form complete verb phrases. (The helping verb is necessary to indicate the tense.) Figure 6.5 indicates the possible combinations of tense and aspect for the verb *to go,* with its participles *going* and *gone.* (Again, the pronoun subjects have been included for completeness' sake.)

Mood

Mood is the grammatical category that shows the degree of certainty attached to a verb. Different grammatical classification schemes identify different categories of verb mood in English, but it seems safe to identify four moods:

INDICATIVE: to make a statement

INTERROGATIVE: to ask a question

IMPERATIVE: to state a command

SUBJUNCTIVE: to express a wish or hypothetical statement

Most sentences in English are in the indicative, sometimes also called "declarative," mood. Interrogatives, or questions, are probably the next most common. Indicative and interrogative statements may occur with any person and in any tense. The grammatical forms to express these

Figure 6.5 *Tense-Aspect Forms of the Verb* To Go

	ASPECT			
	SIMPLE	PROGRESSIVE	PERFECTIVE	PERFECTIVE-PROGRESSIVE
TENSE				
PAST	I went	I was going	I had gone	I had been going
PRESENT	I go	I am going	I have gone	I have been going
FUTURE	I will go	I will be going	I will have gone	I will have been going

moods are fairly obvious. Figure 6.6 shows sample indicative and inter-rogative forms for the verb *to go* with the second-person pronoun *you*. (All examples are in the simple aspect.)

Imperative mood statements, or commands, always take the present tense with the second-person subject understood: "(You) Go!" Impera-tive commands can only be issued to the person spoken to. Require-ments for others are stated in the indicative mood: "All people must go."

The subjunctive mood is used to express wishes, hypothetical state-ments, and contrary-to-fact statements. When the subjunctive is used to state a wish or a hypothetical statement (i.e., a possibility), its form is the same as the uninflected infinitive (without the *to*):

It is important that he *go*.

It is my wish that she *attend* college.

It is necessary that you *be* on time to class.

Though the subjunctive's hypothetical *meaning* is quite common in En-glish, this *form* is rare in English and is getting rarer all the time.

The contrary-to-fact form of the subjunctive is familiar in fixed ex-pressions with the verb *were*, as in the following:

If I *were* you, . . .

If she *were* here, . . .

Other than these fixed expressions, however, the form has all but disap-peared from speech. Even in written English, many people do not recog-nize the subjunctive form and do not use it in their writing. You will not be wrong if you join the majority of users in expressing subjunctive meaning with indicative forms, as in the following revisions of the above examples (note the use of helping verbs in the first and third examples):

He *should go*.

I hope that she *attends* college.

Figure 6.6 *Indicative and Interrogative Forms of* To Go

	MOOD	
	INDICATIVE	INTERROGATIVE
TENSE		
PAST	You went.	Did you go?
PRESENT	You go.	Do you go?
FUTURE	You will go.	Will you go?

You *must be* on time to class.

If I *was* you, . . .

If she *was* here, . . .

Shifts in Tense, Aspect, and Mood

The verb system is sufficiently complicated that writers must constantly make choices about verb forms as meaning develops from clause to clause. Verbs change shape from sentence to sentence as the author comments on when something happened, to what extent it was completed, and who was involved. The trick is to control the choices to make meaningful distinctions, rather than making unmotivated, haphazard changes in the verb forms.

Tense Shifts

A common problem facing writers is how to represent the time of events being described—for example, whether to choose past or present tense in reporting the results of a past-time experiment. Shifting tense is often considered to be an error in writing. Here we will say that an *unmotivated* (or unconscious) shift in tenses can be an error, but a *motivated* (or purposeful) shift in tenses is not.

What is an example of an unmotivated shift in tense in writing? One example is starting a story in past tense and suddenly shifting into present tense:

Last week I *was walking* along a street when this man *walks* up to me and *says* . . .

We do this in speech all the time, but in formal writing it's considered to be an error.

A common kind of tense shift in professional writing involves the use of *will* in shifting to the future tense. This shift often occurs when a writer is documenting procedures and is describing what *will* happen after a step is performed, as in the following example:

After you *press* the Alt and P keys together, the computer *will send* your file to be printed.

The question here is how much time elapses between the user's pressing the keys and the computer's sending the file off to be printed? Not much. In fact, virtually none. So, we urge you to consistently use the present tense when documenting procedures. Notice that there is little difference in meaning if we apply this guideline to the previous example:

> After you *press* the Alt and P keys together, the computer *sends* your file to be printed.

Moreover, the sentence now reads more smoothly.

We have said that unmotivated tense shifts are an error in writing but that *motivated* tense shifts are not. What makes a tense shift motivated? To illustrate a motivated tense shift, we have to talk some more about just what is represented by verb tense.

Tense does not exactly represent time. Perhaps it is more useful to think of tense as representing the perspective of the speaker with respect to the event being described. One common use of tense shift is to represent past-time events in present tense in a presently existing report or document (often the one the reader is holding). Hence the use of present tense in the following sentence:

> This study *describes* the effect of the new chip design on overall part performance.

The meaning of the present tense here is that, even though the study has been done in the *past*, it is doing its work in the present time, *now*, as the reader reads. The effect of the choice of the present form is to give added urgency and a sense of present relevance to the study as it is read. So this is one example of a motivated tense shift.

A second example of a motivated tense shift occurs in reporting the conclusions of investigations or experiments. The writer may have described all the steps of the experiment in the past tense. Suddenly, in reporting the conclusion of the experiment, the writer shifts into the present:

> The results *indicate* that the new chip design *improves* overall part performance.

Presumably, this conclusion is based on some experimental results in which the new chip design *improved* (note: past tense) part performance. Representing that finding in present tense suggests that the writer is making a generalization: not only did the new design improve performance in the past, but it will continue to do so in the present and future.

You can represent some pretty subtle differences by shifting tenses. Consider what happens to the preceding example when we shift everything to past tense:

The results *indicated* that the new chip design *improved* overall part performance.

Doesn't it sound like the conclusions of the study are more restricted? Perhaps further experiments will demonstrate that the new design will lessen part performance or that it won't affect part performance at all. What is the effect of shifting only the first verb into past tense?

The results *indicated* that the new chip design *improves* overall part performance.

Doesn't this shift make the conclusion stronger?

EXERCISE 6-2

Choose the appropriate verb tenses in the following passage. You do not need to choose the same tense consistently if you have a reason for making a tense shift.

A meeting was held on Wednesday, November 21, to discuss proposed changes to the software interface. The proposal (was/is) as follows:

- Replace the current character-based interface with a graphical user interface.
- Reduce the number of functions performed by the interface.
- Simplify the hierarchical structure of the remaining menus.

Most of the attendees felt that the proposal (was/is) not acceptable in its entirety. They felt that making some changes to the interface (was/is) acceptable but that the move to reduce the functionality of the interface (was/is) not acceptable. After discussing the other elements of the proposal, the attendees settled on a compromise version. This version (was/is) as follows:

- Replace the current character-based interface with a graphical user interface.

- Combine the number of functions performed by the interface.

- Clarify the hierarchical structure of the remaining menus.

Aspect Shifts

As with tense, so do some writers carelessly move back and forth between aspect forms without regard to the subtle differences in meaning. This is especially true with regard to unmotivated shifts between the simple past and present perfective forms:

I *lived* in Austin for six years.

I *have lived* in Austin for six years.

In the first example, the action is complete; that is, the speaker is no longer living in Austin. But in the second example, the action—while begun in the past—is not yet complete; that is, the speaker is *still* living in Austin.

Another frequently unmotivated shift of aspect is that from simple past to past perfective forms:

I *went* to the store to get a newspaper.

I *had gone* to the store to get a newspaper...

Here both actions are completed, and both are in the past. But while the first statement simply describes a point in time, the second one is not merely a synonym for the first. The use of past perfective opens the single point of past time into a time *span* for some later action:

...when I suddenly *noticed* that my gas gauge was on empty.

The subtleties of aspect shift are similar to those of tense shift, and while unmotivated shifts of either are to be avoided, *motivated* shifts of aspect can achieve similar effects to those of motivated tense shift. The relevant kind of aspect shift here is from the simple past to the present perfective aspect. To continue with our previous example from the section on motivated tense shifts:

The results *indicated* that the new chip design *improved* overall part performance.

Here, everything is in the simple past tense. The sentence makes no claim about the present truth (or relevance) of the finding. But when we shift the first verb from simple past to present perfective, a subtle change of meaning occurs:

> The results *have indicated* that the new chip design *improved* overall part performance.

The present perfective, while representing completed action, represents that action as being *relevant in the present.* The shift to present perfective in this example suggests the present relevance of the conclusion. In fact, it seems to impel us to re-express the second clause in the present tense:

> The results *have indicated* that the new chip design *improves* overall part performance.

The choice of present tense would not be an effective choice if the writer were citing those studies in order to overturn them. The best choice then would be to maintain the former conclusion in the past tense, while representing the newer conclusion in present tense:

> The results *have indicated* that the new chip design *improved* overall part performance. However, in this paper I *show* that the chip design used in those earlier studies, far from improving overall performance, actually *lessens* it.

EXERCISE 6-3

Choose the best tense-aspect forms of the verbs in parentheses in the following paragraph. Be aware of the pattern of your choices as you proceed: Have you been consistent? What do your choices suggest about the present relevance of the "C language" discussed in the paragraph?

Creating a portable software package (required/has required/ requires) finding a portable language that (was/is) fully supported on all required systems and that (made/makes) developing and maintaining the code at least easier than it (was/is) with assembly language. Also, the source code (needed to be/should be/needs to be) more readable than assembly language programs and thus easier to maintain.

C (met/has met/meets) all these requirements with flying colors.
As an added bonus, using a high-level language (made/has made/
makes) the programmers on this project approximately twice as
productive as if they (coded/had coded/code) in assembly language.

Unmotivated Shifts in Mood

A final shift of verb form to guard against is the unmotivated shift from imperative mood to indicative mood when writing instructions or procedures. Writers often make this shift to introduce variety into their text. Readers, on the other hand, often interpret these indicative-mood statements as descriptions rather than instructions. Consider the following sentence from a computer operating manual:

> The computer is powered on by pressing the switch on the back of the unit. After a one-minute warm-up period, a blinking cursor will appear on the screen.

Is the first sentence of this example a description of how the computer works (and where the power switch is located) or an instruction to turn on the computer? It is evident from the second sentence that the authors intended the first sentence to be read as an instruction. The second sentence presumes that an action has occurred to turn the computer on. Thus, the use of indicative mood in the first sentence is ambiguous. How can you avoid such a problem? By keeping the instruction in the imperative mood. Consider this revision, which also uses the more effective present tense to describe the action of the computer itself:

> Power on the computer by pressing the switch on the back of the unit. After a one-minute warm-up period, a blinking cursor *appears* on the screen.

Now the intended action is clear. And the action is clearly separate from the consequence, a separation reinforced by the shift from imperative to indicative mood.

In Summary

This chapter has discussed some common problems that writers have with verbs, the "nucleus" of clauses. Specifically, we have looked at problems in the areas of subject-verb agreement, unmotivated shifts of tense, and careless use of aspect and mood. Turning those problems around into prescriptions for effective style, we might offer the following pieces of advice:

- When writing long subject constructions, make sure that your main subject agrees in person and number with the main verb. Be especially wary of subject constructions beginning with indefinite pronouns like *each, all, every,* and so on. (See Chapter 8, "Pronoun Problems," for more work on this.)
- Avoid overuse of future tense in professional writing. Try substituting present tense.
- Be sensitive to how shifts in tense and aspect affect the degree of certainty attached to findings in reports. Use simple present tense to report the content of presently existing reports as in, *The report states....* Use simple present tense or present perfective to represent findings that are still considered to hold true as in, *Studies have shown....*
- When writing instructions, use imperative-mood statements to instruct a reader to do something. Do not confuse imperative instructions that describe what a reader is *to do* with indicative-mood statements describing how something *works.*

As the core of a clause, verbs need to be used correctly and *strategically.* If that core is out of whack (or missing), the whole clause will be off-center. The correct and strategic use of verbs will help your reader not only to recognize clause boundaries—which is a helpful technique in understanding new or difficult material—but also to understand your attitude about the actions expressed in those clauses.

EXERCISE ANSWERS

Exercise 6-1 Answers

Subjects are *italicized;* agreeing verbs are bracketed. Corrected versions appear beneath. Some examples have additional suggested revisions printed beneath because the first corrected construction still sounds "funny." Some sentences may not need correction.

1. An *overview* of all the approaches that have been analyzed to date [were presented] by test engineering.

An overview of all the approaches that have been analyzed to date was presented by test engineering.

Test engineering presented an overview of all the approaches that have been analyzed to date.

2. The functional *requirements* for data communications services, audio communications services, and video communications services to accomplish the planning for, and execution of, a mission operation [are described] herein.

   Described herein are . . .

3. The *list* of requirements [are divided] into two classes.

   The list of requirements is divided into two classes.

   There are two classes of requirements.

4. There [is] during December certain *discounts* promoted by retailers.

   There are during December certain discounts promoted by retailers.

   During December, *retailers promote* certain discounts.

5. *Each* of the five options [is] unacceptable. (no change)

6. I feel that fresh *approaches* to the solution of this difficult engineering problem [is] essential.

   I feel that fresh approaches are essential to solve this difficult engineering problem.

   I feel that fresh approaches to the solution of this difficult engineering problem are essential.

7. Despondent over the losses but determined to recoup their investments, the Mullins and Howe *lawyers* in the swank 5th Avenue office [gambled] everything on a single desperate play. (no change)

8. Left without any cash reserves [was] *three* of their best clients.

   Left without any cash reserves were three of their best clients.

   Three of their best clients . . .

9. *Facilities* [has been notified] about the sink.

   The Facilities Department has been notified about the sink.
   or
   We have notified Facilities about the sink.

Exercise 6-2 Answers

The version below begins in past tense to represent the original proposal, which no longer stands. The version shifts to present tense to represent the amended proposal, which still stands.

A meeting was held on Wednesday, November 21, to discuss proposed changes to the software interface. The proposal *was* as follows:

- Replace the current character-based interface with a graphical user interface.
- Reduce the number of functions performed by the interface.
- Simplify the hierarchical structure of the remaining menus.

Most of the attendees *felt* that the proposal *was* not acceptable in its entirety. They *felt* that making some changes to the interface *was* acceptable, but that the move to reduce the functionality of the interface *was* not acceptable. After discussing the other elements of the proposal, the attendees settled on a compromise version. This version *is* as follows:

- Replace the current character-based interface with a graphical user interface.
- Combine the number of functions performed by the interface.
- Clarify the hierarchical structure of the remaining menus.

Exercise 6-3 Answers

The past-tense version focuses on the past-time experience of the group. (Note, however, that this version does not indicate whether the group is still using C.)

Creating a portable software package *required* finding a portable language that *was* fully supported on all required systems and that *made* developing and maintaining the code at least easier than it is with assembly language. Also, the source code *needed to be* more readable than assembly language programs and thus easier to maintain.

C *met* all these requirements with flying colors. As an added bonus, using a high-level language *made* the programmers on this project approximately twice as productive as if they *had coded* in assembly language.

The present-tense version focuses on the present nature of the requirements and the solution that C provides:

Creating a portable software package *requires* finding a portable language that *is* fully supported on all required systems and that *makes* developing and maintaining the code at least easier than it is with assembly language. Also, the source code *needs to be* more readable than assembly language programs and thus easier to maintain.

C *meets* all these requirements with flying colors. As an added bonus, using a high-level language *makes* the programmers on this project approximately twice as productive as if they *code* in assembly language.

As an added twist, a present-perfect version of the second paragraph (with either the past-tense or present-tense version of the first paragraph) focuses on the experience of the group in adopting this solution, which is still being implemented:

C *has met* all these requirements with flying colors. As an added bonus, using a high-level language *has made* the programmers on this project approximately twice as productive as if they *had coded* in assembly language.

chapter 7

Placing Modifiers Effectively

In This Chapter

The last three chapters discussed the basic core of a sentence: the subject-predicate combination known as a *clause*. This chapter discusses the "add-on" portions of a sentence: the words, phrases, or clauses that act as modifiers of the clause. In this chapter, you will learn:

- How to place modifiers effectively
- How to avoid some common errors resulting from ineffective placement of modifiers—specifically, ambiguous modifiers, dangling modifiers, and long modifiers separating the simple subject and predicate

Modifiers that are effectively placed are not only easier to understand in themselves but also make the entire clause structure easier to understand.

A Basic Principle for Placing Modifiers Effectively

The basic principle for effectively placing modifiers may be stated as follows: modifiers should be placed as close to what they modify as possible. Consider the placement of the word *only* in the following sentence:

I *only* want to order a new computer.

As it stands, this sentence is ambiguous because it may mean three things: It may mean that the writer is minimizing the action he or she wants to perform (and you can imagine the defensive tone of voice it would be said in: "*What!?* All I want to do is...."). But it may also mean that a *new* computer is the *only* kind of computer the writer wants to order. If that is the intended meaning, the word *only* should be placed closer to *computer*:

I want to order *only* a new computer.

or

> I want to order a new computer *only*.

The third possible meaning is that it is only *this* writer who wants to order a new computer (*I alone want to order...*); other people in the department want to do something different. If that is the intended meaning, the word *only* should be moved before the subject to more clearly modify the subject (and it alone):

> *Only* I want to order a new computer.

Placing the word *only* more carefully leads to a less ambiguous reading of the sentence than that caused by the original placement. This example demonstrates the basic principle of placing modifiers close to what they modify: If you don't, your readers may get a different meaning from the one you intend.

Ambiguous Modifiers

In the example sentences, the word *only* modifies the word or phrase immediately before or after it. This is true of all words that modify nouns: Most adjectives and modifying nouns occur immediately *before* the noun they modify. Prepositional phrases, relative clauses (remember those from Chapter 4?), and some adjectives (like *alone* or *only* in the above example) occur immediately *after* the noun they modify. But *all* noun modifiers occur immediately before or after the noun (or noun phrase) they modify. We will call these modifiers **adjectivals** because of their function of modifying nouns.

In contrast, modifiers of verbs (adverbs, prepositional phrases, and subordinate clauses, all of which we will call **adverbials**) aren't quite so restricted. They can "float" to other places in the clause. Adverbs especially may occur at the very beginning or very end of the clause, as well as in the general vicinity of the verb they modify. Consider the placement of the adverb *yesterday* in the following sentences:

> *Yesterday* I shipped the parts to Apex Computers.
> I shipped the parts *yesterday* to Apex Computers.
> I shipped the parts to Apex Computers *yesterday*.

There's no ambiguity in these examples; they all mean the same thing: the parts were shipped *yesterday.*

Ambiguity arises when it's not clear from the position of the modifier what the modifier is modifying. This usually happens with modifiers that can act as *either* adjectivals or adverbials—which was the source of our problem with the word *only.* In the initial sentence *I only want to order a new computer,* it wasn't clear whether *only* was an adjective modifying the pronoun *I* or an adverb modifying the verb phrase *want to order a new computer.*

Prepositional phrases are notoriously ambiguous as modifiers because they can act as either adjectival or adverbial modifiers. As adjectival modifiers, they are tightly bound to the noun they immediately follow; as adverbial modifiers, they are more free to "float." And often their position in a clause makes it difficult or impossible to tell what's being modified. To demonstrate this problem with prepositional phrases, let's consider a new version of the preceding unambiguous sentence:

Yesterday I shipped the parts *from Marketing* to Apex Computers.

The prepositional phrase *from Marketing* is ambiguous in its scope of modification. Is it an adjectival modifier of the immediately preceding noun *parts* telling us where the parts originated? Or is it an adverbial modifier of the verb *shipped* telling us where the parts where shipped from? The position of the prepositional phrase makes it impossible to decide what kind of modifier it is.

Another example of this same kind of ambiguity occurs in the following sentence:

The quality team decided to collect data on wasted materials *at their last meeting.*

Again the problem is the placement of the prepositional phrase *at their last meeting:* Does it modify the immediately preceding noun *materials* or is it a "floating" adverbial modifier of the verb, telling *when* the team decided to collect the data?

In this last example, you are more likely to decide that the adverbial reading is correct, because of the (probably unintended) humor of the adjectival reading of the sentence if the team was collecting data on materials that were wasted during the last meeting!

Many misplaced modifiers create potentially humorous readings. Consider the following examples:

Wanted: Woman to sew buttons *on the fourth floor*.

Occasionally we will find someone *in a building* that's not supposed to be there.

In these examples, the initial confusion is resolved by the time you finish reading the modifier. But why make the reader go back and reanalyze the grammatical structure? It is better to place the modifier correctly the first time.

How to Resolve Ambiguous Modifiers

To clarify the grammatical structure (and the intended meaning) from the beginning, you can resolve ambiguous modifiers in two ways. One way is to flip the modifiers, putting prepositional phrases as *close* as possible to their modified element (and *away* from the potentially confusing position):

Yesterday I shipped the parts to Apex Computers *from Marketing*.

The quality team decided *at their last meeting* to collect data on wasted materials.

Wanted *on the fourth floor*: Woman to sew buttons.

Occasionally we will find someone that's not supposed to be there *in a building*.

The second way to edit the sentences is to put the ambiguous modifier up at the *front* of the sentence, followed by a comma:

At their last meeting, the quality team decided to collect data on wasted materials.

In addition to working well with ambiguous prepositional phrases, this solution also works well for ambiguous modifying clauses:

They decided to ship the parts for the new pump *after we threatened to stop all orders*.

Does this sentence mean that someone is waiting for you to threaten to stop all orders before they ship? It's unlikely. Instead, it probably means the following:

After we threatened to stop all orders, they decided to ship the parts for the new pump.

This second way of editing the sentences has the advantage of arranging the clause in the order that events actually occurred: As you will find out by moving "floating" adverbial modifiers around, only modifiers of time (*After we threatened...*), purpose (*In order to save time...*), and condition (*If you want to succeed...*) can be moved to the front of the main clause. Other modifiers—whether of the noun or of the verb—cannot be moved so easily.

Our preference is for putting adverbial modifiers of time, purpose, and condition up front and following them with a comma. And as you will see in Chapter 21, "Managing Sentence Emphasis," this arrangement of a sentence allows you to end strong with the main clause at the end. This discussion leads to a second principle of effective placement of modifiers: Modifiers of time, purpose, and condition should occur at the front of the clause they modify.

EXERCISE 7-1

In the following exercise, modifying phrases are underlined. When the sentences contain modifiers embedded within modifying phrases, the embedded modifiers are double underlined. Identify the underlined elements as modifiers of either the noun (adjectival) or the verb (adverbial). For adjectival modifiers, identify the *word* being modified. For adverbial modifiers, identify the *type* of modifier (i.e., modifier of time, purpose, or condition).

Next, edit the sentences for more effective placement of modifying elements. Is there more than one way to order the modifiers? Experiment with different ways: Which order is more (or most) effective? Notice which modifiers of the verb can be moved to the front of the sentence and which cannot.

1. Do not block the back <u>of the terminal</u> <u>to maintain ventilation</u>.

2. The monitor will display a <u>blinking</u> <u>block</u> cursor <u>after a one-minute warm-up period</u>.

3. Turn the unit off and on <u>again</u> <u>if the cursor fails to appear in the home position <u>of a clear screen</u></u>.

4. The cursor advances <u>after a key is pressed</u> and <u>corresponding</u> characters appear.

5. <u>For <u>best</u> results</u>, the unit should be placed <u>on a <u>flat</u> surface</u> and <u>at a comfortable <u>height</u></u> <u>for the user</u>.

Dangling Modifiers

Another kind of modifier problem is created by a main clause that hides what is being modified. Consider the following sentence:

> Driving through midtown Atlanta, the IBM tower can be seen.

What's wrong with this construction? Because of the placement of the modifier next to the subject, the reader's first tendency is to read the main clause as if the IBM tower is doing the driving! In fact, the driver has been hidden by the passive structure of the clause. (For more information on passives and their functions, see Chapter 18, "Recognizing Active and Passive Voice," and Chapter 19, "When to Prefer the Passive Voice.")

This problem is called a **dangling modifier.** The modifier is said to "dangle" because it has nothing to attach to; the implied subject of the modifier (in this case, whoever was *driving through midtown Atlanta*) is not the same as the explicit subject of the main clause (in this case, *the IBM tower*).

How do you correct a dangling modifier? Not (as in the preceding sections) by moving it to the front of the sentence—it's already there! In the case of dangling modifiers, you usually leave the position of the modifier alone. Instead, you can do one of two things: Either change the structure of the *modifier* (making it into a complete clause) or change the structure of the *main clause.*

The first option, changing the structure of the modifier, involves making the subject of the modifier explicit, as in the following example:

> *While we were* driving through midtown Atlanta, the new IBM tower could be seen.

The second option, changing the structure of the main clause, involves making its subject the same as the implied subject of the modifier. In the current example, that means recapturing a deleted doer of the action from the passive construction:

> Driving through midtown Atlanta, we could see the new IBM tower.

Either way, we end up with a sentence whose meaning is clear on the first reading.

EXERCISE 7-2

Rewrite the following sentences to avoid the "funny" reading caused by the dangling modifier. For each modifier, ask yourself, "Who is doing the action?"

1. After warm-up, you should see a blinking cursor.

2. To ventilate properly, magazines should be placed away from the back of the unit.

3. There are eighty character positions per line. A new line begins after entering the eightieth character.

4. Although helpful for many specialized tasks, the machine can be powered on without consulting the product manual.

Modifiers That Separate Subject and Predicate

One further place where modifiers cause problems within a clause is just after the subject, especially if the modifier is a long one. Frequently, modifiers in this position cause problems in subject-verb agreement (see Chapter 6, "Common Problems with Verbs"), or punctuation errors with misused commas (see Chapter 9, "Commas"), or just an awkward reading as the reader's short-term memory gets stretched to remember the main subject.

Examples of a long modifier separating subject and predicate occur in the following sentences:

A common problem with the power supply *in all the failed units that have been analyzed to date* is overheating.

An overview of *all the failed units that have been analyzed to date* was presented by test engineering.

By the time we get to the main verbs, we may well have forgotten *what* is overheating or *what* was presented. The solution in these cases—and in many others like them—is to flip the subject and the subject complement or object, so that the long modification occurs at the end of the predicate, as in the following:

Overheating is a common problem with the power supply *in all the failed units that have been analyzed to date.*

Test engineering presented an overview of *all the failed units that have been analyzed to date.*

With the subject-verb relation established early in the sentence, the reader can follow the modifiers to the end of the sentence. A further improvement in emphasis and clarity would be gained in the first example by moving the context-setting modifiers to the front of the sentence:

In all the failed units that have been analyzed to date, a common problem with the power supply is overheating.

A common (but erroneous) solution to the problem of long subject modifiers is to place a single comma between the subject and predicate. While this usage reflects the pause that one would take in speaking such a sentence, it is an error in writing to use a single comma to separate the subject and predicate. Thus, the following sentences are incorrect:

WRONG: A few of the power supplies *that appeared to have problems with intermittent outages during testing,* were really OK.

WRONG: A lot of the sentences *that may have problems with punctuation or structure,* look fine to me.

They should be rewritten without the comma as follows:

A few of the power supplies *that appeared to have problems with intermittent outages during testing* were really OK.

A lot of the sentences *that may have problems with punctuation or structure* look fine to me.

There are, however, better ways to manage the modification. One is to substitute a subordinate clause to replace the relative:

Although a few of the power supplies appeared to have problems with intermittent outages during testing, they were really OK.

While a lot of the sentences may have problems with punctuation or structure, they look fine to me.

Making the relative clause into a subordinate one allows you to move the modifier from a position that interrupts the subject-verb relation to one at the front of the sentence, which sets the stage. It also allows you to end strong, with a short, emphatic main clause that delivers the real news.

EXERCISE 7-3

Each of the following sentences contains subject phrases with a long modifying construction before the verb. Shorten the subject modifiers as much as possible by moving them out of the way, correcting the grammar and punctuation as necessary:

1. The practice of seeking some initial training and getting feedback on performance before I take on new and unfamiliar assignments, will yield less anxiety and make for an easier transition.

2. Every time a shortage of supplies that you have responsibility for occurs, you should contact purchasing.

3. The desktop documents that the students created using the new page composition program tended to mimic the features of traditional paper text.

4. Finding new arguments that convince home computer buyers of their need for multimedia machines is easy.

In Summary

In terms of your own writing, probably the most important aspect of this chapter is the basic principle for placing modifiers effectively: Modifiers should be placed as close to what they modify as possible.

We have seen how *not* following this principle creates a good deal of confusion, and how it is also the source of the confusion for dangling modifiers, in which the reader looks (in vain) for the closest noun to be the subject of the modifier.

We also looked at some situations where the modifiers should be moved *away* from what they immediately modify because that position causes ambiguity. This led to a second principle for effective placement of modifiers: Modifiers of time, purpose, and condition should precede the clause they modify. Putting these modifiers at the front of the sentence reflects the actual order of events in the real world: people do things at a certain time, for a certain reason, and under certain conditions.

Finally, we looked at another principle of effective style: Keep the main subject and verb close together, even if it means reorganizing the sentence to put long subjects in subject complement or object position at the end of the predicate. Though doing this may seem to take us directly 180 degrees from where we began, it is actually right where we started, because long subject modifiers often make it difficult for the reader to tell immediately *what is modifying what.* And that's the ambiguity we started out to avoid!

EXERCISE ANSWERS

Exercise 7-1 Answers

The following sentences are edited for more effective placement of modifying elements. Changes from the original are in underlined italics.

1. _To maintain ventilation_ (adverbial modifier of purpose), do not block the back of the terminal (adjectival modifier of *the back*).

2. _After a one-minute warm-up period_ (adverbial modifier of time), the monitor will display a blinking block (adjectival modifiers of *cursor*) cursor.

3. _If the cursor fails to appear in the home position of a clear screen_ (adverbial modifier of condition), turn the unit off and on again (adverbial modifier of time).

4. _After a key is pressed_ (adverbial modifier of time), the cursor advances and corresponding (adjectival modifier of *characters*) characters appear.

5. For best results (this adverbial modifier of purpose is already in the appropriate location at the front of the sentence), the unit should be placed on a flat surface (adverbial modifier of location; cannot move) and at a comfortable height (adverbial modifier of location; cannot move) for the user (adjectival modifier of *height*).

Exercise 7-2 Answers

The following sentences have been rewritten to avoid the "funny" reading caused by the dangling modifier. Changes from the original are underlined and *italicized*.

1. After warm-up, _the screen should display_ a blinking cursor.

2. To ventilate properly, _the back of the unit_ should be kept clear of magazines.

3. There are eighty character positions per line. A new line begins after _you enter_ the eightieth character.

4. Although helpful for many specialized tasks, _the product manual does not have to be consulted in powering on_ the machine.

Exercise 7-3 Answers

In the following sentences, long modifiers between subject and verb are shortened as much as possible.

1. Before taking on new and unfamiliar assignments, I will have less anxiety and an easier transition if I seek some initial training and get early feedback on my performance.

2. You should contact purchasing every time you run short of supplies that you have responsibility for.

3. Although the students used the new page composition program, their documents tended to mimic the features of traditional paper text.

4. It is easy to find new arguments to convince computer buyers that they need multimedia machines.

chapter 8

Pronoun Problems

This chapter reviews several common errors involving pronouns. Just as subjects need to agree with verbs, so pronouns need to agree with the words they stand for and with the part they play in a sentence. Agreement among sentence elements concerns correctness, not preference. We are talking here about rules that call attention to themselves when violated—errors that readers notice and that can call into question your effectiveness as a writer.

In this chapter, you will learn:

- How to choose pronoun forms based on their case roles in sentences: as subjects, objects, and possessives
- How to choose between *who* and *whom* (and why you might want to make the distinction)
- How to maintain consistency in number (singular vs. plural), person (first, second, and third), and gender (masculine, feminine, and neuter)
- How to avoid sexist usage

It is particularly important that you be an active reader in this chapter. As you read, identify those agreement errors that you sometimes commit. Use a pencil to mark such errors in the margins of the text. Make a note if you have questions after reading a passage or doing an exercise. Likewise, try to notice those errors that you recognize as a reader of other people's writing. You need to be a discriminating reader; recognize your own strengths and weaknesses. Then you can set priorities for your own learning.

The Pronoun System

Pronouns are words that usually stand for nouns or other pronouns and sometimes for verbs. Because pronouns take the place of other words or phrases, they need to agree with what they refer to. **Antecedent** is a useful term here, meaning the word the pronoun refers to (from Latin "one that goes before"). We commonly say that pronouns agree with their antecedents (as *their* agrees with *pronouns* in this sentence since both are plural).

Personal pronoun is the term used for those pronouns that refer to participants in the conversation or text. **First person** refers to the one speaking or writing; **second person** refers to the one being spoken to, the listener or reader; and **third person** refers to those being spoken about and not immediately present. (The term *person* is a grammatical distinction rather than a semantic one; we use personal pronouns to refer to animals or things as well as people.) If you examine a chart of the personal pronoun system, you will notice that pronouns reflect quite a few distinctions in their different forms (see Figure 8.1). One thing you may notice in this chart is that the personal pronoun system is not totally regular. For example, the second-person forms (*you*) are the same for singular and plural. And the gender distinctions in third-person singular (*he, she, it*) are not reflected elsewhere in the chart. Such irregularities in the system frequently lead to errors, as we will discuss below.

In addition to these personal pronouns, there are other types of pronouns that perform various functions:

> **DEMONSTRATIVE PRONOUNS:** (*this, that, these, those*) point to things being referred to.

> **RELATIVE PRONOUNS:** (*who* and *whom, which, that*) tie dependent clauses to independent clauses.

Figure 8.1 *Personal Pronoun Forms*

	SINGULAR	**PLURAL**
FIRST PERSON		
SUBJECT	I	we
OBJECT	me	us
POSSESSIVE	my, mine	our, ours
SECOND PERSON		
SUBJECT	you	you
OBJECT	you	you
POSSESSIVE	your, yours	your, yours
THIRD PERSON		
SUBJECT	he, she, it	they
OBJECT	him, her, it	them
POSSESSIVE	his, her, its	their

INTERROGATIVE PRONOUNS: (*who* and *whom, which, what*) help form questions.

INDEFINITE PRONOUNS: (*each, every, any, all, everyone, anyone, anything, someone, everybody, somebody, both, many, most, few, either, neither*) allow us to refer to a group or an individual without specifically naming someone or something.

REFLEXIVE PRONOUNS: (*myself, yourself, himself, herself, itself, ourselves, yourselves, themselves*) allow us to show the subject of the clause acting upon itself.

Although there is no need to memorize the various types of pronouns in this list, the list can give you a sense of how complicated pronouns are in their many forms and functions. With all these distinctions in the pronoun system, and all the irregularities, is it any wonder that even careful writers make mistakes when choosing the correct forms? In this chapter, we will take a closer look at four aspects of pronouns that often give writers trouble: case, number, person, and gender. Below, we will discuss each distinction and identify some of the common kinds of errors associated with each.

Case: Subject or Object?

Pronouns, like nouns and noun phrases, often serve in subject or object roles in sentences. When they do, pronouns carry some indication of **case:** the role the word plays in the sentence. Notice in Figure 8.1 that each pronoun has **subject, object,** and **possessive** case forms. If a pronoun is the subject of the sentence, it will have one case form. If it is an object, it will have another. Thus, the first- and third-person singular forms change in these example sentences according to the role the pronouns play:

s   o
He asked *me* for a raise.

s   o
I ignored *him* during the meeting.

Pronouns are tricky in these case changes because they force you to make choices based on grammatical roles. If you have studied a foreign language, you know that some languages are much more demanding than English in this respect. Adjectives and nouns in Russian, for instance, have different word endings that show case roles. In Spanish, possessive pronouns must agree in gender and number with the nouns they modify. The case system in English once included a complex set of word endings for nouns, but most of these distinctions are now lost. Pronouns, however, continue to carry case distinctions.

When a pronoun works as the subject of a sentence, it must be in its subject form; when it is an object, it must be in its object form. We can see both forms in the following sentences:

s   **o**
She kissed *her*.

s   **o**
They discovered *them* in a little-used file drawer.

These are straightforward sentences in the S-V-O pattern. Notice in each example that the object form is used when the pronoun receives the action, but the subject form is used when the pronoun is the acting subject of the sentence.

English grammar recognizes several sorts of objects. We have primarily been concerned with objects of the verb, but prepositions also take objects:

s   **o**
They brought the reports to *him*.

s   **o**
They struck a deal with *me*.

Another common sentence type contains two objects: a **direct object** and an **indirect object:**

s   **IO**   **DO**
He offered *me* an apology.

s   **IO**   **DO**
He gave *her* a fine evaluation.

In this construction, the direct object tells *what* received the action and the indirect object tells *who* received the action. To choose the correct form of a pronoun, you need to recognize when the pronoun is on the receiving end—whether it is a direct object, an indirect object, or an object of a preposition—and so must be in the object case. When a pronoun stands for the one doing the action, it is in the subject case.

Linking Sentences

People often choose the wrong form of the pronoun in **linking sentences,** which are built around some form of the verb *to be* or another verb that suggests existence but not action. Since there is no action in the verb, there cannot be a direct object. (Without action, nothing can receive the action.) The following linking sentences show the correct pronoun choice:

> It is *I.*
>
> It was *he* who left the package.
>
> This is *she*.

The pronouns after the linking verb are in subject form. They are subject complements, essentially identical to the subject. They are not acted upon and cannot be considered objects. These sentences sound a little "funny" to many speakers. The S-V-O pattern is strong, so speakers expect what comes after the verb to be an object (and thus be in the objective case, not the subjective case). If you like informal English, you will say *It's me* rather than *It is I*. We don't want to make too much of this distinction. Such constructions are primarily spoken rather than written, and a lot of people wouldn't notice if you make a mistake. But it is the sort of thing careful language users sometimes worry about.

Common Problems with Personal Pronouns

One interesting thing about case in English is that, while pronouns are marked for subject and object roles in a sentence, nouns are not. Compare the following sentences:

> s   s
> *Art Winkelman* and *I* are collaborating on the report.

> o   o
> Please send any comments to either *Art* or *me*.

The noun *Art* doesn't change form to reflect its role in a sentence. But what happens if you replace *Art* with the appropriate pronouns in the above sentences? Does the form change from sentence to sentence?

> *He* and I are collaborating on the report. Please send any comments to either *him* or me.

Most of the time, you probably don't have any problem picking correct pronoun forms, especially in simple constructions. But when pronouns are part of compound phrases, they often give people trouble. In sentences like the ones above, you can always drop one part of the compound phrase and make your choice. If you are not sure whether to write *Art and me* or *Art and I,* try dropping *Art* and your decision will usually be easy.

If you have problems with this construction, it is probably because you listened to your mother when she told you to say *Bill and **I** want to go to the movie,* not ***me** and Bill.* And so you learned to use *I* in any compound construction, whether the pronoun really was in subject position or not. This is common in language use, a form of **hypercorrection** that occurs when people learn a rule and then apply it where it doesn't belong.

Another common confusion about personal pronouns is the use of the reflexive pronouns (*myself, yourself,* etc.). Reflexive pronouns are not the more "polite" form of object pronouns, any more than subject forms are more "formal" or "polite" sounding. Instead, reflexives have a very precisely defined usage: when the subject of the verb acts upon itself, as in the following:

I wrote *myself* a note to edit the last section of the report.

Notice that in this example, the subject is *I,* and the subject acts upon itself, so the pronoun form is *myself.* That is the only time you need to use reflexive pronouns. Such is not the case in this example:

WRONG: When your weekly timesheets will be late, please notify *myself* at least three days in advance.

CORRECT: When your weekly timesheets will be late, please notify *me* at least three days in advance.

Using reflexive pronouns as a more "polite" subject or object pronoun is another example of hypercorrection.

The following exercise should help focus your attention on commonly troublesome phrases.

EXERCISE 8-1

For each example, first determine whether the pronoun role is subject or object, and then choose the appropriate pronoun case.

1. Sharon and (*I* or *me*) gave instructions to the new employees.

2. The new employees first told Bill and (*I* or *me*) what area they desired for their first assignments.

3. George forwarded the requests to (*she* or *her*).

4. Patti told the employees to deliver their personnel forms to either Becky or (*I* or *me*) in the front office.

5. (*She* or *her*) and Bill then reviewed procedures for completing the health insurance applications.

6. Just between you and (*I* or *me*), I don't think there will be any problems.

7. The suit forced Jenkins and (*he* or *him*) to redefine the corporation's limits of responsibility.

8. Mary asked Bill and (*me* or *myself*) to stay late to finish our work.

9. Invited to the company party were Betsy and (*I* or *me* or *myself*).

The Special Case of *Who* and *Whom*

Some writers make a careful distinction between *who* and *whom* based on the distinction between the subject form (*who*) and the object form (*whom*). The choice is based on the same principle you applied in Exercise 8-1. If the pronoun is the subject of its clause, use the subject form:

> *Who* delivered the parts?
> I will reward the one *who* sells the most cars.

Notice in each example sentence that *who* is the one doing the delivering and selling: *who* is the subject of each clause and therefore it takes its subject form.

If the pronoun is in an object position, choose the object form:

> To *whom* do you wish to speak?
> *Whom* did he reprimand?

Don't be fooled by the position of the word in these examples. You rightly expect to see subjects up-front. But questions always change around the normal word order so what comes up front in a question isn't necessarily the subject. If you rephrase these questions as statements, *whom* is clearly in object position:

> You wish to speak to *whom*? (object of preposition)
> He reprimanded *whom*? (direct object of verb)

It is worth noting that the distinction between *who* and *whom* is dropping out of the language, especially the spoken language—though more slowly than anyone might expect. In the process, the word *who* is taking over the functions of *whom*. If you enjoy being perfectly correct, you should choose to learn and maintain the distinction in your speech and writing. But be careful. Some people half learn the distinction and use *whom* where it doesn't belong because they think it sounds more formal. Be perfectly correct if you want to but don't be hypercorrect. If you want to go with the flow of the language, forget *whom* and use *who* in all spoken situations. Only the purists will correct you, and you can explain that you have on your side the gradual changes that shape language. Most people don't notice the use of *who* where *whom* is called for, but they do notice the incorrect use of *whom*.

Writing, however, tends to be more formal than speaking, so you would be wise to maintain the distinction more carefully in your formal written documents. Situations where you find yourself choosing *who* versus *whom* in written documents are, thankfully, somewhat infrequent.

EXERCISE 8-2

Choose the right form in these examples by distinguishing subject from object roles.

1. (Who or Whom) gave you those beautiful flowers?

2. (To who or To whom) do I owe thanks?

3. I wonder (who or whom) has the answer.

4. Francis will give the tickets to (whoever or whomever) wants to go to the opera.

5. (Who or Whom) did you offend?

Possession

In addition to subject and object forms, each pronoun has a **possessive** form. You know that nouns typically signal possession by the addition of *'s* or *s'* (*John's report; the employees' report*). Pronouns, too, have special forms that indicate **possession:**

I gave *my* section of the report to Art.

I got *Art's* section to read at the same time.

Unlike nouns, however, pronouns do *not* signal possession by the addition of *'s* or *s'*. None of the possessive pronouns in Figure 8.1 (*my, our, your, his, her, its, their*) has an apostrophe in it.

Some writers have trouble distinguishing between possessive pronouns and pronouns in **contracted** forms. Compare the forms in Figure 8.2. One source of confusion may be the asymmetrical use of the apostrophe (') in possessive and contracted forms for nouns and for pronouns: nouns use apostrophes for both possessive and contracted forms; pronouns use apostrophes only for contraction. An additional source of confusion is that certain of these pronoun forms sound alike: *your* and *you're, its* and *it's, their* and *they're, whose* and *who's*.

If you're one of those writers who tends to confuse possessive and contracted pronoun forms, here's a rule of thumb that may help: Any time you use a pronoun with an apostrophe, you should be able to paraphrase it with its uncontracted form, as follows:

It's a nice day outside.

can be paraphrased as:

It is a nice day outside.

Figure 8.2 *Possessive and Contracted Pronouns*

	SINGULAR	**PLURAL**
FIRST PERSON		
POSSESSIVE	my	our
CONTRACTION	I'm	we're
SECOND PERSON		
POSSESSIVE	your	your
CONTRACTION	you're	you're
THIRD PERSON		
POSSESSIVE	his, her, its	their
CONTRACTION	he's, she's, it's	they're
INTERROGATIVE/ RELATIVE		
POSSESSIVE	whose	whose
CONTRACTION	who's	who're

But that won't work for:

WRONG: Make sure the machine is properly placed on it's stand.

so that sentence should be written as:

Make sure the machine is properly placed on *its* stand.

Figure 8.2 shows possessive and contracted forms for the various pronouns.

EXERCISE 8-3

1. Write a sentence that uses *its* and *it's* in the same sentence.

2. Write a sentence that uses *who's* and *whose* in the same sentence.

3. Write a sentence that uses both *your* and *you're* in the same sentence.

4. Write a sentence that uses *their, they're,* and *there* in the same sentence.

Agreement of Number, Person, and Gender

Like nouns, pronouns carry number; that is, they can be singular or plural. In Figure 8.1, the middle column contains the singular forms; the right-hand column contains the plural forms. If a pronoun's antecedent is a plural noun, the pronoun itself must be plural. In other words, the two words must agree in number.

Unlike nouns, pronouns also carry person. English has three persons:

FIRST PERSON: the one or ones speaking (*I* or *we*)

SECOND PERSON: the one or ones spoken to (*you*)

THIRD PERSON: the one or ones spoken about (*he, she, they*)

These distinctions among persons help establish and maintain interpersonal roles in writing, whether the writer is referring to self (*I* or *we*), referring directly to the reader or listener (*you*), or referring to someone or something else (*he, she, it, they*). When you write, you are often faced with the decision whether to represent yourself as an individual (*I*), as a group or company (*we*), or in the third person (*the author, the company*).

Notice that number and person are closely tied. You can't make a choice of form from Figure 8.1 without choosing both person and number at the same time. And if you choose from the third-person, singular pronouns, you are also forced to make a choice of **gender:** masculine, feminine, or neuter. Once you make choices, it is your job to be consistent both within sentences and throughout a whole piece of writing.

In Chapter 13, "Clear Reference," we offer advice about using pronoun reference across sentences and throughout whole texts. Pronouns are a powerful tool for creating smooth-flowing, well-connected text. Pronouns also play a large role in how personal your writing feels to readers, how closely involved they feel with the language on the page. Later, we will discuss questions about when to project personality in writing through referring to yourself and your readers (Chapter 20, "Projecting Personality"). Here, though, we want to focus on pronoun errors associated with the choices offered by the system of person.

Singular versus Plural Pronouns

Making sure that singular pronoun subjects agree with singular verb forms is not too difficult for the personal pronouns. But the indefinite pronoun forms cause a lot of problems. In English, many of the indefinite pronouns are considered singular. (See Figure 8.3.) You are not alone if certain singular indefinite pronouns feel plural to you: perhaps *anybody* or *everybody, everyone* or *either.* But to be correct, these pronouns must be treated as singular:

Each of the struts *displays* cracks at the interior angle.

but

Few of the struts *display* cracks at the interior angle.

Similarly, *everybody* is treated as singular in this example:

Everybody needs to file weekly progress reports.

But the word *some* is treated as plural:

Some need to update their quarterly progress reports.

You need to maintain consistency in both person and number among pronouns, verbs, and their antecedents. You especially need to pay attention to the person and number of the subject construction so that you can choose the correct verb form. In the above example, the word *Each* in *Each of the struts* is the head word of the subject construction. Don't

Figure 8.3 *Indefinite Pronouns*

SINGULAR	PLURAL
each	most
either	all
neither	few
anyone	many
anybody	several
everybody	some
everyone	both
no one	
nobody	
somebody	
someone	
something	

allow yourself to be misled by the intervening plural modifier of the subject—the prepositional phrase *of the struts.*

Like the distinction between *who* and *whom,* the treatment of indefinite pronouns as singular is falling away from the language. Especially in speech, it is common to hear such constructions as the following:

Everyone should take their time cards to the office.

Each client deserves to have their interests respected during negotiations.

Notice the inconsistency here: the subject takes a singular verb form (ending in *-s*) but a plural referent *their.* Similar constructions can be found in the writing of well-educated professionals. So it is not a simple matter to say *X* is correct, but *Y* is an error. To some careful writers, singular indefinite pronouns demand singular reference. Other writers argue that the language is changing; they see little point in wasting time defending a usage that is frequently contradicted in speech and writing.

Gender Distinctions

Notice that only one cell in all of Figure 8.1 contains pronouns that reflect gender: the third-person, singular pronouns. Notice, too, a gap in the system that writers must struggle with repeatedly: there is simply no form to indicate a singular pronoun reference of unknown gender.

You have no doubt noticed the problems caused by having to choose among masculine, feminine, and neuter singular pronouns. Which of the following constructions do you favor?

Each employee must submit his time card on a weekly basis.

Each employee must submit his or her time card on a weekly basis.

Each employee must submit their time card on a weekly basis.

Employees must submit their time cards on a weekly basis.

The first example will annoy many readers who object to sexist usage, and the third example will annoy many who consider it ungrammatical to refer to a singular subject with a plural pronoun.

It is a rule in English (as in many other languages) that pronouns must be the same gender as the person or thing they refer to. In other words, pronouns must agree in gender with their antecedents, as in the following sentences:

Jane Adams, the manager of the personnel department, has been with the company for six years.

She has shown remarkable skill in navigating the department through the company's rapid expansion in size.

The problem arises when we want to refer to an indefinite someone— some one person of unstated gender. Traditionally, English speakers have used the masculine, singular pronouns (*he, him,* or *his*) for so-called "generic" references. Thus, in the past, most writers would have preferred the first alternative above:

Each employee must submit his time card on a weekly basis.

These writers might say that they know that an employee can be either male or female but that the pronoun *his* should be taken to refer, indiscriminately, to either sex. And some style guides still offer this line of reasoning to defend the use of generic reference.

However, with everyone's increased sensitivity to sexism in the workplace, a writer can no longer presume that *he* or *his* refers to both men and women. In place of this generic *he,* careful writers now find alternatives that do not carry the implication of bias.

You need a red flag that pops up in your mind each time you are tempted toward sexist pronoun use. English offers various ways to rewrite sentences to eliminate gender bias, so you are never really forced to choose sexist usage. Note how each of the following sentences is rewritten to eliminate the bias:

Sexist usage: Every person has a right to represent himself in a court of law.

Nonsexist usage: Every person has a right to self-representation in a court of law.

Sexist usage: Nobody should have to keep his opinion a secret during these deliberations.

Nonsexist usage: Nobody should have to keep an opinion secret during these deliberations.

Sexist usage: The average employee worries about his yearly evaluation.

Nonsexist usage: The average employee worries about yearly evaluation.

Sexist usage: Anybody who plans to work overtime should report to his supervisor beforehand.

Nonsexist usage: If you plan to work overtime, report to your supervisor beforehand.

Sexist usage: A nurse has to rely on her best judgment during emergencies.

Nonsexist usage: Nurses have to rely on their best judgment during emergencies.

These examples suggest several strategies for avoiding sexist usage. Sometimes you can simply drop the reference, sometimes recast the sentence in plural form, sometimes change to second person, and sometimes do some creative rephrasing. You have probably noticed that some writers alternate, using a feminine reference in one situation and a masculine one in the next. The fact is, though, that readers notice such strategies, and it is usually best if readers concentrate on the message and not the grammar of a text.

Consider it a personal challenge to eliminate sexist usage from your writing and speech. When you are good at it, your readers will pay attention to what you say rather than get hung up on how you say it.

While we are on the subject, sexism creeps into language in ways other than through the pronoun system, though that is where it tends to be most obvious. Sexism is also part of the general vocabulary—*chairman, businessman, stewardess, mankind, the common man.* Sometimes cultural stereotypes show up in unexamined assumptions that phrasing reveals:

Do you have a gal who could type this?

That's a man-sized job.

Employees and their wives are welcome to attend the banquet.

She's a career girl with high aspirations.

All of these sentences carry bias that writers should notice and avoid. Do you have a feeling for where these examples suggest bias? Can you offer other examples of language that carries a gender bias?

EXERCISE 8 - 4

Some of the following sentences mix singular pronouns with plural antecedents, or *vice versa*. Others mix singular subjects and plural verbs, or *vice versa*. A few have sexist usage. And just to make sure you don't fall asleep, some are perfectly correct as they stand. Correct the errors of pronoun agreement.

1. Each of the new employees want to contribute to the quality circle.

2. Everyone needs to take their lunch break between 11 A.M. and 1 P.M.

3. Neither the boss nor the employees know how to correct the problem.

4. If an employee is unhappy about having to take a drug test, he can always find work elsewhere.

5. Considering the expense, I think neither the first alternative nor the second is disastrous.

6. The recording secretary on each committee should follow the standard form and submit the minutes at the next meeting, with her initials affixed.

7. One of the comptrollers needs to offer his ideas on streamlining the procedures.

8. The cleaning ladies offered the chairman of the environmental oversight committee a number of useful suggestions for storing and handling toxic substances.

9. The practice run had so many errors that the director issued new procedures and demanded that every technician follow it.

10. If either the final approval or the test results is late, we will probably be off our target date by at least a month.

In Summary

This chapter has covered a lot of ground because pronouns probably cause more problems than other parts of speech. You should now have the language to talk about pronoun problems: person, number, gender, possession, antecedent, and case. You should also have some decision-making strategies for using pronouns correctly. For example, you should be able to choose between *who* and *whom* or *he* and *him* on the basis of whether a word is in subject or object position. You should also know that indefinite pronouns—like *anyone* and *everyone*—are treated as singular and take singular antecedents. And you should be more aware of how sexism creeps into language.

Pronoun usage offers a good opportunity to understand why people have trouble with grammar. The pronoun system in English is not quite regular, and it preserves some distinctions that have been lost in other parts of speech. People make mistakes for good reasons, and you can take some pleasure in observing how other speakers and writers handle the inevitable mistakes that arise as they make choices within an imperfect system.

Putting It All Together

The following exercise asks you to identify and correct a variety of grammatical errors—fragments and run-on sentences, inconsistent or misplaced modifiers, verb tense and agreement errors, and errors in pronoun usage. As you edit these minutes, also be on the alert for the use of sexist language.

TO: All Employees

FROM: George Mason, Secretary

            Committee on Plant Safety

SUBJECT: Minutes of Committee on Plant Safety Meeting

DATE: June 23, 1996

The Committee on Plant Safety met on June 11, 1996. To plan their annual awards and to select they're chairman and recording secretary for the coming year.

Two employees of the company for helping Sterling Industries achieve their safest year since 1988 was selected for recognition.

Each of the employees will be awarded a plaque and a $50 bond for there contributions. Betty Sandoval, of the Highlands manufacturing unit, will receive an award for a suggestion of her's that a system of signal lights be installed on the assembly line to regulate the flow of materials, Betty's newly installed system of signal lights give the loader's an advanced warning when backups are about to occur.

Mr. Tom Rollins, of the Health Center, will receive recognition for his self-initiated campaign to reduce smoking in the workplace. Under Mr. Rollins plan, every employee can now request that his immediate work area be smoke free. An employee can only still smoke on their breaks in specially designated areas. Working patiently for two years to see these new guidelines through the Committee, the new plan was a real contribution to everybodies health.

The Committee elected Ms. Nancy Stoner as incoming chairman, Neil Argonne was elected as secretary. The Committee wishes both she and he a productive year.

The meeting was adjourned at 10:30 A.M. The next meeting being scheduled for August 15 at 10:00 A.M. Neil noted that anyone with an agenda item should submit them by August 7.

EXERCISE ANSWERS

Exercise 8-1 Answers

The correct pronoun choices are *italicized*.

1. Sharon and *I* gave instructions to the new employees.
2. The new employees first told Bill and *me* what area they desired for their first assignments.
3. George forwarded the requests to *her*.
4. Patti told the employees to deliver their personnel forms to either Becky or *me* in the front office.

5. *She* and Bill then reviewed procedures for completing the health insurance applications.

or

Bill and *she*...

6. Just between you and *me*, I don't think there will be any problems.

7. The suit forced Jenkins and *him* to redefine the corporation's limits of responsibility.

8. Mary asked Bill and *me* to stay late to finish our work.

9. Invited to the company party were Betsy and *I*.

Exercise 8-2 Answers

The following pronouns correctly match their subject/object roles.

1. *Who* gave you those beautiful flowers?

2. *To whom* do I owe thanks?

3. I wonder *who* has the answer.

4. Francis will give the tickets to *whoever* wants to go to the opera. (This is a really tricky one. *Whoever* is the object of the preposition *to* but also the subject of its clause. Grammarians tell us that its role as subject of its clause takes precedence.)

5. *Whom* did you offend?

Exercise 8-3 Answers

Answers will vary by individual. You might compare your answers to those of others.

Exercise 8-4 Answers

Errors of agreement and sexist usage have been removed from the following sentences.

1. Each of the new employees *wants* to contribute to the quality circle.

2. Everyone needs to take a lunch break between 11 A.M. and 1 P.M.

3. Neither the boss nor the employees know how to correct the problem. (This is acceptable as it stands, with the plural form *know*, since *employees* is the noun closer to the verb *know*.)

4. An employee who is unhappy about having to take a drug test can always find work elsewhere.

5. Considering the expense, I think neither the first alternative nor the second is disastrous.

(No error; the *neither/nor* correlative construction with two singular phrases takes the singular verb form *is*.)

6. The recording secretary on each committee should follow the standard form, initial the minutes, and submit them at the next meeting.

7. One of the comptrollers needs to offer *some* ideas on streamlining the procedures.

8. The *cleaning staff* offered the *chair* of the environmental oversight committee a number of useful suggestions for storing and handling toxic substances.

9. The practice run had so many errors that the director issued new procedures and demanded that every technician follow *them*.

10. If either the final approval or the test results *are* late, we will probably be off our target date by at least a month.

Putting It All Together Answers

Corrections are marked on the minutes.

TO:	All Employees
FROM:	George Mason, Secretary
	Committee on Plant Safety
SUBJECT:	Minutes of Committee on Plant Safety Meeting
DATE:	June 23, 1996

The Committee on Plant Safety met on June 11, 1996~~. Tt~~to plan their annual awards and to select their~~y're~~ [or its] chair~~man~~ and recording secretary for the coming year.

Two employees of the company ~~for helping Sterling Industries achieve their safest year since 1988~~ were~~as~~ selected for recognition for helping Sterling Industries achieve its safest year since 1988. ~~Each of the~~Both employees will be awarded a plaque and a $50 bond for their~~re~~ contributions. Ms. Betty Sandoval, of the Highlands manufacturing unit, will receive an award for ~~a~~her suggestion~~of her's~~ that a system of signal lights be installed on the assembly line to regulate the flow of materials~~.;~~ ~~Betty's~~Ms. Sandoval's newly installed system of signal lights gives the loader~~'~~s an advanced warning when backups are about to occur.

Mr. Tom Rollins, of the Health Center, will receive recognition for his self-initiated campaign to reduce smoking in the workplace. Under Mr. Rollins' plan, every employee can now request that his or her immediate work area be smoke free. An employee can ~~only~~still smoke on ~~their~~breaks, but only in specially designated areas. Mr. Rollins ~~W~~worked~~ing~~ patiently for two years to see these new guidelines through the Committee~~;;~~ the new plan wa~~i~~s a real contribution to everybody's~~ies~~ health.

The Committee elected Ms. Nancy Stoner as incoming chair~~man,~~ and Mr. Neil Argonne ~~was elected~~as secretary. The Committee wishes both ~~she and he~~ a productive year.

The meeting was adjourned at 10:30 A.M. with ~~T~~the next meeting ~~being~~scheduled for August 15 at 10:00 A.M. ~~Neil~~Mr. Argonne noted that anyone with ~~an~~agenda items should submit them by August 7.

"Professional writing uses punctuation to show what *is*— and what is *not*— important."

Punctuation does in writing what people do with their voices in speaking. When we speak, we signal lots of information about our message to our listeners by varying the pitch and volume of our voice, as well as by pausing between units of speech. Because we cannot be everywhere to read our texts aloud to various readers, we use punctuation to provide the same signals. Punctuation tells readers where to pause and for how long, where to raise their voice pitch and where to lower it, where to get louder and where to get softer.

This perspective on punctuation often makes more sense to people than the hundreds of confusing rules most of us learned in school, so Unit 3 is arranged according to this perspective. We start first with those punctuation marks that show where to pause and for how long: Chapter 9 deals with commas, which indicate the shortest degree of pause. Chapter 10 deals with punctuation marks of medium pause: semicolons and colons. Chapter 11 deals with hyphens, which indicate where *not* to pause between groups of words because they work as a unit. Finally, Chapter 12 deals with those marks of punctuation (dashes and parentheses) that signal where to lower voice pitch and volume in communicating extra information.

In this unit, we cross the boundary from correct usage to effective style. Some punctuation choices (as you read in Chapter 5, "Sentence Completeness") are clearly about correct versus incorrect usage. And as you will note—especially in Chapters 9 and 10—punctuation is a clue to the grammatical structure of a sentence, indicating how the various clauses and phrases are tied together. But many punctuation choices are about signaling your meaning most effectively and completely to your reader. Ineffective choices will slow the reader down and confuse him or her; effective choices, in contrast, will make the meaning of your message so clear that the reader may never even be aware of the punctuation choices you have made.

chapter 9

Commas

This chapter shows how **commas** can help your reader easily recognize what information is important and what is secondary. In this chapter, you will learn four guiding principles for placing commas:

1. Use a comma to set off an introductory dependent clause or phrase from an independent clause.
2. Use a comma with a coordinating conjunction to separate compound independent clauses.
3. Use a pair of commas to set off interrupting modifiers (or a single comma when the modifiers come at the end of a sentence).
4. Use a comma to separate items in a series.

These four principles for using commas can be presented in the following sentence patterns:

1. [Introductory Dependent Clause or Phrase], [Independent Clause].
2. [Independent Clause], [Coordinating Conjunction] [Independent Clause].
3. [Part of a Clause], [Interrupting Modifier], [Rest of the Clause].
   or
   [Independent Clause], [Interrupting Modifier].
4. [Item 1], [Item 2], and [Item 3]

You should also use a comma to avoid situations where readers are likely to "go down the wrong path" as they read a sentence. In such instances, a comma can show readers what goes with what, and they will not be forced to backtrack to establish the appropriate reading.

If you follow these general principles, you will control most of the uses of commas that careful writers observe. Additionally, you will help your readers to follow your sense and to appreciate your emphasis.

Conventional Commas

Commas are governed by a number of conventional uses—for example, with dates, with addresses, and with numerals. Many of these conventions are matters of house rules, so you should consult your organization's style book.

To take one example, it is impossible to generalize about the use of commas or even about the order of elements in a date, especially given the difference between practice in the United States (month/day/year) and practice in the rest of the world (day/month/year). Traditional usage in the United States writes out the name of the month and requires a comma between the day and the year. A second comma is required after the year when the date is embedded in a sentence, but current usage tends to do without one or both of these commas. Similarly, some writers are now dropping all commas in addresses, a change encouraged by the United States Postal Service in its rules for machine-readable addresses.

Some current language users seem intent on streamlining their writing by dropping commas everywhere. When practice is changing, the best you can do is to observe usage around you; look at the correspondence of careful writers in your organization and follow the recommendations of your style manual.

There are, however, some comma usages that are not matters of house rules but rather matters of grammar. The comma guidelines discussed in this chapter are based on sentence structure. Each guideline helps a reader figure out how to read sentences. These guidelines are stable, useful, and worth knowing.

Commas with Introductory Elements

When a dependent clause or a long modifying phrase begins a sentence, usage demands a comma between the introductory element and the independent clause (as in this sentence):

> When a dependent clause or a long modifying phrase begins a sentence, usage demands a comma between the introductory element and the independent clause.

Notice how the comma marks the start of the main part of the sentence and signals to the reader that the subject construction follows. Recall that the subject establishes the theme or focus of the sentence—what the sentence is about. As they read, readers need to establish in their minds the subject-predicate construction, the base of the sentence. Marking the beginning of the independent clause helps the reader locate the subject, determine the focus, and thereby process the sentence.

Notice how the comma after the introductory element in each of these examples helps you locate the subject of the sentence—what the sentence is about:

> After purchase by the Portfolio, the rating of an issue of municipal securities may cease to be a determining factor in buy/hold decisions.

> If an issuer, bank, or dealer should default on its obligation to repurchase an underlying security, the Portfolio might be unable to recover all or a portion of any loss sustained from having to sell the security elsewhere.

> Although the Portfolio does not currently intend to do so on a regular basis, it may invest more than 25 percent of its assets in Municipal Securities that are repayable out of revenue streams generated by the Portfolio's investment adviser.

> Under normal market conditions, at least 80 percent of the Portfolio's total assets will be invested in obligations issued by or on behalf of states, territories, and possessions of the United States.

If you read these examples aloud, you will hear the natural pause at the comma. In each example, the comma cues the reader to notice the subject—who or what is doing the acting. You should also notice that the introductory information beginning each sentence could be deleted. You would still have a complete sentence in each case, even without the introductory modification.

The rule about following an introductory element with a comma is tempered somewhat by the length of the introductory element. In the last example above, *Under normal market conditions* is fairly short, so the comma might be omitted. You won't be wrong in such a case if you use a comma; and you might argue that, even with short phrases, the comma helps the reader figure out the sentence structure.

The corollary to this rule is that when dependent clauses or modifying phrases come at the end of a sentence, the comma is unnecessary but optional, as in the following example:

> Such securities will appreciate in value when interest rates rise but will decrease in value when interest rates decline.

In this example, neither of the dependent clauses beginning with *when* takes a comma. Commas here would interrupt the flow of the sentence and interfere with the reading. Since the sentence begins with the subject, a comma cannot signal the beginning of the independent clause. Likewise, you would probably not choose to place a comma before the final *because* phrase in this example:

> The Portfolios' investments are considered to be the safest available because of their short maturities and high quality ratings.

Nor would you use a comma in this example before the long final phrase beginning with *in:*

> Such notes are issued with a short-term maturity in anticipation of the receipt of tax payments or other revenues.

Try turning either of these last two examples around, however, and you will need a comma to set off the modifying element that is now introductory:

> Because of their short maturities and high quality ratings, the Portfolio's investments are considered to be the safest available.
>
> In anticipation of the receipt of tax payments or other revenues, such notes are issued with a short-term maturity.

Sentences with introductory clauses or phrases are very common and stylistically useful. They let you put background or modifying information in a subordinate slot at the beginning of a sentence, allowing you to direct the reader's focus to the more important information in the independent clause. If you recognize the structure and use commas, you can avoid a frequent mistake in comma usage while helping your reader to read more efficiently.

EXERCISE 9-1

Place commas in the following sentences where required to set off introductory modification.

1. If you want to protect yourself against steep declines in the stock market you should invest 20 to 30 percent of your money in government-issued bonds.

2. Because the value of bonds tends to increase during periods of inflation they can counter the effects of falling stock portfolios.

3. Trading in futures has proven risky because of the unpredictability of foreign markets.

4. While a few investors prefer to make all investment decisions many others are happy to have the mutual-fund managers decide on the best strategies.

5. Some of the more desirable mutual funds represent particularly good investments since they do not impose a front-end load and do not have high management fees.

Commas with Compound Clauses

In the discussion of run-on sentences in Chapter 5, you saw how two independent clauses can be punctuated with a semicolon:

> The minimum initial investment is $1,000; the minimum subsequent investment is $100.

Either of these two clauses could stand alone as a sentence, but they are so closely related that you might choose to connect them with a semicolon. An alternative would be to join them with a coordinating conjunction, such as *and* or *but:*

> The minimum initial investment is $1,000, and the minimum subsequent investment is $100.

or

> The minimum initial investment is $1,000, but the minimum subsequent investment is $100.

Other coordinating conjunctions include *or, yet, for,* and *so.* (An easy way to remember all the coordinating conjunctions is with the acronym *FANBOYS: For, And, Nor, But, Or, Yet, So.*) Coordinating conjunctions can tie together any two equivalent grammatical elements (words, phrases, clauses). In this case, the coordinating conjunctions are tying together two independent clauses. The comma and its coordinating conjunction act as a fulcrum between two independent clauses, a balance point in the sentence between equal parts. That's why the conjunctions are called *coordinating:* they coordinate two equal parts.

Notice that the comma comes before the conjunction, not after. Don't be tempted to bracket the conjunction with commas:

WRONG: A Portfolio may borrow money as a temporary measure for extraordinary or emergency purchases, but, no Portfolio will borrow for leverage purposes.

You should not use a second comma after *but*. Learn to resist using pairs of commas to surround similar connectives, like *yet, so, but,* or *and.* Sometimes, you can get away with a coordinating conjunction and no comma when the two clauses are very short:

Bonds are going up and stocks are going down.

Even here, however, conservative usage would call for a comma.

A few handbooks suggest that when both independent clauses are short, it is permissible to punctuate the sentence with only a comma and no coordinating conjunction:

The minimum initial investment is $1,000, the minimum subsequent investment is $100.

However, if you punctuate such sentences with only a comma and no coordinating conjunction, you risk creating a run-on sentence (or at least the impression of a run-on). (See Chapter 5, "Sentence Completeness.") Your reader won't know if you are being daring or if you are simply ignorant of the difference between a run-on sentence and a correctly punctuated compound sentence. It is probably best to avoid taking such chances when writing in work situations.

Here are several other examples of compound sentences:

Trading of such commercial paper is conducted primarily by institutional investors through investment dealers, *and* individual investor participation in the commercial market is very limited.

The Portfolio will only make commitments to purchase Municipal Securities on a when-issued or delayed-delivery basis with the intention of actually acquiring the securities, *but* the Portfolio reserves the right to sell these securities before the settlement date if deemed advisable.

The laws of several states and local taxing authorities vary with respect to the taxation of such income, *and* each shareholder is advised to consult a tax adviser as to the status of the account under state and local tax laws.

Remember that in all of the examples in this section, the comma and the coordinating conjunction join two independent clauses (groups of words with connected subjects and predicates in each clause). Don't be misled by a sentence such as this:

> The Tax-Exempt Portfolio intends to continue to qualify under the Internal Revenue Code as a regulated investment company and will not be liable for federal income taxes to the extent its earnings are distributed.

Don't put a comma before the *and*. What follows *and* is not an independent clause. It is the second half of a compound predicate construction, revealed here when we strip the sentence to its base clause:

> The Portfolio intends to continue and will not be liable.

You should not separate two parts of a compound predicate with a comma. If you have sentences with very long compound predicates, you probably should consider breaking up the sentence rather than using commas to try to keep the reader on track.

One final note concerns style, not correct usage. Many writers overuse *and* when relations of ideas might be better indicated by other coordinating conjunctions or subordinating conjunctions. Stringing together sentences with *and* is easy, but not particularly effective, especially when more than one *and* is working at more than one level in a sentence (coordinating clauses on the one hand and phrases on the other). Too many *and*s should tip you off to look for the underlying relations and to rephrase the sentence with subordinating conjunctions such as *because, since, if,* or *whenever.* (Chapter 21, "Managing Sentence Emphasis," shows how to subordinate less important ideas.)

EXERCISE 9-2

Place commas where necessary in the following sentences to balance two coordinate independent clauses.

1. The price/earnings ratio is only fair but the price per share is bound to go up in the next few months.

2. It is a risky strategy to speculate on new computer manufacturing businesses yet there has never been any shortage of people willing to take a chance on the potentially large profits.

3. The money you pay as an up-front load on your investment will never increase your earnings and the portion of the earnings your fund takes for management expenses will never go into your pocket.

4. In general, most advisers will tell you to look for a no-load fund and to be wary of funds with high management fees.

Commas with Parenthetical Modifiers

When modifying elements interrupt a clause, use a pair of commas to set off the interrupting, or **parenthetical,** elements. Notice how the modifying phrase in this example interrupts the subject and predicate:

> A security purchased on a when-issued basis, like all securities held by the Tax-Exempt Portfolio, is subject to changes in market value.

Similarly, comments that are interjected, qualifying phrases, or other parenthetical interruptions should be set off with commas. Here again, your voice should tip you off: When you read such phrases, your intonation dips down, showing that the element is not an essential part of the clause.

Read each of the following sentences aloud, exaggerating the drop in your voice that signals parenthetical intonation:

> Checks will be mailed monthly, within five business days of the reinvestment date, to you or any person you designate. (Notice the interruption of *Checks will be mailed monthly to you.*)
>
> Certain miscellaneous deductions, such as investment expenses, tax-preparation fees, and employee business expenses, will be deductible by individuals only to the extent they exceed 2 percent of adjusted gross income. (Notice the split of the subject *deductions* from the verb *will be deductible.*)
>
> A Portfolio will not purchase illiquid securities, including time deposits and repurchase agreements, if, as a result thereof, more than 10 percent of such Portfolio's asset would be invested in such securities.
>
> The Fund will, however, hold special meetings as required for such purposes as electing trustees.

In each example, the parenthetical elements that are set off by commas could be deleted without changing the meaning of the sentence. The modifiers interrupt the sentence to add minor details and elaborations, but they do not form part of the base clause.

Commas with End-of-Sentence Modification

English allows modifiers to move rather freely about the sentence. When modifying phrases are attached loosely to the end of a sentence, they are called **loose** or **cumulative,** as in the following example:

> Brokerage houses offer the advantage of access to libraries of current information, a useful convenience, especially considering the expense of some newsletters and trading reports.

Notice how the modifying phrases are simply appended, loosely attached, not really part of the base clause. The modification is clearly parenthetical since it could be deleted without disrupting the meaning of the sentence. Your voice will tip you off to the need for commas to set off such loose modification. Here are other examples of loose modification at the ends of sentences:

> Military buildups and the threat of war always give investors the jitters, a feeling that anything might happen.
>
> True balance in a portfolio protects an investor over the long term, offering security from short-term ups and downs.
>
> Many new investors approach their brokers with extreme anxiety, nervously fingering their clothing, hoping not to embarrass themselves.

Sentences like the last one suggest the writer is casually adding detail to detail. If your intention is to appear logical and decisive, loose or cumulative modifiers are probably not a good idea. If your intention is to appear open to suggestion, as though you are still making a decision, such modification works well.

E X E R C I S E   9 - 3

Use commas in the following sentences to set off modification that parenthetically interrupts the flow of the sentence or that is loosely attached to the end of the sentence.

1. Some mutual funds especially those featuring overseas stocks or foreign currencies can provide attractive returns when investments in U.S. companies are not doing well.

2. It is not wise however to sink all investments in any particular type of fund.

3. Mutual funds on average have outperformed the Dow Jones average an indication of the expertise of the fund managers.

4. The prospectus for a fund always assures the reader that long-term earnings while not providing any guarantee do justify confidence in the fund's management strategies.

5. The fund claims a strong performance record over the past fifteen years an honest claim one based on substantial data.

No Commas with Restrictive Modification

Up to this point, we have been discussing modifiers that are not essential to a clause. Parenthetical or cumulative modifiers represent added details within a clause, details that can be included or omitted. Such modification—called *nonrestrictive*—can often be moved around, set off by commas or parentheses, or deleted. In contrast, a special sort of modification—called *restrictive*—is essential to the clause because it restricts the phrase it modifies:

> The Tax-Exempt Portfolio seeks the maximum current income that is exempt from federal income taxes.

In this example, the modifying clause *that is exempt from federal income taxes* limits or restricts the meaning of income. The Portfolio does not seek all income; it seeks only *income that is exempt from federal income taxes*. The modifying clause changes the meaning of *income* by restricting it; if the modifying clause were deleted in this example, the meaning of the sentence would change dramatically.

Such **restrictive modification** is essential to a sentence because it limits the meaning of the word or phrase it modifies. Unlike nonrestrictive (or parenthetical) modification, restrictive modification is *not* set off with commas. Doing so would change the meaning of a sentence.

Restrictive modifiers often take the form of the special sort of dependent clause known as a **relative clause.** Relative clauses modify nouns and begin with one of the relative pronouns *who, which,* or *that:*

> The book *that* is on the table is called *Fundamentals of Cost Accounting.*
>
> The tax adviser *who* is employed by H & R Block saw about fourteen clients each day.

The relative clauses beginning with *that* and *who* modify the nouns they follow. Notice that there is no pause before or after the relative clause because the whole phrase—headword plus modifier—works as a single unit of meaning.

Commas usefully signal whether relative clauses are restrictive or nonrestrictive. Let's look at a couple of simple examples to see why this is so. Compare these two sentences:

> Accountants who are careless don't last long in the business.
>
> Accountants, who are careless, don't last long in the business.

Which of these examples suggests that *all* accountants are careless? Which example suggests that only *some* accountants are careless? The sentence with restrictive modification (the first example) suggests that only some accountants don't last long, those *who are careless.* Notice how the modification restricts the whole group of accountants to only a subgroup. Restrictive modification shouldn't be set off with commas because doing so changes the meaning of the sentence (as in the second example).

Here's another example:

> My father, who was an accountant for TransUnion Corporation, testified during mileage-arbitration cases on international rail shipping.
>
> My father who was an accountant for TransUnion Corporation testified during mileage-arbitration cases on international rail shipping.

Which sentence suggests that the writer has more than one father? In all likelihood, the second sentence is punctuated incorrectly. The modification should be nonrestrictive and therefore take commas, unless the writer has more than one father.

Such apparently minor differences in punctuation can have important consequences. When the Republican National Committee was writing its platform in 1984, a draft version suggested that Republicans "oppose any attempts to increase taxes which would harm the recovery and reverse the trend to restoring control of the economy to individual Americans." Does this mean that Republicans oppose *any* attempts to increase taxes or only certain attempts? As it stands, they oppose only those tax increases *which would harm the economy.* Other taxes, apparently, would not be opposed. But that's not what they meant. Try putting commas around the modifier (actually only one comma, after *taxes,* since the sentence ends with the modifying phrase):

> Republicans oppose any attempts to increase taxes, which would harm the recovery and reverse the trend to restoring control of the economy to individual Americans.

The sentence now indicates that *any* attempts to increase taxes would harm the economy. With the comma, the modification is nonrestrictive, or parenthetical. Without a comma, the modification is restrictive. The difference is an important one, particularly in legal, scientific, or technical writing. The pause signaled by the comma also signals a subtle but important change in meaning.

Careful readers will have noticed another issue here. Traditional usage dictates the use of *that* for restrictive clauses and *which* for nonrestrictive, as in the following examples:

Taxes that place an undue burden on the poor and elderly have been eliminated in the reform measures.

Personal property taxes, which place the major burden on homeowners, are often used as a primary source of school funding.

Like many such distinctions, this one appears to be fading, with more and more writers simply using *which* in both instances. Careful writers and editors will continue to maintain a distinction between *that* and *which*. The commas remain important; omitting the punctuation in these examples changes the meaning. The lack of commas shows what is important or essential (the restrictive modification) and the use of commas sets off what is less important (the parenthetical, or nonrestrictive, modification).

A Note about Prepositional Phrases

One final note about restrictive modifiers: After reading this chapter, people sometimes have a tendency to be "comma crazy," placing commas everywhere they might pause (even slightly) when speaking. One place they often want to start putting commas is before and after prepositional phrases. But prepositional phrases usually contain important (restrictive) information, so they are usually connected to what they modify *without* commas.

The only place where you might put commas around prepositional phrases is where the phrase is clearly acting as an interrupter or verbal aside, as in the following example:

She has been, on the whole, an exemplary employee.

But you would not put commas around either of the prepositional phrases in the following example:

Her office is in the corner of the building.

Commas with Items in a Series

It is a real rule in English to use commas to separate items in a series, as follows:

the costs of stocks, bonds, currencies, and gold (a series of single-word nouns)

A diversified portfolio protects against large losses, offers long-term appreciation, and earns some current income. (a series of verbs with objects)

The seller gives the order, the broker wires the transaction, and the bank credits the account. (a series of independent clauses)

Such examples are clear enough. The only question is whether to place a comma before the *and* that introduces the final element. This final comma tends to be a matter of house style. Traditional usage calls for a comma. It is never wrong, and it can often help to avoid confusion about just how many elements there are in the list.

Sometimes you may be unsure whether to use commas with a series of modifiers that come before a noun. Use commas when the modifiers work independently. A test of independence is to see whether the modifiers can be used separately:

an unusual, sudden drop
an unusual drop
a sudden drop

A second example of independent modifiers would be:

five, young, untested managers
five managers
young managers
untested managers

In these examples, each modifier appears to modify the noun independently, and commas are thus appropriate. Notice the following example won't pass this test:

a somewhat risky strategy

Although you can say *a risky strategy,* you cannot say *a somewhat strategy.* In this phrase, *somewhat* modifies *risky,* and *somewhat risky* modifies *strategy.* Thus, the modifiers are not independent and should not be separated by commas.

Commas That Help Avoid Confusion

Whenever a comma can help avoid confusion on the part of the reader, use one. You have undoubtedly had the experience of reading along and finding yourself on a syntactic sidetrack:

> To be considered eligible expenses must be documented in writing on the day the expense is incurred.

If you are like most readers, you construed *eligible expenses* as a phrase, but then you hit the predicate *must be documented* and realized you had no subject for the verb. So you had to back up and pause after *eligible* to get the phrasing right. A comma after *eligible* would be helpful, even though the introductory phrase is quite short.

Here are a couple of other examples where adding a comma would help a reader figure out the sentence structure:

> Although nontaxable dividends still must be disclosed on federal income tax returns.
>
> In spite of the tax beating they took their deductions in the following year.
>
> When we first started talking about recycling a lady in her mid-seventies told me she would like to help.

It is an easy matter to insert commas that show the reader how to read each sentence correctly the first time through:

> Although nontaxable, dividends still must be disclosed on federal income tax returns.
>
> In spite of the tax beating, they took their deductions in the following year.
>
> When we first started talking about recycling, a lady in her mid-seventies told me she would like to help.

Such careful uses of commas help readers avoid the momentary confusion that comes from "reading down the wrong track." Unfortunately, it is not easy for writers to recognize such opportunities, because the writer tends to give the passage the correct, intended reading automatically. Here, editors or peer reviewers can be of great help if they pay attention to those subtle instances where they find themselves having to back up and read the sentence again to get the phrasing correct.

In Summary

You now have four principles for placing commas:

1. Use a comma to set off an introductory dependent clause or phrase from an independent clause.
2. Use a comma with a coordinating conjunction to separate compound independent clauses.
3. Use a pair of commas to set off interrupting modifiers (or a single comma when the modifiers come at the end of a sentence).
4. Use a comma to separate items in a series.

These principles can protect you from the most common comma errors. More importantly, they can help you write prose that is easier to read and that clearly represents sentence construction. The four principles can be represented visually as follows:

1. [Introductory Dependent Clause or Phrase], [Independent Clause].
2. [Independent Clause], [Coordinating Conjunction] [Independent Clause].
3. [Part of a Clause], [Interrupting Modifier], [Rest of the Clause].
   or
   [Independent Clause], [Interrupting Modifier].
4. [Item 1], [Item 2], and [Item 3]

To these four principles introduced at the beginning of the chapter we have added a fifth principle in the final section:

5. Use a comma wherever it helps you to avoid confusion on the part of your reader.

It is difficult to visually represent this principle as we have represented the other principles. Although we can't diagram confusion for you, we all are able to recognize it when we see it.

EXERCISE 9 - 4

Place commas in the following passage. Above each comma, indicate whether it reflects principle 1, 2, 3, 4, or 5.

If you are planning to invest in any mutual fund you should consult

the prospectus. The prospectus must offer certain information stipulated by the Securities Exchange Commission and this information can help you compare the performance of various funds. Although they are not very easy to read many prospectuses have been rewritten by their funds to present the information in plain English and in clear informative tables.

One common investment goal for mutual funds an investment encouraged by the Federal government through 403b payroll-deduction plans is retirement income. Long-term appreciation of capital protection of the principal and some income return are the goals and a low-to-moderate level of risk is tolerable. If the fund value fluctuates somewhat in the short term that is not necessarily a problem since steady long-term growth can still characterize the fund. The best indicator of long-term performance at least the one indicator that most investors rely on is the fund's performance over the past five or ten years. Many of these funds show five-year performances in the 20 to 30 percent range a nice rate of return. It should be noted however that these returns often represent the early performance of the fund when there were relatively few investors. As the fund grows in number of investors maintaining such high rates of growth becomes increasingly difficult. Remember that all performance indicators suggest the future growth of the fund but no indicators of course offer any guarantee about the future. Some risk of capital is always involved whenever you invest in the market.

If you are near retirement you will want to consider funds that primarily provide income. Income funds seek investment issues that pay relatively high dividends or earn relatively high rates of interest. A large investment in an income fund such as the distribution from a retiree's profit sharing can provide steady income while preserving capital. The income on such funds which is typically 10 to 15 percent certainly makes income funds a better choice than bank accounts money-market funds or CD certificates.

EXERCISE ANSWERS

Exercise 9-1 Answers

The necessary commas with introductory modification are indicated below:

1. If you want to protect yourself against steep declines in the stock market [insert comma here] you should invest 20 to 30 percent of your money in government-issued bonds.
2. Because the value of bonds tends to increase during periods of inflation [insert comma here] they can counter the effects of falling stock portfolios.
3. Trading in futures has proven risky because of the unpredictability of foreign markets. (No comma is necessary because the modifying phrase falls at the end of the sentence, after the independent clause.)
4. While a few investors prefer to make all investment decisions [insert comma here] many others are happy to have the mutual fund managers decide on the best strategies.
5. Some of the more desirable mutual funds represent particularly good investments since they do not impose a front-end load and do not have high management fees. (No comma is necessary because the modifying phrase falls at the end of the sentence, after the independent clause.)

Exercise 9-2 Answers

Commas that balance coordinate independent clauses are indicated on the following page:

1. The price/earnings ratio is only fair [insert comma here] but the price per share is bound to go up in the next few months.

2. It is a risky strategy to speculate on new computer manufacturing businesses [insert comma here] yet there has never been any shortage of people willing to take a chance on the potentially large profits.

3. The money you pay as an up-front load on your investment will never increase your earnings [insert comma here] and the portion of the earnings your fund takes for management expenses will never go into your pocket.

4. In general, most advisers will tell you to look for a no-load fund and to be wary of funds with high management fees. [no commas necessary with a compound predicate]

Exercise 9-3 Answers

Commas are indicated below to set off modification that parenthetically interrupts the flow of the sentence or that is loosely attached to the end of the sentence:

1. Some mutual funds [insert comma here] especially those featuring overseas stocks or foreign currencies [insert comma here] can provide attractive returns when investments in U.S. companies are not doing well.

2. It is not wise [insert comma here] however [insert comma here] to sink all investments in any particular type of fund.

3. Mutual funds [insert comma here] on average [insert comma here] have outperformed the Dow Jones average [insert comma here] an indication of the expertise of the fund managers.

4. The prospectus for a fund always assures the reader that long-term earnings [insert comma here] while not providing any guarantee [insert comma here] do justify confidence in the fund's management strategies.

5. The fund claims a strong performance record over the past fifteen years [insert comma here] an honest claim [insert comma here] one based on substantial data.

Exercise 9-4 Answers

Each comma in the following passage is labeled as to whether it reflects principle 1, 2, 3, 4, or 5.

1

If you are planning to invest in any mutual fund, you should

consult the prospectus. The prospectus must offer certain information

2

stipulated by the Securities Exchange Commission, and this informa-

tion can help you compare the performance of various funds.

1 or 5

Although they are not very easy to read, many prospectuses have

been rewritten by their funds to present the information in plain

4

English and in clear, informative tables.

3

One common investment goal for mutual funds, an investment

encouraged by the Federal government through 403b payroll deduc-

3   **4**

tion plans, is retirement income. Long-term appreciation of capital,

4   **2**

protection of the principal, and some income return are the goals,

and a low-to-moderate level of risk is tolerable. If the fund value

1

fluctuates somewhat in the short term, that is not necessarily a

problem since steady long-term growth can still characterize the

3

fund. The best indicator of long-term performance, at least the one

3

indicator that most investors rely on, is the fund's performance over the past five or ten years. Many of these funds show five-year perfor-

mances in the 20 to 30 percent range, a nice rate of return. It should

be noted, however, that these returns often represent the early

performance of the fund when there were relatively few investors. As

the fund grows in number of investors, maintaining such high rates

of growth becomes increasingly difficult. Remember that all perfor-

mance indicators suggest the future growth of the fund, but no

indicators, of course, offer any guarantee about the future. Some risk

of capital is always involved whenever you invest in the market.

If you are near retirement, you will want to consider funds that

primarily provide income. Income funds seek investment issues that

pay relatively high dividends or earn relatively high rates of interest.

A large investment in an income fund, such as the distribution from a

retiree's profit sharing, can provide steady income while preserving

capital. The income on such funds, which is typically 10 to 15

percent, certainly makes income funds a better choice than bank

accounts, money-market funds, or CD certificates.

chapter 10

Semicolons
and Colons

No punctuation marks are more frequently confused than **semicolons** (;) and **colons** (:). Their names do not suggest their forms, and the marks themselves look very similar. But there are important differences, and the careful writer will use both marks with some frequency. When you finish this chapter, you should know:

• How to punctuate two independent clauses with a semicolon
• How to decide when semicolons are needed, when commas suffice, and when the two marks of punctuation should be used together to show sentence structure
• How to use colons to introduce lists
• How to use colons to point toward information at the end of a sentence that completes or expands on an idea

Semicolons with Balanced Independent Clauses

You might think of semicolons as a balancing mark of punctuation, a sort of fulcrum that balances two independent clauses:

Radiology is understaffed; pharmacy is overstaffed.
∧

On both sides of the fulcrum, the clauses are balanced, independent, full clauses. Either side could stand alone as a complete sentence:

Radiology is understaffed. Pharmacy is overstaffed.

But the two clauses are closely related, and it may be stylistically effective to join them using a semicolon.

You can also use a semicolon to join two clauses that are longer and not as balanced, as in the following:

> Radiology has two prospective employees currently enrolled in technician training at the community college; they should be finished by August.

Though not tightly balanced, the two clauses are still closely related in idea. They are both independent clauses that could be punctuated as separate sentences with capital letters and periods, but it may make better sense to keep them together. The choice would be based on surrounding sentences and the effects the writer desires for the whole passage.

The semicolon is a "halfway" mark between a comma and a period. It is a stronger mark of punctuation than a comma; however, it is weaker than a period in that the two clauses it joins together are still inside the same sentence. In addition, it signals a closer relationship between clauses than a period does. As pointed out in Chapter 5, a semicolon can correct serious problems of sentence structure: run-ons and comma splices. Two independent clauses cannot be joined with a comma, but they can be joined with a semicolon:

> **WRONG:** Two student interns from the laboratory technician program look very strong, we will probably try to hire them.

> **RIGHT:** Two student interns from the laboratory technician program look very strong; we will probably try to hire them.

Semicolons are frequently used with certain modifying words called **conjunctive adverbs,** such as *however, therefore, in fact, moreover, besides, also, then,* and *still.* Like coordinating conjunctions, these words tend to modify a whole clause or show the relation of one clause to the next. But unlike coordinating conjunctions, they cannot join independent clauses with only a comma. Conjunctive adverbs require a semicolon or period between the clauses that they introduce. The correct punctuation when using conjunctive adverbs looks like this:

> The ambulance responded immediately to the call for assistance; *however,* the address called in was wrong, and the team was very late arriving on the scene.

> The victim appeared to be in shock; *in fact,* she had sustained a severe concussion.

> One of the passengers in the car had no obvious injuries but appeared confused; *therefore,* she was taken to the hospital for observation.

This is a highly useful sentence pattern, one worth learning and using. An alternative would be to separate the two independent clauses with a period and a capital letter:

> One of the passengers had no obvious injuries but appeared confused. Therefore, she was taken to the hospital for observation.

A clue to identifying conjunctive adverbs is that, unlike the subordinating conjunctions that introduce dependent clauses, conjunctive adverbs can move around inside clauses:

> The ambulance responded immediately to the call for assistance; the address called in was wrong, *however,* and the team was very late arriving on the scene.
> The victim appeared to be in shock; she had, *in fact,* sustained a severe concussion.
> One of the passengers in the car had no obvious injuries but appeared confused; she was, *therefore,* taken to the hospital for observation.

The movability of conjunctive adverbs suggests their status as interruptive modifiers and differentiates them from true conjunctions. Like other interruptions, these conjunctive adverbs are set off with commas (or a comma working with a semicolon). When true coordinating and subordinating conjunctions join clauses, a comma is all that is necessary to separate the clauses:

> The ambulance responded immediately to the call for assistance, *but* the address called in was wrong.

Here the coordinating conjunction *but* joins independent clauses.

> *While* the victim appeared to be in shock, she had, in fact, sustained a severe concussion.

Here the initial clause is made dependent by a subordinating conjunction.

> *Because* one of the passengers appeared confused, she was brought to the hospital for observation.

Here again the initial clause is made dependent by a subordinating conjunction. Note also that the true conjunctions in these examples—*but, while,* and *because*—cannot be moved.

Using Semicolons and Commas to Show Relationships

Sometimes semicolons can work together with commas to show various groupings within sentences:

> A new electromagnetic imager, ordered last October, should arrive this week; and a second electrocardiograph will be ordered in December.

Normally, you wouldn't need a semicolon since the coordinating conjunction *and* is sufficient to join two independent clauses. But because the first independent clause has internal commas, the semicolon is useful for showing the major division in the sentence between the two independent clauses.

A fairly specialized case of this use of the semicolon as a "strong comma" can help you separate distinct items presented in lists. In the following examples, notice how the semicolon effectively handles separation of items in a list, at a level above commas. Here, semicolons and commas work together to show what goes with what:

> Training sessions on the new, portable defibrillator will be held on July 17, in College Station, Texas; on August 2, in Moline, Illinois; and on September 13, in Fresno, California.
>
> Several new employees joined our staff in September: Ann Jenkins, Patient Care Coordinator for Pediatrics; Stan Smith, Patient Account Representative; and Sharon Dooley, Risk Management Coordinator.

You may not write such sentences very often, but their structure is a good one to keep in reserve.

EXERCISE 10-1

Place semicolons and commas in the following sentences where needed.

1. Medical records will begin to put all its accounts on computer this week by the end of the month the transfer should be complete.

2. The new records system still requires that we keep backup paper records however the number of trips to the morgue (where inactive files are stored) should be sharply reduced.

3. For a few weeks we will have significant training hours added to the daily workload but we should be able to handle this without adding any temporary employees.

4. A larger problem one we need help with is providing tutorials and quick reference cards on the new system.

5. The existing documentation is grossly inadequate it is essentially notes from the programmers.

6. We need to develop the following supporting documentation immediately: short tutorials that provide background in accessing entering and reporting data quick reference cards brief reminders of the functions of the control keys for frequent operations and on-line help panels simple messages that indicate the status of the system.

Using Colons in Sentences

In contrast to thinking of semicolons as balancing markers, you might think of colons as pointing devices. They suggest "more to come." What follows the colon provides a complementary detail or examples, or it completes or amplifies an idea:

> The employee-of-the-month works in ways that continually represent the largest goal of the hospital: providing *quality* health care.
>
> Tom Wilkins, environmental technician, displays a range of characteristics that make him deserving of recognition: a team spirit, a creative approach to problems, and a cheerful disposition.
>
> Providing quality health care means more than just doing your job: it means doing everything in your power to make certain a patient receives the best medical treatments available from people who are concerned and attentive caregivers.

Notice in these examples that the words following the colon can be a phrase, a series of phrases, or a whole sentence. Unlike the semicolon, the colon does not need balanced grammatical elements on either side.

In the following example, the colon follows an independent clause, pointing toward a series of noun phrases that are balanced and coordinated by commas and semicolons:

> Several new employees joined our staff in September: Ann Jenkins, Patient Care Coordinator for Pediatrics; Stan Smith, Patient Account Representative; and Sharon Dooley, Risk Management Coordinator.

When the element that follows a colon is a complete sentence, you have the option of punctuating it as one (that is, by either capitalizing the first letter following the colon):

> Providing quality health care means more than just doing your job: It means doing everything in your power to make certain a patient receives the best medical treatments available from people who are concerned and attentive caregivers.

The use of capitalization in such sentences provides a little more emphasis to the text that follows the colon.

You need to exercise some caution when using colons to punctuate sentences. For example, it is a good idea to resist a colon that would separate a verb from its objects:

> **Wrong:** Stan Smith will handle: worker's compensation cases, indigent claims, and uninsured patients.

> **Right:** Stan Smith will handle worker's compensation cases, indigent claims, and uninsured patients.

The sentence reads more smoothly without the colon. Generally, you should avoid using punctuation that separates a subject from its verb or a verb from its object.

Colons with Vertical Lists

A very common structure, one used especially in business and technical writing, is the **vertical list.** Individual points are sometimes bulleted, sometimes numbered, and sometimes simply listed. A typical pattern is to introduce the list with an independent clause followed by a colon and to capitalize the first word of each item in the list:

> Seven incident reports were filed during February:
> • Three falls
> • Two cases of wrong medication
> • Two cases of equipment failure

Traditional handbooks and style guides recommend the use of colons only after full clauses, as in the last example. That advice is not always followed, especially with list structures, and you are likely to see phrases rather than independent clauses introducing lists:

February incident reports included:
- Three falls
- Two cases of wrong medication
- Two cases of equipment failure

In this structure, the listed items are actually direct object phrases that complete the predicate to create an independent clause. It is a matter of preference whether this incomplete clause is acceptable before the colon. It could easily be turned into an independent clause:

February incident reports included the following:

You won't leave yourself open to criticism or correction by knowledge-able editors if you use colons in sentences only after independent clauses.

There are several possible ways to punctuate items in a list. In the following example, the entire list is punctuated as a complete sentence beginning with a capitalized *Seven* and having an *and* before the last item. Notice that, unlike the previous example, this version has commas after the first two items and ends with a period:

Seven incident reports were filed during February:
- three falls,
- two cases of wrong medication, and
- two cases of equipment failure.

Another pattern lists each individual item in a complete sentence:

Seven incident reports were filed during February:
- Three patients fell while ambulating in the hallways.
- Two patients were administered the wrong medications.
- Two cases of equipment failure were reported in the emergency room.

We would be hard-pressed to say which of these patterns is "the right way" to punctuate vertical lists. List structures of all sorts are becoming very common, and the rules for punctuating them vary widely. As with other aspects of language use where patterns are changing, you would do well to consult an in-house style guide, compare recommendations in various handbooks, and keep a close eye on the practice of good writers in your organization. More important than determining "the right way" is to be consistent within your own writing and with the writing of your organization.

EXERCISE 10-2

Use semicolons or colons to show relationships between information in the following sentences. Add commas, capital letters, and periods where necessary.

the Safety Committee decided to revise the form used for incident reports since the old form caused problems one problem was that employees frequently left out important information the other problem was that inappropriate information was often included information that would expose the hospital to risk the new form has three sorts of information factual details about the time and place of the incident a narrative describing the incident and a final section that identifies people and units involved there is no section that invites employees to identify causes

it is not useful for employees to speculate on causes it is appropriate however to provide sufficient factual detail for example if a patient were administered the wrong medication the incident report should include the following name of patient date and time of incident supervising nurse medication prescribed and medication administered

employees are encouraged to make recommendations for changing procedures so as to avoid future incidents forms are available to initiate procedural changes from the Safety Committee Employee Education will offer training in the use of the new incident report form the training is required for all full-time employees

In Summary

In this chapter, you have learned how semicolons and colons fulfill two contrasting functions, with semicolons balancing equal grammatical elements and colons pointing toward elements that complete or amplify an idea. Both are useful punctuation marks, and it is unfortunate that many writers avoid using them due to uncertainty about how to do so correctly. Both marks are used in highly patterned ways. Once you learn to recognize the sentence patterns, you can create polished sentences that accurately reflect the subtleties and complexities of your thinking.

EXERCISE ANSWERS

Exercise 10-1 Answers

Semicolons and commas have been inserted in the following sentences where needed:

1. Medical records will begin to put all its accounts on computer this week; by the end of the month, the transfer should be complete.

2. The new records system still requires that we keep backup paper records; however, the number of trips to the morgue (where inactive files are stored) should be sharply reduced.

3. For a few weeks, we will have significant training hours added to the daily workload, but we should be able to handle this without adding any temporary employees.

   or

   For a few weeks, we will have significant training hours added to the daily workload; but we should be able to handle this without adding any temporary employees. (This semicolon recognizes the existing comma at a lower level of division within the sentence.)

4. A larger problem, one we need help with, is providing tutorials and quick reference cards on the new system.

5. The existing documentation is grossly inadequate; it is essentially notes from the programmers.

6. We need to develop the following supporting documentation immediately: short tutorials that provide background in accessing, entering, and reporting data; quick reference cards, brief reminders of the functions of the control keys for frequent operations; and on-line help panels, simple messages that indicate the status of the system.

Exercise 10-2 Answers

There are many correct ways to punctuate this exercise. Here is one way:

Tthe Safety Committee decided to revise the form used for incident reports since the old form caused problems. Oone problem was that employees frequently left out important information; the other problem was that inappropriate information was often included, information that would expose the hospital to risk.

Tthe new form has three sorts of information:

- Factual details about the time and place of the incident
- A narrative describing the incident
- A final section that identifies people and units involved

Tthere is no section that invites employees to identify causes.

Iit is not useful for employees to speculate on causes. Iit is appropriate, however, to provide sufficient factual detail. Ffor example, if a patient were administered the wrong medication, the incident report should include the following: name of patient, date and time of incident, supervising nurse, medication prescribed, and medication administered.

Eemployees are encouraged to make recommendations for changing procedures so as to avoid future incidents; forms are available to initiate procedural changes from the Safety Committee. Employee Education will offer training in the use of the new incident report form; the training is required for all full-time employees.

chapter 11

Hyphens

This chapter treats a single mark of punctuation: the **hyphen** (-). In essence, hyphens join closely related words that work as a unit. The words joined are some combination of nouns and their modifiers.

Hyphens are sometimes confused with a similar looking punctuation mark, the **dash** (—). Dashes (the longer mark) allow phrases to be set off from a surrounding sentence. Think of them in this way: Hyphens join; dashes separate.

Hyphens are found on all keyboards, but dashes are not. To form a dash when your keyboard has no special character for it, type two hyphens with no spaces before, between, or after. Alternatively, determine how your word processor inserts a dash (usually through inserting a special character from the symbol font or by a combination of keystrokes). Neither a dash nor a hyphen uses spaces—surrounding words are immediately adjacent to the punctuation marks.

When you finish this chapter, you should know:

- How to use hyphens to join modifiers that work as a unit to modify a noun
- How to decide whether two nouns that work together should be written as one word, as a hyphenated word, or as two words

Using Hyphens with Compound Modifiers

You will recall from the discussion in Chapter 4, "Parts of Sentences and Parts of Speech," that noun phrases are typically composed of a main word (or head noun) plus one or more modifiers. In the following examples, the noun that serves as the main word of the phrase is italicized:

a long, slow *trip*

five, young, undergraduate *interns*

complex, interchangeable, moving *parts*

Notice that in each of these phrases, each modifier directly modifies the head noun. Thus, it makes sense to refer to a *long trip,* or *young interns,* or *interchangeable parts.* The commas signal that each modifier independently modifies the head noun.

This kind of modification differs from a second sort in which two words work *together* to modify the head noun of a phrase. In the following examples, compound modifiers work as a single unit:

high definition television
decision making procedures
direct drive turntable
four wheel drive
well deserved raise
five speed transmission

In each of these examples, the two words that modify the main word cannot be split. It makes no sense to speak about a *direct turntable* or a *five transmission.* Because these modifiers work as single units, the convention is to hyphenate them:

high-definition television
decision-making procedures
direct-drive turntable
four-wheel drive
well-deserved raise
five-speed transmission

Similarly, hyphenated modifiers can consist of three or four word strings:

hand-to-hand combat
ground-to-air transmission
off-the-cuff remark

Notice that the examples given thus far cover modifiers that come *before* the main word of the phrase. When modifiers follow the head noun, no hyphens are used:

a *strong-willed* leader

but

a leader who is *strong willed*
the *barnacle-encrusted* bilge tanks

but

the bilge tanks were *barnacle encrusted*

The usefulness of hyphens is obvious in situations where language becomes complicated and technical. Compare the effort it takes to read and understand the first example below as compared to the second example:

zero wait state free electron ground based laser

zero-wait state free-electron ground-based laser

The phrase is easier to understand when the words that act as modifying units are hyphenated. Of course, when modification piles up in such lists, commas can help, too:

zero-wait state, free-electron, ground-based laser

These commas work here because each of the hyphenated modifiers directly modifies the head noun *laser*.

The one sort of compound modifier that does not take a hyphen is *-ly* adverbs:

a highly deserved promotion

extremely divisive arguments

Similarly, certain common adverbs that intensify meaning, such as *very*, *much*, and *quite*, do not take hyphens.

The use of hyphens with modifying phrases is a mark of consideration for the reader. Such hyphens let you show the subgroupings in complex phrases and allow your readers to process your sentences with greater efficiency and accuracy.

EXERCISE 11-1

Place hyphens in the following sentences. Look for pairs of modifiers that work together as a unit.

1. Ground based tracking systems have a number of serious limitations.

2. Their signal to noise ratio tends to be compromised by atmospheric disturbance, and high frequency voltage surges cause false readings.

3. Signal loss is common in station to station transmissions, since ground level sources of high voltage static energy are everywhere.

4. Continuous coverage is difficult to achieve because of the curvature of the earth.

5. The only solution to the coverage problem is a long series of receivers placed at approximately 750 mile intervals.

6. Using ground to satellite transmissions, each station in turn passes the signal to the next ground based station, somewhat like a bucket brigade.

7. A much better solution to providing continuous tracking is provided by medium height satellites.

8. Three such satellites can provide continuous coverage; their distance from the earth gives each satellite long range tracking abilities.

Other Hyphenated Forms

Hyphens are sometimes used with prefixes when those prefixes maintain a separate quality:

> non-entity
> vice-chancellor
> ex-wife

As the prefix becomes fully established as part of the word, the hyphen tends to be dropped, as in the following examples:

> co-operation has become cooperation
>
> non-returnable has become (or is becoming) nonreturnable

Recall that hyphens join. Hyphens show that certain well-established noun/modifier phrases work as single, inseparable units. In each of the following examples, a head noun has closely attached modifiers:

> Johnny-on-the-spot
> brother-in-law
> poet-in-residence

The same principle is active here as with pairs of modifiers—the terms work as a single unit, behaving much as a single word behaves.

Hyphens with Compound Nouns

Like many languages, English frequently allows two words to be compounded—to work as a single unit. Nouns are most often compounded, usually with other nouns, sometimes with adjectives or verbs. Thus, we have well-established words in our vocabulary that are made up of words that have been compounded:

bedroom	skyscraper
cheeseburger	icebox
textbook	killjoy

Notice that these **compounds** carry primary stress on the first part of the word, with a secondary stress on the second part of the word. (The *stressed* part of a word is the part that is spoken more loudly and forcefully.) You can hear the shift in stress when you contrast the pronunciation of compounds with the pronunciation of a modifier/noun pair:

a *greenhouse* vs. a *green house*

a *bluebird* vs. a *blue bird*

The compound has a heavier stress on the first word than on the second. When, instead of a compound, you simply have two unattached words, they both tend to receive equal stress. You can hear the same distinguishing stress in nouns with prefixes: contrast *viceroy* with *vice-chancellor*. *Viceroy* is closer to being fully compounded; *vice-chancellor* maintains a bit more separation between the two parts. Stress signals the extent to which two words are integrated into a single unit of meaning.

Many noun compounds are written as a solid word (*skyscraper,* for example); other pairs use a hyphen to join the two words into a compound:

man-eater	one-half
zero-derivation	kilowatt-hour

All writers spend time trying to decide between writing compounds as two words, as hyphenated pairs, or as solid words. Is it *lawn mower, lawn-mower,* or *lawnmower?* (*Webster's New Collegiate Dictionary* suggests *lawn mower.*) If you look up *lawn mower,* you will find it has its own entry, which suggests it is being treated as one word, a compound noun.

There are no absolute rules to govern hyphen usage with compounds. Rather, the choice is based on common usage, and common usage tends to vary. Government agencies, publishers, and some large companies follow a specific style manual that answers many hyphenation questions. *The Chicago Manual of Style,* for example, offers a useful, detailed table demonstrating and explaining preferred spellings for a number of compounds. By consulting this writer's guide, you can learn, for example, that *-ly* modifiers are not hyphenated (adverbs such as *especially, really,* or *fully*). The complexity and length of the *Chicago Manual's* section on hyphens, however, suggest that deciding about hyphen usage will continue to be difficult.

When in doubt, consult a dictionary. Many compounds, like *lawn mower,* are sufficiently established that they receive their own entries in dictionaries—they are treated as single words. Keep in mind, though, that new compounds are formed all the time. When words tend to co-occur, they tend to be hyphenated as a unit. Over time, the tendency is for the hyphen to disappear and for the compound to be punctuated as a single word.

In general, there is a tendency in modern English to use fewer marks of punctuation, and this tendency exerts a pressure on writers to drop hyphens and fuse compounds as single words. Knowing that many writers prefer to write compounds as solid words rather than as hyphenated words can sometimes help you make a decision. The hyphen represents a point of accelerated language change, and reference works frequently can't keep pace with language users. When reference works fail you, keep your reader in mind and hyphenate in ways that help your reader understand what goes with what.

Hyphens to Show Word Breaks across Lines

Hyphens are frequently used to break long words at line ends to give the right margin a smooth appearance. Such hyphens also keep lines from being filled out with excess spaces when both left and right margins are justified. Careful use of hyphenation at line ends is a particularly important part of fitting text to tight columns, as in newspaper layouts or three-column page layouts. Otherwise, the word wrapping would generate too much meaningless white space.

For most workplace writing, it might be better to turn off both right justification and automatic hyphenation in your word-processing program. A ragged-right margin is not necessarily a bad thing; some research suggests it actually helps readers keep their place. And it probably helps readers to keep whole words intact rather than breaking them for visual appearance sake. If you are seeking a more typeset look, you can have your word processor hyphenate and wrap long words at the ends of lines. But you should still check a dictionary for correct syllabification, since word processing programs are likely to make some mistakes on syllable breaks.

Hyphens and Ambiguity

Occasionally, hyphens can help you avoid **ambiguity** (that is, having two possible meanings in a sentence). A phrase like *ten foot candles* will make a reader pause to decipher its meaning, even if only one reading really makes sense: *ten foot-candles.* (A *foot-candle* is a unit of measurement of light.)

Although the hyphen has been dropped from most *co-* words, like *cooperation* or *coordinate,* it is usefully retained in a shortened form like *co-op,* since *coop* would likely be misread, even when the context would allow only one meaning. It is never wrong to help a reader figure out puzzling prefixed expressions by retaining hyphens. *Re-entry* and *meta-analysis* are other examples in which a hyphen can help a reader avoid the momentary confusion of figuring out how to pronounce a double *a* or *e.*

Similarly, a few prefixed verbs would be confusing without a hyphen:

to *recover* from an illness

but

to *re-cover* the pool
to *reapply* for a loan

but

to *re-apply* the epoxy coating

Moreover, a hyphen can signal phrase structure when prefixes are part of compound phrases:

two- and four-door
pre- and posttest
cross- and multidisciplinary approaches

In such instances, hyphens really do help a reader figure out which words belong together. Alternately, you could write *pretest and posttest* and *crossdisciplinary and multidisciplinary approaches.*

EXERCISE 11-2

Add hyphens where necessary to clarify modification or to signal compound noun phrases. In a few places, a comma might also help to show the phrase structures.

1. Research based layout principles can help page designers create easy to read text.

2. We know, for example, that ragged right margins are a little easier to read than the flush right margins of text that has been fully justified.

3. In a double column format, however, fully justified text has much better visual appeal than ragged right text.

4. A range of type size is legible, but a good all purpose font for text is 10 point type.

5. Using 12 point leading with a 10 point font opens up the text, making it look more inviting.

6. Line length is an important variable, with forty to sixty characters per line being acceptable; longer lines invariably create line scanning troubles for readers.

7. Well formed letters generally avoid an extremely high x height (the distance from the base of the letter to the mean line).

In Summary

You have learned in this chapter that hyphens show what goes with what. Hyphens are especially useful in technical writing, when modifiers stack up before the head noun in a phrase. They can provide instant clarity, showing the reader how to read a phrase. Because hyphens are so helpful to readers, their use with compound modifiers is spreading.

The situation with compound nouns is a little different. You can observe language change taking place within noun compounds as pairs of words become more closely associated, first hyphenated and then written as one word. English is the language of the world's scientific and technical community, and this community has a rapidly expanding vocabulary. A major way that English generates the words it needs is to combine existing words to create new terms. These terms may first be hyphenated, and then, as they become more common, written as one word. Such a situation requires writers to be alert to the evolving status of compounds.

EXERCISE ANSWERS

Exercise 11-1 Answers

Hyphens have been added to reflect modifiers that work together as a unit.

1. Ground-based tracking systems have a number of serious limitations.

2. Their signal-to-noise ratio tends to be compromised by atmospheric disturbance, and high-frequency voltage surges cause false readings.

3. Signal loss is common in station-to-station transmissions, since ground-level sources of high-voltage static energy are everywhere.

4. Continuous coverage is difficult to achieve because of the curvature of the earth.

5. The only solution to the coverage problem is a long series of receivers placed at approximately 750-mile intervals.

6. Using ground-to-satellite transmissions, each station in turn passes the signal to the next ground-based station, somewhat like a bucket brigade.

7. A much better solution to providing continuous tracking is provided by medium-height satellites.

8. Three such satellites can provide continuous coverage; their distance from the earth gives each satellite long-range tracking abilities.

Exercise 11-2 Answers

Hyphens have been added to clarify modification or to signal compound noun phrases.

1. Research-based layout principles can help page designers create easy-to-read text.

2. We know, for example, that ragged-right margins are a little easier to read than the flush-right margins of text that has been fully justified.

3. In a double-column format, however, fully justified text has much better visual appeal than ragged-right text.

4. A range of type size is legible, but a good all-purpose font for text is 10-point type.

5. Using 12-point leading with a 10-point font opens up the text, making it look more inviting.

6. Line length is an important variable, with forty-to-sixty characters per line being acceptable; longer lines invariably create line-scanning trouble for readers.

7. Well-formed letters generally avoid an extremely high x-height (the distance from the base of the letter to the mean line).

chapter 12

Dashes and Parentheses

This chapter shows you how to use various marks of punctuation that set off information from the rest of a sentence. The marks are used in pairs and most commonly include **dashes** (—), **parentheses** ( ), and **commas** (,) but also include sets of characters for specialized purposes (square brackets and braces). These punctuation marks allow you to control the status of information in a sentence, showing that some information is more important or more central than other information.

Punctuation calls the reader's attention to certain groupings of words. Sometimes the punctuation says, "Notice that the enclosed information is not part of the main clause. It explains, modifies, or adds detail, but it is not essential to the sentence." Sometimes the punctuation says, "I am going to tell you something, but it is not really central to what I am saying. It is a digression or an explanation you may or may not need."

When you finish this chapter, you should know:

- How to use dashes and parentheses to separate a phrase or clause from the rest of a sentence
- How to choose among dashes, parentheses, commas, and colons to set off information
- How to add other punctuation to phrases that are enclosed by dashes and parentheses

Dashes and Parentheses

Dashes and parentheses separate. They allow you to break into an ongoing sentence to present information that qualifies, completes, or exemplifies some idea:

The three new interns—Mary Beth, David, and Lisa—will be arriving before the month is out.

If you feel you are in a rut (and who doesn't feel this way from time to time?), a course can sometimes help you discover new ways to solve old problems.

The two missing parts—a mercury switch and a backing plate—were discovered in the bin behind Bench 32.

Learning how to do quick (but careful) proofreading can sometimes prevent embarrassment.

In each of these examples, the phrases or clauses enclosed by dashes or parentheses add extra information to the sentence. The information is not essential, but it is useful. It could be dropped, and the sentences would still be grammatically complete.

If you read the sentences aloud, you will notice that your voice drops when you hit the first dash or parenthesis and that it doesn't come back up until you get beyond the second dash or parenthesis and back into the sentence. (Try it: read each example above and exaggerate the changes in your voice pitch.) Setting off inserted information with dashes or parentheses reflects what speakers normally signal through intonation and phrasing.

Commas can also work in similar ways to set off information that is not part of the base clause:

The company airplane, a 1995 Cessna, has proven too costly to maintain and will be sold.

This use of commas is discussed in Chapter 9, "Commas," as an instance of nonrestrictive modification; phrases that are not essential (that is, nonrestrictive) should be set off with commas. Dashes and parentheses can work equally well with such modifiers:

The company airplane—a 1995 Cessna—has proven too costly to maintain and will be sold.

The company airplane (a 1995 Cessna) has proven too costly to maintain and will be sold.

EXERCISE 12·1

Use dashes or parentheses to rewrite the following pairs of sentences as single sentences. You will frequently be able to delete words, but try not to lose any information.

1. The medical evacuation team had a busy weekend.

   Two rock climbers were stranded in the Pecos and a woman was trapped in her car after a crash.

2. Emergency services are contracted by the hospital.

   Emergency services include ambulance calls and disaster responses.

3. Three times each year, all equipment is tested and serviced.

   All equipment is checked out in February, June, and October.

4. One of the recently purchased pieces of equipment increases the unit's ability to respond to cardiac calls.

   A portable fibrillator was recently purchased.

5. Two new trauma centers were recently opened in the greater Chicago area.

   Rosemont, near the Horizon, and Wheaton both have new trauma centers.

Choosing among
Commas, Dashes, and Parentheses

Any of the three marks—commas, dashes, or parentheses—can work equally well to set off nonrestrictive modifying phrases. If you are like most readers, you probably feel that dashes and parentheses are somewhat stronger in their effects than commas. They certainly make the separation more visually prominent. You might think of these paired marks of punctuation as delimiters, marking the boundaries of a phrase group.

Dashes and parentheses give a writer options for controlling information at various levels within sentences. In many cases—with lists, with longer phrases, or when commas are used elsewhere in a sentence—commas simply won't do the job. Dashes and parentheses, because they are stronger marks of punctuation, can be called upon to signal serious disjunctures in sentences:

> The most recent conviction—it was his third citation for DWI—landed him in jail for six months.

Here a full independent clause is embedded in the base clause. Commas are insufficient to set off an independent clause.

Phrases can also be set off from a base clause:

> The three dates in question (October 28, November 3, and November 12) are all open for scheduling production runs.

In this example, the parentheses are useful for visually setting off the list, which itself has internal commas.

Square brackets ([. . .]) can also be used to group and set off certain phrases within longer structures. Square brackets enclose words that have been added by the writer to someone else's words to make quoted speech intelligible:

> Sources close to the White House quoted the President as saying, "All appropriate measures have been taken to ensure they [the terrorists] will be brought to justice."

Brackets are also used inside parentheses (since the rules of punctuation [rules you can find in most style guides] do not allow parentheses inside parentheses). Curly brackets ({ . . . }), also called *braces,* tend to have specific uses in mathematical formulas. In fact, mathematics has strict rules of precedence for these "fences," as follows: {[( )]}. If you have a sense for how bracketing works in math, you can apply it to sentence structure.

Setting Off Information at the End of a Sentence

Generally, dashes, like parentheses, are used in pairs to set off interrupting material. Sometimes, however, it is useful to separate information that comes at the end of a sentence—information that modifies or extends the meaning of the sentence or that completes some idea expressed in the sentence. Because such dashes come at the end of the sentence, only a single dash is used. A period ends the sentence:

> Jenkins was accused of withholding information from the tax investigators—information concerning account transfers between January 12 and 14.

> We were surprised to see new housing starts decline during March—it is normally a robust period of new growth.

> Employees will be pleased to note the enhanced benefits under the new carrier—a lower deductible, an optional eye-care plan, and an automatic disability provision.

Sometimes a writer has the option of choosing to use a colon (:) rather than a comma, a dash, or parentheses at the end of a sentence:

The union voted to send a representative to the national meeting in Hawaii, a meeting viewed by some as a junket.

The union voted to send a representative to the national meeting in Hawaii—a meeting viewed by some as a junket.

The union voted to send a representative to the national meeting in Hawaii (a meeting viewed by some as a junket).

The union voted to send a representative to the national meeting in Hawaii: a meeting viewed by some as a junket.

The choices among dashes, parentheses, commas, or colons (with end-of-sentence phrases) offer subtle stylistic control. They give writers control over tone, with parentheses most forcefully lowering the status of the information and commas most gently lowering the status of information. Dashes tend to be perceived as somewhat less formal (more dashing?) than other marks, but they have serious uses in technical and scientific writing. While commas and dashes may or may not be used in pairs to set off information, parentheses must always be used in pairs and colons never are. Colons only work to point toward information at the end of the sentence or toward items in a list. They wear the most formal garb.

Judgments about the relative force of these delimiters are admittedly subjective, and not all readers respond in the same ways to the different punctuation marks. The choice among commas, dashes, parentheses, or colons is based on the writer's answer to a logical question: How closely related is the information to the rest of the sentence?

Other Punctuation with Parentheses and Dashes

When a parenthetical phrase comes at the end of a sentence, the end punctuation goes outside the parentheses:

The new dental plan provides twice-yearly checkups with no out-of-pocket charges to the insured (a very popular benefit).

Notice that there is no comma before the parenthetical phrase. The only exception to the "no commas before parentheses" rule is with enumerated lists:

The policy defines (1) the limits of liability, (2) the obligations of the claimant, and (3) the provisions for claiming a total loss.

If a full sentence is enclosed within parentheses, it should be punctuated as one, with a capital letter and a period inside the parentheses:

> The new dental plan provides twice-yearly checkups with no out-of-pocket charges to the insured. (This benefit has proven to be highly popular, especially for those employees with large families.)

Look carefully at the punctuation in the example above. Notice that both sentences are fully punctuated. The first ends with a period before the parenthetical sentence begins. The parentheses then fully enclose a sentence with an initial capital letter and a period at the end, inside the closing parenthesis.

If the sentence context requires it, a comma can follow the closing parenthesis:

> Because of the change in liability laws (Section 1.12.a), this office no longer accepts claims for accidents that occur away from the workplace during nonwork hours.

The comma is required here to mark the end of the introductory modification and the beginning of the independent clause.

However, when a dash falls where a comma would ordinarily separate clauses, the comma is omitted:

> Because of the unusually high incidence of Legionnaire's Disease—it was the third outbreak in as many months—the resources of the county health department were stretched to their limits.

The dash in this example takes the place of the comma that ordinarily would follow the introductory dependent clause.

EXERCISE 12-2

Combine each of the following groups of sentences into one sentence. Use the range of punctuation discussed in this unit: dashes, parentheses, commas, and colons.

1. At a recent trade show, one product stood out.

The product was SoilAbsorb.

2. SoilAbsorb is a synthetic polymer.

It can absorb up to 800 times its weight in water.

3. SoilAbsorb has polymers. These polymers retain water.

The water that is retained would normally drain from the soil.

4. SoilAbsorb works in the root zone of the plants.

It reduces water loss through percolation and evaporation.

5. Plants still have a source of moisture.

Plants don't need watering for weeks.

6. SoilAbsorb provides other benefits.

It stabilizes nutrients, herbicides, and pesticides.

Fewer chemical applications are needed.

7. SoilAbsorb can increase the size of plants by up to 35 percent.

SoilAbsorb can save 50 to 70 percent on plant watering.

In Summary

Dashes and parentheses offer you ways to downplay information that is not as important as other information in a sentence. They let you manage information by showing the reader (visually) which information is primary and which is secondary.

Some writers avoid dashes, feeling they are too informal. Other writers have not learned the broad principle of setting off information that interrupts or adds details. Learning to control the presentation of information through punctuation is worth the effort. Such punctuation keeps every sentence from looking the same—from looking like an undistinguished string of words. Punctuation allows you to display the emphasis and thus to control the ways your reader understands your meanings.

Putting It All Together

The following exercise presents a set of "kernel" sentences—short, single clause, simple sentences. Your task is to combine these sentences using the various punctuation marks discussed in the four chapters of this unit. Use each of the punctuation marks discussed in Chapters 9 to 12: commas, semicolons, colons, hyphens, dashes, and parentheses.

The earlier chapters are relevant, too. You don't want to create any run-on sentences or reference problems, and you want to maintain strong clauses with actions centered in the verbs and strong S-V-O patterning. You will need to alter the order of information and insert paragraph breaks to make the resulting passage coherent.

Push yourself to use structures you don't normally use and play with the variety of sentence patterns that the full range of punctuation allows.

The Food and Drug Administration (FDA) approves applications for new drugs.

Pharmaceutical companies file New Drug Applications (NDAs) to gain approval for marketing new drugs.

The filing and approval process has its roots in the thalidomide crisis of the post war period.

Some women had fertility problems.

These women were unable to become pregnant.

Women took thalidomide to become pregnant.

They became pregnant.

Their babies had deformed limbs.

The FDA realized something.

More rigorous procedures were needed for drug testing.

More rigorous procedures were needed for drug approval.

The FDA imposed new requirements on drug companies.

Drug companies were required to test new drugs.

The drug tests were conducted under controlled conditions.

The results of tests were submitted to the FDA.

The FDA reviews the applications for new drugs.

All drugs pose some risk.

The FDA conducts a benefit/risk analysis.

The FDA considers the safety results of drug testing.

The FDA will not approve a drug that presents too many risks.

The FDA reviews the efficacy of a proposed drug.

The FDA will not approve a drug that does not have good efficacy data.

The approval process takes a long time.

Time is measured from submission of an application by the drug

company to time of approval from the FDA.

A typical NDA has about 200,000 pages of information.

The FDA takes about eighteen months to make its decision.

The NDA must be evaluated by a panel of expert medical officers.

The NDA is evaluated by technical experts.

The NDA is evaluated by statisticians.

The stakes are high.

A new drug at peak sales can earn one million dollars a day or more.

The drug companies pressure the FDA for faster review times.

The drug companies pressure the FDA for simpler application

requirements.

The FDA remembers earlier experiences.

The FDA is not anxious to have another experience.

The experience they remember is thalidomide.

EXERCISE ANSWERS

Exercise 12-1 Answers

Here are possible sentences. There are many ways to combine the sentences in the exercise.

1. The medical evacuation team had a busy weekend—two rock climbers were stranded in the Pecos and a woman was trapped in her car after a crash.

2. Emergency services (including ambulance calls and disaster responses) are contracted by the hospital.

3. Three times each year—in February, June, and October—all equipment is tested and serviced.

4. The portable fibrillator (a recent equipment purchase) increases the unit's ability to respond to cardiac calls.

5. Two new trauma centers were recently opened in the greater Chicago area—in Rosemont (near the Horizon) and in Wheaton.

Exercise 12-2 Answers

As with other exercises, the answers here are only suggestions. Many other solutions are possible.

1. At a recent trade show, one product stood out: SoilAbsorb.

2. SoilAbsorb—a synthetic polymer—can absorb up to 800 times its weight in water.

3. Polymers in SoilAbsorb retain water—water that would normally drain from the soil.

4. SoilAbsorb works in the root zone of the plants (by reducing water loss through percolation and evaporation).

5. Plants still have a source of moisture: they won't need watering for weeks!

6. SoilAbsorb provides other benefits—it stabilizes nutrients, herbicides, and pesticides, so fewer chemical applications are needed.

7. SoilAbsorb can increase the size of plants (by up to 35 percent) and can save on plant watering (by 50 to 70 percent).

Putting It All Together Answers

Here is one version of the exercise passage, rewritten to use all the punctuation marks in a variety of sentence structures. We hope you like your version better!

The Food and Drug Administration (FDA) approves New Drug Applications (NDAs), filed by pharmaceutical companies to gain approval for marketing new drugs. The filing and approval process has its roots in the thalidomide crisis of the post-war period.

Some women (with fertility problems) were unable to become pregnant, took thalidomide and became pregnant, but had babies with deformed limbs. The FDA realized something: more rigorous procedures were needed for drug testing and approval.

The FDA imposed new requirements on drug companies. Drug companies were required to test new drugs under controlled conditions, with the results submitted to the FDA.

The FDA understands that all drugs pose some risk. When it reviews new drug applications, the FDA analyzes risk vs. benefit, considering the results of both safety and efficacy testing. The FDA will not approve a drug that presents too many risks; nor will the FDA approve a drug that does not have good efficacy data.

The approval process takes a long time—about eighteen months (measured from time-of-submission of the NDA by the drug company to time-of-approval by the FDA). A typical NDA has about 200,000 pages of information, all of which must be evaluated by a panel of medical officers, technical experts, and statisticians.

The stakes are high: A new drug at peak sales can earn one million dollars a day or more. And so the drug companies pressure the FDA for simpler application requirements and faster review times.

But the FDA remembers earlier experiences: they are not anxious to have another experience like thalidomide.

"Professional writing uses a *clear* and *concise* vocabulary."

The following five chapters will help you develop a prose style that gains strength through effective word choice and phrasing. Many writers, for a variety of reasons, develop habits that interfere with a clear, concise style. Perhaps some writers think they will be perceived as smart if they use complex vocabulary; perhaps some have been part of a technical group for so long that they forget that others don't speak their language.

Frequently, a reference that is clear in a writer's mind is not equally clear in a reader's, but unless a writer is consciously choosing forms for clear reference, the ambiguities may persist. Chapter 13, "Clear Reference," highlights the importance of reference in maintaining coherence across sentences and paragraphs. In most cases, a clear professional style results when writers start to put their readers' needs foremost.

Some writers have attended the "thesaurus school of writing" and like to substitute more abstract or longer words for shorter and more concrete terms. Sometimes it is easier to use more words rather than fewer: words have a way of spilling out in preformed phrases once the ink starts to flow. Chapter 14, "Lean Words versus Redundant Words," will help you slim down your style by encouraging you to pay close attention to word choice.

A natural process that often occurs within groups at work is the development of specialized vocabulary. However, when writers must address audiences outside their own groups, these specialized terms (known as *jargon*) often interfere with communication. Close-knit work groups also tend to develop the habit of speaking and writing in familiar phrases and shorthand acronyms that are clear only to the insiders. These issues of "insider language" and jargon are discussed in Chapter 15, "Technical Vocabulary versus Jargon." Similar concerns are introduced in Chapter 16, "Preferring a Verbal Style," and Chapter 17, "Unpacking Noun Compounds." In these chapters, the concern is with the overuse of noun forms of verbs and noun compounds that has sprung up everywhere in technical, scientific communities.

Clear writing demands that writers break out of their self-centered worlds. Good writers can role-play, sometimes acting as writer and sometimes (imaginatively) acting as reader in an attempt to bring the reader's understanding of the subject closer to the writer's understanding. The choice of vocabulary is an important aspect of building bridges to the reader.

chapter 13

Clear Reference

Every stretch of language longer than a few words establishes patterns of **reference.** Phrases refer to previous phrases; words refer to other words. Sometimes the references are to objects or actions in the world around the text. Often, phrases refer to information in other sentences in the text itself. To be effective, references need to be understood in similar ways by both writer and reader.

Problems of reference arise when a reader cannot determine what a phrase refers to. When such problems occur in conversations, a listener can ask for clarification: "Now wait a minute. Which purchase order are you talking about?" In contrast, written language must stand on its own because the writer is not around to clarify intended meanings.

Chapter 8, "Pronoun Problems," discussed certain sorts of reference problems with pronouns. A pronoun like *he* or *it* must have a clear antecedent (the word that comes before the pronoun to which the pronoun refers). Similarly, demonstrative pronouns (words that point, like *this, that, these,* and *those*) must have a clearly defined scope of modification. If you write *this problem,* the reader must be able to determine which particular problem or part of a problem situation you are referring to. Synonyms, too, can cause reference problems. If a writer switches terms—from *computer* to *CPU* to *machine,* for example—a reader might be unsure whether some meaningful distinction is being drawn or whether the writer is simply shifting terms to achieve variety in phrasing.

While Chapter 8 restricted its attention to problems of pronoun use within sentences, this chapter takes a broader look at patterns of reference across sentences and between a text and the situation that surrounds it. In this chapter, you will learn how to:

- Recognize and control common errors in pronoun reference across sentence boundaries
- Make principled decisions about when and how to use synonyms
- Use reference to bring clarity and coherence to your writing

The more complicated your subject matter—especially when writing about scientific and technical matters—the more important it is to control patterns of reference. It becomes increasingly important not just to avoid common errors of reference but also to make intentional use of patterns of reference across sentences to bring coherence to your paragraphs and documents.

Systems of Reference

A generous portion of any grammar system is devoted to establishing and maintaining reference relations within and across sentences. A partial list would include the following:

Personal Pronouns (*he, she, it, they,* etc.):
Sally Robinson, the training director, argued with *her* manager for more safety training for the maintenance engineers. *She* was convinced that one of the problems was that *they* had not yet begun complying with some of the recent changes in OSHA regulations governing the handling of toxic compounds.

Demonstrative Pronouns (*this, that, these, those,* etc.) and the **definite article** (*the*):
In textile industries, workers are studying math so they can eliminate measurement errors that cause material to end up on the cutting room floor. Avoiding these errors can easily result in cost savings on raw materials of 15–20 percent and bring additional benefits in pride and self-esteem to the workers who attend the classes.

Indefinite Pronouns (*each, every, any, all, both, many, few, either, neither,* etc.):
Most managers willingly acknowledge the importance of training for front-line workers. Few, however, are ready to commit the planning and resources necessary for a successful on-site program.

Root Word Inflected for Different Parts of Speech (for example, *manage, manager, management* or *develop, developer, development*):
Coproduction facilities can lead to tremendous savings in energy costs. For example, a producer of wood or paper might enter into a business relationship with an energy utility, so the excess energy produced by the utility can be used by its business partner. The energy might be excess electricity or by-products of electric generation (typically, steam or heat).

Synonyms (substitution of a word with similar meaning in subsequent reference):

Many workers are motivated by the <u>self-respect</u> they gain by working as a contributing, valued team member. <u>Self-esteem</u> is consistently rated by psychologists as an enabling component of the psyche. Those who <u>respect</u> themselves are most ready to accept responsibility and to take on challenging assignments.

Antonyms (use of words with opposite meanings in subsequent sentences):

The <u>upside</u> of training is that productivity is bound to increase. The <u>downside</u> is that workers become more susceptible to raiding from other firms.

Whole-to-Part Relations (reference to a system and its parts across sentences; in this example, references to various components of performance appraisal):

A clear understanding of the process can help businesses use <u>performance appraisals</u> to enhance employee satisfaction and productivity. <u>Setting clear goals</u> is a first step: the broad statements that define successful job performance. Each of the goals should be supported by <u>specific, measurable objectives</u>. These objectives should be built into <u>individual performance plans</u>, with clear milestones for how and when each objective will be measured. Frequent <u>attention to the plan</u> during the year, with some sort of <u>tracking of progress,</u> can prevent disastrous year-end confrontation.

Reduced Phrases (shortened phrases that refer to longer preceding phrases; sometimes clauses reduced to phrases; in this example, the italicized phrases reduce the longer, underlined constructions in previous sentences to short phrases):

Many managers tend <u>to ignore employees until they suddenly jump on them for some simple mistake.</u> *To do so* encourages employees to try to avoid unpleasant confrontations rather than concentrate on strong overall performance. <u>Keeping lines of communication open, discussing performance frequently, and openly acknowledging and praising strong performance</u> build a much better working environment. *Such forms of managerial attention* work toward a model of performance based on long-term, productive interaction.

Some Problems of Reference across Sentence Boundaries

Reference problems arise when there are inappropriate shifts in number or person from sentence to sentence or when there is no clear, unambiguous antecedent for a reference.

Number refers to whether words are singular or plural. When you choose pronoun forms, you need to maintain consistency in number. Singular pronouns have singular antecedents; plural pronouns take plural antecedents.

Person refers to the interpersonal roles in language, whether the writer is referring to self (*I* or *we*), referring directly to the reader or listener (*you*), or referring to someone or something else (*he, she, it, they*). Be especially careful about using third-person pronouns across paragraph boundaries (including headings) or using third person when there is more than one possible antecedent.

EXERCISE 13-1

The following sentences contain inappropriate shifts of number or person. Make whatever changes are necessary to regain consistency in interpersonal relations within the sentences.

1. Writers need to be careful about pronoun choice. You can't just make choices based on single sentences. They need to consider what comes before and after a sentence.

2. An expert editor checks for consistency of pronoun reference from sentence to sentence. They want to be sure that all references are consistent in both person and number.

3. Some technical publications editors will provide different levels of editing depending on where a publication is in the publishing cycle. She might edit only for grammatical correctness, or for compliance with agency specifications, or for document consistency in terms and format.

4. In our publications group, we prefer that writers schedule their editing sessions rather than just bringing in your manuscript and expecting a fast turnaround. It is not so difficult for someone to plan ahead and avoid last minute rush jobs. If you want quality work, a writer needs to allow sufficient time for final copyediting and correction.

5. Some people believe that the use of first and second person is inappropriate in formal writing. One may remember an English teacher who asked them to avoid *you* in their essays. But we don't want to always avoid second-person reference. It can help you create solidarity with your reader. They will feel like you are talking directly to them. Don't listen to absolute rules. Decide when the use of first or second person is appropriate. As a writer, one needs to make informed choices, not depend on absolute rules.

Reference Problems across Paragraphs

Problems of pronoun reference also occur when crossing the boundary from one paragraph to another (or from a heading to the text accompanying it). Paragraph breaks represent topic boundaries, and it is best to restate topics explicitly rather than relying on the reader's frame of reference. Restating topics also helps readers who are not reading sentence-to-sentence, but skimming a document to pick up main points.

A good rule of thumb is to restate a full noun phrase rather than using a pronoun at the beginning of a paragraph. Otherwise, the pronoun reference may not be immediately clear, and the reader may have to waste valuable reading time looking back to the preceding paragraph instead of reading onward. The following passage demonstrates the confusion that results when a pronoun reference is *not* restated at the beginning of a new paragraph:

> The documents in this delivery include the last four sessions for the traffic-controller training course, as well as the sessions for the supervisor and training staff. This delivery, combined with the previous delivery on June 1, represents all the sessions for the training courses for all personnel.
>
> It has been separated into seven books as follows:

What does *it* in the second paragraph refer to? It takes some rereading to figure out that *it* refers to *this delivery.* It would be much clearer to simply restate that reference at the beginning of the paragraph.

Ambiguous Reference

Writers need to be careful each time they choose a demonstrative pronoun like *this* or *that, these* or *those.* These words point to something previously mentioned. When the reference works well, the pointing creates links between sentences that help writing achieve a coherent flow. When the pointing is not carefully controlled, however, it can cause momentary confusion for the reader. To make sense, writers need to be certain the antecedent is clear to the reader.

Frequently, an ambiguous reference can be clarified by adding a noun to the demonstrative pronoun:

> **Vague:** Training initiatives can help employees understand and avoid sexual harassment in the workplace. *This* can contribute to a healthy work environment.

> **Clear:** Training initiatives can help employees understand and avoid sexual harassment in the workplace. *This training* can contribute to a healthy work environment.

Sometimes substituting a specific noun phrase for the pronoun will clear up any ambiguity:

> **Vague:** Several companies in the Austin area are able to provide solid courses in diversity training for workplaces with employees from various ethnic, sociocultural, or linguistic backgrounds. *These* can be viewed as assets to a company rather than liabilities. *They* can contribute to improved communication with clients or bring diverse perspectives to problems that beg for creative thinking.

> **Clear:** Several companies in the Austin area are able to provide solid courses in diversity training for workplaces with employees from various ethnic, sociocultural, or linguistic backgrounds. *Employees of diverse backgrounds* can be viewed as assets to a company rather than liabilities. *People from different ethnic or cultural groups* can contribute to improved communication with clients or bring diverse perspectives to problems that beg for creative thinking.

Sometimes writers fail to make clear the **scope of reference** (that is, what a phrase refers to). In the following example, it is unclear what *this problem* refers to—cross-cultural communication, the hospital attempt, or the need to understand border Spanish:

> **Vague:** The hospital has been attempting to provide training in cross-cultural communication skills because clinical people in each wing need to speak and understand the border varieties of Spanish that are common to the Southwest. *This problem* is compounded by both subtle and obvious stereotypes that disrupt communication across groups.

> **Clear:** The hospital has been attempting to provide training in cross-cultural communication skills because clinical people in each wing need to speak and understand the border varieties of Spanish that are common to the Southwest. *The difficulties of communicating with our patients who speak border Spanish are* compounded by both subtle and obvious stereotypes that disrupt communication across groups.

The solution to problems of reference across sentences is to be explicit: to use more words, or fuller phrases, or more exact terms so that readers can immediately determine the antecedent of a pronoun.

EXERCISE 13-2

The sentences in the following paragraphs are connected by references that may not agree with their antecedents, that may have no clear antecedent, that may be ambiguous, or that may have undetermined scope of reference. Fill out the phrases or provide specific terms that will lead to a clear reference in each case:

Effective teams recognize and expect to experience conflict. They seek to eliminate destructive personal conflict and promote constructive, substantive conflict. This problem arises when group members take criticism personally or when they let personal likes and dislikes poison the group process. For example, it could happen when someone decides, "I simply can't work with so-and-so." This can disrupt the group process and prevent the group from moving forward.

At other times, a group will experience substantive conflicts when there appear to be several possible routes to a goal and no clearly superior solution. They may be unable to compromise because they cannot take another member's viewpoint. They may refrain from voicing disagreement early in the process until the group explodes in unproductive anger. This is actually easiest to do in the early stage of the process.

A group that functions well will expect conflict and use it to advance the purposes of the group. They will encourage members to voice divergent opinions and resist making a decision until several avenues have been explored. This leads to a sense that the group keeps possibilities open, that everyone contributes to the eventual decisions, and that the final outcomes reflect a truly participative group process.[1]

Repeating Terms and Using Synonyms

One consequence of writing essays in school is that many adults carry away rules that are not very useful in the workplace. One such rule is that it is preferable not to repeat the same word within a sentence or within adjacent sentences in a paragraph. Trying to avoid repetition leads to a substitution process, with clarity corrupted by "elegant variation." Sometimes, students are taught to consult a thesaurus and to substitute fancier, "fifty-cent" words for their plain English equivalents. Thus, *meeting* becomes *convocation, assemblage, symposium,* or *colloquium.* Or an *attendance problem* is subsequently referred to as *this disturbing situation, the aforementioned difficulty,* or *a troubling neglect of school policy.*

The reasoning behind this stylistic rule is that a truly creative writer has many ways of saying the same thing and therefore can avoid boring the reader. The tradition goes back a long way in schools to rhetorical training in *copiousness.* The rhetorical value of elegant variation was one of display, of showing learning through fancy vocabulary.

These days, however, it is much more important to achieve economy and clarity in expression than it is to achieve copiousness or fullness. The problem with always choosing to use **synonyms** instead of repeating words shows up quite clearly in texts that describe computers. A writer might have several terms for *monitor,* including *display, CRT, screen, flat panel,* or a product name like *the NTR 1437.* Switching terms might confuse a reader, who will wonder if different terms refer to different objects. It is far better to choose a single, useful term of reference

[1] Loosely adapted from Rebecca Burnett, Chapter 5, "Collaboration in Workplace Communication," pp. 85–114 in *Technical Communication,* 3rd ed. Belmont, CA: Wadsworth, 1994.

and to scrupulously avoid changing terms. Keeping a reader on track, able to move through a document quickly and correctly, is much more important than impressing a reader with a range of terms.

EXERCISE 13-3

Disrupt the following paragraphs by substituting synonyms wherever possible for the repeated nouns *company/companies, workers, employees, managers, layoffs*. See if you can make the passage unintelligible.

The massive layoffs of the early 1990s have, in many cases, backfired, leaving companies in worse shape than ever. One recent study of large companies showed that while the profits of nearly all large companies fell between 1989 and 1991, the profits of companies that had layoffs fell much more. Another study showed that nearly two-thirds of managers saw no productivity gains for layoff programs during the late 1980s. When a company announces a massive layoff, employees turn paranoid. Many threatened employees immediately begin looking for other opportunities, and they may spend significant portions of their workdays on the phone, following leads and checking out rumors. The morale and self-esteem of the employees fall and their productivity goes down.

Many companies find that their best employees are the first to leave under layoff programs. The talented employees evaluate the often generous separation packages that are tendered and figure the odds on moving into another position while "taking the goods" are in their favor. The companies themselves tend to be bad at identifying unproductive workers, and the company tends to identify employees or work groups who are politically powerless, who can be let go with the least fuss. After the layoffs, managers frequently find themselves facing an increased workload and end up hiring the very same people who were let go.

Special Uses for Synonyms

We said above that you should, in general, avoid synonyms when making repeated reference to the same things. That does not mean, though, that you are totally restricted from ever repeating a word. When referring to the same noun, some variation is acceptable, especially with product names. You usually have the following options:

- Use the complete product name: for example, *the Bose® Jewel Cube speakers.*
- Use a shortened form of the product name: for example, *the Jewel Cube speakers.*
- Use a specific common noun synonym: for example, *the speakers.*
- Use the appropriate personal pronoun: for example, *they.*

Furthermore, when referring to common verbs, it is acceptable to use synonyms—especially to avoid repeating the same verb over and over, like *use.* Note, however, that for verbs describing specific technical actions or processes, you probably need to repeat the same verb throughout—for example, *photoetch.*

Using Reference to Build Coherent Paragraphs

Maintaining a clear pattern of reference across sentences is one of the best ways to create coherent paragraphs. Just as a reader needs to determine the subject of a sentence, so determining the topic of a paragraph brings unity and focus to a paragraph. In the following paragraph, notice how each sentence refers to elements in the preceding sentences (new topics are italicized, while references back to them are circled and underlined):

(1) One factor that is confounding the economic recovery is termed *downsizing* or *rightsizing.* (2) These synonymous terms the latter with a little more positive spin than the former, describe a consequence of reengineering *industries* to become more competitive. (3) The tendency in these industries is to change *management* practices so that control is extended downward in the organization to lower levels in the hierarchy. (4) Where middle managers once directed work processes, now self-managed teams are empowered to make decisions about inventory, staffing, and cost control. (5) The middle managers who once bloated the staffing charts are finding themselves an endangered species. (6) In their place, *front-line workers* are taking on responsibility for inventory and process control. (7) These front-line workers are working smarter, bringing their brains and strategic skills to the task of reengineering their workplace.

We could identify more chains of reference in this short paragraph, but the point is not to be exhaustive. Rather, we simply want to note that the language provides many ways to link sentences through patterns of reference. Paying attention to the links between sentences can help you see why some paragraphs seem to flow smoothly and coherently, while others seem choppy, illogical, or hard to follow.

In Summary

Any text sets up patterns of reference across sentence boundaries and makes reference to objects, people, ideas, or events outside the text. As a writer, it is your task to pay attention to the references and to make sure that each reference in the text points clearly and unambiguously to its antecedent.

Reference problems most frequently arise at the beginnings of sentences when a writer uses a pointer word like *this, that, these,* or *those.* The best way to avoid problems with these terms is to be explicit, to use a full, specific noun phrase to answer the question, "This *what?*" Reference problems can also be cured by a careful attempt to be consistent in how people or things are referred to.

The many resources for setting up patterns of reference allow you to create prose that is orderly, logical, and coherent. To gain control of reference, pay particular attention to sentence beginnings and ask what the link is to the previous sentence. If there is no clear link, see if you can make some explicit link at the beginning of your sentence that refers to the previous sentence. Chapter 23, "Maintaining Flow from Sentence to Sentence," will expand upon this discussion, but you have already seen in this chapter how written passages are threaded together with patterns of reference.

EXERCISE ANSWERS

Exercise 13-1 Answers

Here are possible solutions for the inappropriate shifts of number or person in the exercise sentences.

1. Writers need to be careful about pronoun choice. They can't just make choices based on single sentences. They need to consider what comes before and after a sentence.

2. An expert editor checks for consistency of pronoun reference from sentence to sentence. The editor wants to be sure that all references are consistent in both person and number.

3. A technical publications editor will provide different levels of editing depending on where a publication is in the publishing cycle. He or she might edit only for grammatical correctness, or for compliance with agency specifications, or for document consistency in terms and format.

4. In our publications group, we prefer that writers schedule their editing sessions rather than just bringing in their manuscripts and expecting a fast turnaround. It is not so difficult for people to plan ahead and avoid last minute rush jobs. If they want quality work, the writers need to allow sufficient time for final copy editing and correction.

5. You may believe that the use of first and second person is inappropriate in formal writing. You may remember an English teacher who asked you to avoid *you* in your essays. But you don't want to always avoid second person reference. It can help you create solidarity with your readers. They will feel like you are talking directly to them. Don't listen to absolute rules. Decide when the use of first or second person is appropriate. As a writer, you need to make informed choices, not depend on absolute rules.

Exercise 13-2 Answers

Here are possible solutions for the exercise sentences. Phrases have been filled out and specific terms provided that lead to clear references. There are, of course, other ways to solve the problems.

Effective teams recognize and expect to experience conflict. They seek to eliminate destructive personal conflict and promote constructive, substantive conflict. Destructive conflict arises when group members take criticism personally or when they let personal likes and dislikes poison the group process. For example, destructive conflict could happen when someone decides, "I simply can't work with so-and-so." Declaring the impossibility of working with a group member can disrupt the group process and prevent the group from moving forward.

At other times, a group will experience substantive conflicts when there appear to be several possible routes to a goal and no clearly superior solution. Some members of the group may be unable to compromise because they cannot take another member's viewpoint. Other group members may refrain from voicing disagreement early in the process until the group explodes in unproductive anger. Bringing disagreement into the discussion is actually easiest to do in the early stage of the process.

A group that functions well will expect conflict and use it to advance the purposes of the group. They will encourage members to voice divergent opinions and resist making a decision until several avenues have been explored. This attitude of open acceptance in the early stages leads to a sense that the group keeps possibilities open, that everyone contributes to the eventual decisions, and that the final outcomes reflect a truly participative group process.

Exercise 13-3 Answers

In an effort to disrupt the following paragraphs, synonyms have been substituted wherever possible for the repeated nouns *company/companies, workers, employees, managers, layoffs*. Individual answers, of course, may differ from this version.

The massive layoffs of the early 1990s have, in many cases, backfired, leaving companies in worse shape than ever. One recent study of large capitalist enterprises showed that while the profits of nearly all large business concerns fell between 1989 and 1991, the profits of the going concerns that had instituted rightsizing fell much more. Another study showed that nearly two-thirds of managers saw no productivity gains for handing out walking papers during the late 1980s. When an enterprise announces a massive reduction in workforce, employees turn paranoid. Many threatened workers immediately begin looking for other opportunities, and they may spend significant portions of their workdays on the phone, following leads and checking out rumors. The morale and self-esteem of the rank and file fall and their efficacy goes down.

Many business concerns find that their best personnel are the first to leave under corporate restructuring. The talented staff evaluate the often generous separation packages that are tendered and figure the odds on moving into another position while "taking the goods" are in their favor. The firms themselves tend to be bad at identifying unproductive workers, and the partnership tends to ascertain the identity of workers or work groups who are politically powerless, who can be let go with the least fuss. After the firings, capitalist pigs frequently find themselves facing an increased workload and end up hiring the very same people who were let go.

chapter 14

Lean Words versus Redundant Words

Writers with a strong sense of style invariably prefer fewer words to more words. When we want to compliment a writer, we say that he or she makes every word count and suggest that not a single word could be deleted without disrupting the writer's meaning.

Weak writers, in contrast, often compose in a loose or flabby style, using more words than necessary to convey their meaning. We would describe their writing as lacking economy.

In this chapter, you will work on eliminating **redundancy**—unnecessary wordiness. When you finish the chapter, you should be able to:

- Distinguish a lean style from a redundant style
- Recognize common structures that lead to redundancy
- Eliminate needless words from your writing

In essence, this chapter asks you to put your prose on a diet. It is a simple enough concept. Applying it consistently can lend economy, clarity, and strength to your writing.

Sources of Redundancy

We discuss below a number of sources of redundancy. Your writing style is unlikely to suffer from all the kinds we describe. As you work through this chapter, think about the kinds of redundancy that actually characterize your writing and resolve to address those specific kinds.

Simple Redundancies

Some words may seem to be acting as modifiers (words that add details to noun or verb phrases). When examined, however, they don't so much qualify meaning as repeat what is already contained in the noun or verb phrases. This is called redundancy.

Each of the following phrases has redundant terms that can be deleted with no loss of meaning:

blue ~~in color~~	oval ~~in shape~~
cool ~~in temperature~~	~~most~~ unique
~~means to~~ impl~~y~~ies	several ~~in number~~
joined ~~together~~	attractive ~~in appearance~~
~~personal~~ opinion	~~final~~ outcome
careful ~~in habits~~	cooperate ~~together~~
~~the reason is~~ because	~~past~~ history
repeat ~~again~~	visible ~~to the eye~~
~~conscious~~ attention	thirty ~~(30)~~ minutes

When you work to eliminate redundancy, you are deleting words that do not add anything to the writing. They are simply deadwood or clutter.

It is probably a good idea to distinguish redundancy from **repetition,** since repetition can be a useful writing strategy. Repeating words or phrases lets you emphasize a point or remind a reader of what you have argued. Repeating key words can help you maintain a **focus** on your topic. Within a paragraph, repeating your focus at the beginning of successive sentences can help you tie one sentence to the next. All of these are useful, strategic uses of repetition. When you eliminate redundancy, you are deleting the accidental or unmotivated repetition, not the intentional repetition. Redundancy is needless repetition.

Circumlocution

A **circumlocution** is a long way of saying something—going around a topic with words (*circum* means "around" and *locute* means "to say"). Circumlocutions sound formal to some writers; to many readers, however, such constructions sound pompous or inflated.

Imagine shorter alternatives to the following phrases:

in the modern world of today

in a manner of speaking

with regard to the fact that

it is possible that there might be

without any regard for the feelings of the people involved in the situation

submit suggestions that you may have in regard to the topic

in view of the foregoing discussion among the assembled participants

You can probably cite more phrases that some writers (or speakers) rely on that add bulk without adding muscle to prose. Preassembled phrases that are simply plugged into prose without much thought are the steroids of stylistic development. True fitness comes from working carefully with individual words.

Freshness of style comes from choosing each word, not from pasting together long, prepackaged phrases. You can develop a strong style by resisting the impulse to paste high-sounding but empty phrases into your sentences.

Intensifiers

Intensifiers are adverbs—words that modify verbs, adjectives, and other adverbs. Often, intensifiers can be cut without losing strength. Sometimes, phrases actually sound more forceful without the intensifiers. Less can be more.

Compare the phrases on the left (with intensifiers) to those on the right (without):

a very important reason	an important reason
a most unusual occurrence	an unusual occurrence
a really innovative idea	an innovative idea
a totally honest manager	an honest manager

The gain in concision is small—a single, short word eliminated. But the gain in overall directness and power is significant.

EXERCISE 14-1

Eliminate the wordiness from the following paragraph.

During the time period of the early 1970s, the progress of economic development ran into various new obstacles that blocked the path and the pace of progress. Productivity started going down into a decline, which seemed to suggest to some observers who looked at the problem that something or other was wrong with the way we were using technology, people and labor, and the organization of work. Other observers blamed the decline in productivity, at least in part, on the infusion of new female and young workers who came into the workplace with less experience and less education than previous workers. Bottlenecks arose in other areas as well that blocked continued increases in productivity. By the period of the 1980s, postwar productivity brought about the result that mass markets were saturated at home in this country, motivating companies to go abroad to other countries, which encouraged globalization of competition. Eventually, after a period of time, global demand around the world became saturated as well, like demand at home in this country, and a number of industries were faced with the situation of a glut in production.

Expletive Constructions

Sentences that begin *It is . . .* or *There are . . .* are termed **expletive constructions.** They can often be rephrased with a gain in economy. Consider the following wordy examples:

> There were good ideas to cut costs and increase productivity that were introduced during the seminar.
> It is clearly the case that the new manufacturing economy demands workers who know how to learn.

These sentences can be rewritten to introduce a real subject instead of a dummy subject:

> The seminar introduced good ideas to cut costs and increase productivity.
> Clearly, the new manufacturing economy demands workers who know how to learn.

Sometimes, an expletive construction is the best way to introduce what it is you want to discuss—it gets your topic on the floor. At other times, expletive constructions help you emphasize or focus your reader's attention on some topic. But more often than not, expletives are not chosen for a good reason and they can be rewritten to good effect.

Overreliance on Prepositional Phrases

Prepositional phases work as modifiers, adding details or qualifications to other parts of the sentence (as discussed in Chapter 7, "Placing Modifiers Effectively"). Relying too heavily on prepositional phrases, however, leads to a style that is wordy and bureaucratic sounding. The modifying content of the prepositional phrase can often be reduced to a single word, resulting in fewer words and greater directness.

In the following pairs of sentences, the first relies on prepositional phrases for modification, the second on single-word modifiers:

Wordy: The report of the Secretary of Labor was comprised of a list of essential skills needed by graduates of public schools in America.

Concise: The Secretary of Labor's report listed essential skills for American public school graduates.

Wordy: The worker in a restructured factory must have in his or her possession skills of the sort that allow him or her to work as a team member in a cooperative fashion.

Concise: The restructured factory demands teamwork.

Wordy: The development of self-esteem among employees is built through a system of recognition for contributions to the business by employees.

Concise: Employees gain self-esteem when management recognizes their contributions to the business.

A style that relies too heavily on prepositional phrases becomes heavy. Eliminating prepositional phrases energizes sentences without sacrificing content. It places the energy in the verb phrase, which is always a good idea for strengthening prose.

Negative Constructions

Sometimes sentences that are negatively phrased can be rephrased in the positive. Doing so takes fewer words and improves clarity. Compare the following pairs of sentences:

Employees should not refuse to accept responsibility for the product before it arrives at the workstation and after it leaves.

Employees should accept responsibility for the product before it arrives at the workstation and after it leaves.

The positively phrased sentence saves a couple of words, but, more importantly, it reflects a positive outlook rather than a negative one.

Incidentally, research favors rewriting negative sentences in positive terms. Readers understand passages that are positively worded more quickly and accurately than they do those that are negatively worded. And sentences with two or more negatives are notoriously difficult to understand:

> It is not true that no new manufacturers have not been able to increase quality while maintaining the line on wages.

This sentence turns your head each time a negative is introduced.

Unlike some of the other revisions suggested in this chapter, changing from negative to positive often changes the meaning in important ways. Compare the following sentences:

> A not uncommon complaint is for managers to find that employees do not have a sense of career path within the organization.

> Managers frequently complain that employees do not have a sense of career path within the organization.

> Managers value employees who have a sense of career path within the organization.

Each sentence gets a little shorter through these revisions. Does the meaning change as the wording becomes more economical and direct? Certainly. Each version becomes more positive, in both grammatical and psychological terms. Generally, writers who cultivate a strong style prefer positive phrasing to negative, and the preference probably helps not only their writing style, but their successful interaction with others.

Complex Verb Constructions

Verb phrases can be either single words or several. Frequently, verbs have **auxiliary** or helping verbs attached before the main verb, words such as *have* or *will*. These auxiliary verbs help indicate when something happened, or whether it might happen, or whether it is completed.

Writers sometimes fall into a pattern of using auxiliaries that could just as easily be deleted. Using simpler verb forms in the predicates leads to greater directness in fewer words. Look at the verb pattern in this paragraph:

> The Japanese industries have been more successful than American ones at exploiting networks. The strength of Japanese automakers has begun with work teams on the factory floor and has extended outward to

> supplier groups and conglomerate groups of principal partners and financial backers. Japanese manufacturers have had stronger relationships with fewer suppliers than have American manufacturers. GM, for instance, has been using 1,500 suppliers per plant. Toyota has been using only 177 suppliers per plant.

Deleting the auxiliaries and going to the more direct present tense results in a gain in economy and immediacy:

> The Japanese industries are more successful than American ones at exploiting networks. The strength of Japanese automakers begins with work teams on the factory floor and extends outward to supplier groups and conglomerate groups of principal partners and financial backers. Japanese manufacturers have stronger relationships with suppliers than American manufacturers do. GM, for instance, uses 1,500 suppliers per plant. Toyota uses only 177 suppliers per plant.

In Summary

Preferring concise writing to wordy writing should become second nature to your writing strategy. You will find pleasure in taking a knife to your own writing to cut away the deadwood.

It is true that schools do not necessarily encourage the habits discussed in this chapter. Students are often told to write 500 words when they may only need 347. So students learn to pad their writing, to fill it out with empty phrases, circumlocutions, and loose sentence structures. You can break those habits by paying attention to word choice. You can decide to make each word count.

A word of caution: Being brief is generally desirable, but being too brief can cause problems. Sometimes a few extra words convey politeness, as when you ask someone do something:

> Would you mind moving over slightly so that John might join us at the table?

The auxiliary verbs (*would, might*) and extra words (*that, slightly, join us*) soften the request—they carry interpersonal meaning. Removing them would lead to directness but also bossiness:

> Move over so John can sit at the table.

The trick is to find a balance—of economy, of clarity, of effect. As a writer, you want to offer sufficient information in an economical style—

a style that feels comfortable and encourages cooperation from your reader. Working with an editor under tight space restrictions is one good way to learn what it means to write in a lean, concise style. It is often easier to write something long than something short—words are cheap, and they come easily once they start rolling. Editors are good at spotting wasted words because they spend their lives with too much copy and too little space. Sometimes managers are explicit about how long a document can be. Writing to the specification of a single page or to some other specific length limit can sharpen your prose style by encouraging you to focus on being concise.

You might apply this chapter by editing a piece of your writing so it is shorter and more economical. Choose a memo of two or three pages and bring it down to one page or choose a report of ten to fifteen pages and try to cut it by one-half or one-third. Your goal is to keep the content but to reduce the word count. You will be amazed at how many words you can delete and how many you can rewrite with greater economy.

EXERCISE 14-2

Use the revision strategies discussed in this chapter to revise the following paragraph for economy. You will be able to strike out some words, but you will find that more gains in economy come from revising phrases and sentences.

It would appear to be the case that the new economy will demand a new set of skills from its workers that will replace the old set of skills. Because of the changes in technology and the changes in production, marketing, and distribution, workers will find it necessary to continually learn new skills and new ways of doing things. The ability to learn will be the basic foundation to all other skills.

Workers will also need strong communication skills as well. It is likely that, with the move toward an information and service based economy, every worker will need to be a good reader and writer. Additionally, workers will need strong oral communication skills to communicate with other workers and with clients and customers. There are several oral communication skills that will be particularly useful. These include strong listening skills, oral skills related to negotiation and problem solving, and the ability to communicate well with others to influence and work with others in previous and subsequent phases of the production process.

Workers in the new economy will need good technical skills. While technology takes over repetitive work processes, humans take over the higher-order functions of controlling the technology so it does what it is supposed to do. The new automation eliminates and does away with repetitive intellectual tasks, just as was the case with earlier automation doing away with repetitive physical tasks. For every repetitive task surrendered, however, it turns out that new human capabilities are demanded that lead to the exploitation of the flexible capabilities of the new technology. As technology grows more flexible and powerful, the corresponding need grows for work teams to be more skillful in order to deploy it effectively and productively.

EXERCISE ANSWERS

Exercise 14-1 Answers

Here is a less wordy version of the paragraph:

During ~~the time period of~~ the early 1970s, ~~the progress of~~ economic development ran into ~~various~~ new obstacles ~~that blocked~~ <u>to</u> ~~the path and the pace~~ progress. Productivity ~~started going down into~~ ~~a~~ decline<u>d</u>, which ~~seemed to~~ suggest<u>ed</u> to some observers ~~who looked at the problem~~ that something ~~or other~~ was wrong with ~~the way we were using~~ <u>our uses of</u> technology, ~~people and~~ labor, and the organization of work. Other<u>s</u> ~~observers~~ blamed the decline in productivity, at least in part, on the infusion of female and young workers ~~who came into the workplace~~ with less experience and ~~less~~ education ~~than previous workers~~. <u>Other</u> bottlenecks ~~arose in other areas as well that~~ blocked continued increases in productivity. By ~~the period of~~ the 1980s, postwar productivity ~~brought about the result that~~ <u>saturated</u> mass markets ~~were saturated~~ at home ~~in this country~~, motivating companies to go abroad. ~~to other countries, which~~ <u>This move</u> encouraged globalization of competition. Eventually, ~~after a period of time,~~ global demand ~~around the world~~ became saturated as well, ~~like demand at home in this country,~~ and ~~a number of~~ <u>many</u> industries ~~were~~ faced ~~with the situation of~~ a glut in production.

Here is a "cleaned-up" version of the paragraph, so you can see how it flows:

During the early 1970s, economic development ran into new obstacles to progress. Productivity declined, which suggested to some observers that something was wrong with our uses of technology, labor, and the organization of work. Others blamed the decline in productivity, at least in part, on the infusion of female and young workers with less experience and education. Other bottlenecks blocked continued increases in productivity. By the 1980s, postwar productivity saturated mass markets at home, motivating companies to go abroad. This move encouraged globalization of competition. Eventually, global demand became saturated as well, and many industries faced a glut in production.

Exercise 14-2 Answers

Here is a revised version of the paragraphs. Words have been deleted, verbs rewritten in present tense, prepositional phrases rephrased, expletives deleted, ideas rearranged, and sentences combined:

The new economy demands a new set of skills from its workers. Changes in technology, production, marketing, and distribution force workers to continually learn new skills. Basic to all other skills is the ability to learn.

Workers also need strong communication skills. In an information- and service-based economy, every worker must read and write well. Additionally, workers need to communicate orally with other workers and with clients. In particular, workers must listen well, negotiate tactfully, and use language to solve problems. Workers must communicate well to influence and work with others in all phases of production.

Workers in the new economy need good technical skills. As technology takes over repetitive work processes, humans take over the higher-order functions of controlling the technology. The new automation eliminates repetitive intellectual tasks, just as earlier automation eliminated repetitive physical tasks. For every repetitive task surrendered, however, new human capabilities are demanded to exploit the flexible capabilities of the new technology. As technology grows more flexible and powerful, work teams need to be more skillful at deploying it effectively.

chapter 15

Technical Vocabulary versus Jargon

"Professional writing uses a *clear* and *concise* vocabulary," reads the theme for this unit. You read in Chapter 14, "Lean Words versus Redundant Words," that writers sometimes inflate their texts by adding words that contribute to the word count but not necessarily to the meaning. This trait is sometimes true of writers of technical documents, when they feel the need to impress readers with their extensive vocabulary.

Other times, in an effort to be concise, writers of technical documents go to the *opposite* extreme of being overly brief: using a single, unusual term (often a long one) in place of several shorter ones; taking for granted the meaning of acronyms; and omitting the "little" words of normal connected speech like *a, an,* and *the*. This kind of writing goes beyond concise to the terse or cryptic end of the scale.

Another reason why writers use jargon is a desire to show "club membership" in a specialized field. Using certain technical terms and acronyms shows that writer to be "in the know." But such language, while convenient among specialists with a common vocabulary, may exclude readers who are not specialists in the same field.

In this chapter, we will return frequently to a piece of advice that you have read before in this book. Applied to the content of this chapter, that advice is as follows: Choose technical vocabulary and acronyms with your reader in mind. When you finish reading this chapter you should have a better understanding of how to reach your reader better by:

- Writing to inform rather than to impress
- Using necessary technical vocabulary while avoiding inappropriate jargon and "technobabble"
- Using invented words (clipped forms and back-formations; blends and acronyms; word-class shifters) in effective ways
- Writing briefly and concisely, while still retaining a smooth flow

Writing to Inform versus Writing to Impress

We once saw a poster on the wall of a writing classroom that read:

Writing to

Impress

DOESN'T

After we got over the initial abruptness of the syntax, we decided that we very much liked the sentiment expressed there. In an effort to impress people and sound sophisticated, writers often pull out all the excesses of "formal" writing they were taught in school, including unnecessarily complex vocabulary and sentence structures. The ironic effect of such writing is frequently the *opposite* of what was intended: the reader either feels intimidated or, more likely, senses that the writer is uncomfortable or is hiding something behind that wall of words. And whatever that something is, it certainly isn't a clear understanding of the topic!

To make our point about the negative effects on the reader of writing to impress, we're going to ask *you* to be the reader of two versions of the same information and then to answer the questions in the exercise following them.

Version A

This Interface Description Document (IDD), which is produced and maintained by the Control Center, provides early control information for the Control Center Design Review. The IDD describes the functional requirements for data, audio, and video communications services for planning and executing mission operations.

Version B

This document is released as an Interface Description Document (IDD) and provides early interface control information in support of the Control Center Design Review (CCDR). The Control Center is responsible for the production, coordination, and control of this IDD. The functional requirements for data communications services, audio communications services, and video communications services to accomplish the planning for and execution of mission operations are described herein.

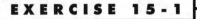

EXERCISE 15-1

After reading the two versions of the introductory paragraph for the IDD, discuss the following questions with your classmates:

1. Which version of the information would you prefer to read? Why?

2. Which writer do you think is more intelligent—the author of Version A or the author of Version B? Why?

3. Which writer do you feel is trying harder to impress you?

If you're like most readers we have asked to compare these two passages, you prefer Version A, and you probably also think that the author of Version A is more intelligent!

Below are some of the differences that readers have cited in preferring Version A to Version B:

- The *tone* of Version A is much friendlier then that of Version B, which uses a lot of imposing legal language.
- The *syntax* of Version A is simpler and more compressed than the "legalese" of Version B, which has lots of unnecessary repetitions and interruptions. Version A says:

This IDD describes the functional requirements for data, audio, and video communications services for planning and executing mission operations.

Version B says:

The functional requirements for data communications services, audio communications services, and video communications services to accomplish the planning for and execution of mission operations are described herein.

- Version B uses empty, formal-sounding phrases, such as *in support of,* which Version A avoids altogether.
- Version A uses a more direct, "verbal" style:

which is *produced* and *maintained* by the Control Center

Version B uses a more abstract, "nominal" style in an attempt to impress:

The Control Center is responsible for the *production, coordination,* and *control* of this IDD.

In this chapter and those that follow, we will use these differences between Version A and Version B to illustrate the problems created by elevated language, technical and legal jargon, and nominal style—and we will show you how to avoid them.

The "Thesaurus School of Writing"

Some writers have evidently attended the "Thesaurus School of Writing." These are writers who draft their texts using common language and then go through those drafts systematically replacing common terms with longer synonyms derived from a thesaurus. Sometimes this language slides into "technobabble," which we will discuss in the next section. Other times it is simply pretentious, without any attendant technical flavor.

Consider the following (*italicized*) examples of "thesaurus writing":

A new line is *initiated* after the eightieth character is entered.

This document is organized into five sections. It is intended to *facilitate* the efficient development and maintenance of the Control Center hardware and software.

Is there a special technical sense to *initiate* and *facilitate* in these examples? Maybe, but we don't think so. No technical meaning would be lost (apparently) by substituting the more common synonyms *begin* and *help:*

A new line *begins* after the eightieth character is entered.

This document is organized into five sections. It is intended to *help* programmers develop and maintain the Control Center hardware and software.

Many times, the longer word adds more syllables but not more meaning. This is especially true of words that seem to add syllables to the same word root. A familiar example of this "more heat but no more light" phenomenon is the amplification of the word *use*. Writers often "dress up" the verb *use* by substituting the word *utilize;* for its noun meaning, they substitute the word *utilization*. Now there is nothing wrong with using a more exact synonym of *use* like *employ* or *require,* but *utilize* means nothing more technical than *use*. Can you think of other examples like this?

In addition to being pretentious, thesaurus writing creates two problems: one for the writer, the other for the reader. For the *writer,* the problem in using an unfamiliar synonym is that he or she may be ignorant of some of its **connotations,** or associated meanings. While the unfamiliar word's **denotation,** or dictionary meaning, may be the same as the common word, its connotative flavor may make it inappropriate as a synonym—and may lead to some unintended shades of meaning apprehended by the reader.

For a *reader* of thesaurus writing, the problem is that he or she may have to stop reading at the inserted synonym to consider its meaning or, in some cases, to consult a dictionary. While we have no qualm with people who want to increase their reading comprehension by increasing their reading vocabulary, we think they should be able to do so *willingly* and on their own schedule—rather than being *forced* to do so in order to understand the meaning of a professional document.

EXERCISE 15-2

The following proverbs have evidently been rewritten by someone who attended the "Thesaurus School of Writing." Translate them back into their common English equivalents.

1. An igneous, sedimentary, or conglomerated mass of mineral substances that advances by means of revolving repeatedly on its axis is not apt to accumulate on its surface any leafy bryophytic organisms.

2. It is conceivable that one may take a large, solid-hoofed herbivorous mammal and direct it to a body of hydrogen and oxygen (chemically combined at the ratio of two molecules of the former to one molecule of the latter), but it does not follow that one can coerce such a mammal to take such material into its oral cavity and pass it down its esophagus.

3. A small vertebrate covered with furry appendages, held in the terminal section of one's forelimb, is of equal relative value to two such organisms located in a small herbaceous plant not exceeding 25 feet in height at maturity.

4. Pulchritude in the human organism descends no further than the subcutaneous layer of the outer dermis.

5. It is foolish for one to enumerate the embryonic members of a common group of domesticated fowl until they have been incubated.

6. Bodies of accumulated liquids whose upper surfaces seem to be in a state of relative tranquillity frequently have currents flowing at great distances below the surface.

7. A container kept under constant surveillance will not reach a state of extreme heat capable of vaporizing liquids.

Appropriate and Inappropriate Technical Vocabulary

We are not suggesting that you avoid all specialized vocabulary when writing about specialized topics. Indeed, *both* Version A and Version B on page 202 use the same technical vocabulary and acronyms: *Interface Description Document (IDD); functional requirements; data, audio,* and *video communications services; mission operations.* Such vocabulary is useful and desirable; it allows for conciseness in writing. What we are trying to stress here is the need for you to consider the *appropriateness* of such vocabulary. Ultimately, that appropriateness (or inappropriateness) depends upon the intended audience of your document.

This is also true about deciding which technical words you use without explanation and which ones you will have to define in context: your decision should depend on the level of technical understanding of the intended audience of your document. To be safe, you may decide—as the writers of Version A and B did—to introduce acronyms in their full forms first. Or you may decide—as we have done in this book—to set technical terms in bold type and to include a glossary of terms at the end. If you find yourself having to define *every* technical term you're using, though, you may be aiming at the wrong audience.

Obviously, you can't anticipate the needs of *all* audiences, nor should you be expected to. But two words of caution are in order: First, writers often *over*estimate how much readers know about a topic; second, documents often have a larger audience than the writer anticipates.

Jargon and "Technobabble"

If it's difficult to say exactly which words are safe to use in a technical document, it's a little bit easier to say which kinds of words should be used sparingly or not at all. For example, **jargon** (defined as a common term used in a specialized sense) should be used sparingly.

A good example of jargon is the word *boot* used in computing. In common use, *boot* is a noun meaning "an extended shoe," and when used less frequently as a verb it means "to kick something out or away." But in computer shoptalk, *boot* is a verb meaning "to start up a personal computer." We even talk about a *cold boot* and a *warm boot* depending on whether the computer is being started from a "cold" (unpowered) state or restarted from a "warm" (already powered) state. (A *warm boot* is a little easier on the computer and a bit faster, so there is an advantage in being able to distinguish between the two procedures.) Most professions have their own specialized language, or jargon, and when you're communicating within that profession, that jargon is entirely appropriate.

Jargon is *inappropriate,* however, when you are communicating with readers outside the profession. A manual can advise a user either to "perform a cold boot" or to "restart the computer by turning the power switch off, then pausing, then turning the power switch back on." Anyone who can locate the power switch has enough context and learning to follow the latter procedure, but some readers are bound to be baffled by the term *cold boot.* If you decide that a jargon term is a useful one, then it is appropriate to define it in context. In the case of *cold boot,* you would need to decide if it is worth spending the time teaching your readers what a *cold boot* is and then reinforcing the learning. Otherwise, you can avoid the jargon, use a few more words, and keep your readers on track. When jargon is used and not defined, it can either confuse readers or signify to them that they are not members of the "in group" being addressed.

There is an erroneous belief that using jargon is more *precise* because it expresses in a single word what would require several words in common terms. This belief is that fewer words are necessarily better. But that's not always so. If the single-word term is an unfamiliar one to most readers, they may spend more time deciphering it, looking it up in a specialized dictionary, or asking someone in the field.

Take, for example, the use of the word *contention* in the following sentence:

> Hardware simulators increase the range of machine types that can be tested, while at the same time reducing hardware contention.

To *contend* in common terms means "to argue for a position or to struggle for a goal," so *contention* as a noun must mean "a struggle" or "a fight." But what's fighting here—the hardware? *Hardware contention* in this example means "scheduling struggles over the use of the hardware." Wouldn't it be quicker to write that in the first place:

> Hardware simulators increase the range of machine types that can be tested, while at the same time reducing scheduling struggles over the use of the hardware.

This rewrite avoids a confusing bit of jargon rather than making readers stop to figure out the meaning of the term. Shorter is not always better, and being precise is not always a higher goal than being clear on the first reading.

Jargon can also slide quickly into **gobbledygook,** language more complicated than the concepts it is used to refer to. Variant dialects of gobbledygook include *legalese* (language more legal sounding than what it means), *bureaucratese* (language more official sounding than what it means), and *technobabble* (language more technical sounding than what it means). These dialects are not mutually exclusive. Writers often intermix legalese with technobabble, as Version B above demonstrates.

It is sometimes hard to tell where appropriate technical vocabulary (and even appropriate jargon) ends and technobabble begins. A good example of this slide occurs with the computer term *interface.* When used as a noun in computing, *interface* means "the place where humans and machines meet or interact," and the use of the term is perfectly acceptable. But when, in an effort to sound more technically "with it," *interface* is used as a verb meaning "to communicate with," it becomes technobabble. The following example is a technobabble use of *interface:*

> Technical coordinators are the customer representatives who *interface* with the company for support on the usage of personal computers.

"Interface" simply adds a more technical-sounding tone to the sentence, not any more technical meaning than the common synonyms *work* or *support:*

> Technical coordinators support customers with questions concerning computer use.

(Notice that we've also substituted the shorter noun *use* for *usage.*)

To eliminate technobabble, you need to concentrate on finding plain alternatives. You always have other choices.

EXERCISE 15-3

The words in the following list seem to be derived from a desire to impress the reader.[1] List more common synonyms for each word in the space to the right. But be careful: some of the words also have a specialized jargon usage. Can you make a case for maintaining some of these words in specialized contexts? Identify which ones and which specialized contexts they belong to.

---

[1]Adapted from Joseph Williams, *Style: Ten Lessons in Clarity and Grace,* 3rd ed., Glenview, IL: Scott, Foresman, 1989.

1. activate

2. apprise

3. contingent upon

4. deem

5. facilitate

6. implement

7. interface (verb)

8. initiate

9. termination

10. utilization

Effective Use of Invented Words

Another characteristic of technical writing is the frequent use of invented words (clipped forms and back-formations; blends and acronyms; word-class shifters). **Clipped forms** are new words derived by cutting off parts of existing words. **Back-formations** are likewise derived by shortening longer words but often by removing a suffix (or supposed suffix) in order to serve as different part of speech. **Blends** are new words formed by combining parts (or all) of other words, and **acronyms** are new words formed by combining just the initial letter (or letters) of various words. Finally, **word-class shifters** are not so much new words as they are words that can shift their part of speech depending on their sentence context.

Each of these invented word groups is discussed below. The advice we will give you about including them in your document is, again, to be sensitive to your readers. Will most of your readers be familiar with the invented word? If not, you either need to define the word in context (if it is an important word for them to understand) or consider replacing it with a more familiar synonym.

Clipped Forms and Back-Formations

Clipped forms are new words formed by shortening longer words. Many clipped forms are used so widely that people neither recognize them as such nor remember the underlying longer word from which they were derived. The word *bus* is one such example; it originally came from the word *omnibus,* from Latin meaning "all." In its first uses as a clipped form, *bus* was written with an initial apostrophe (*'bus*) to show the part of the word that had been lopped off. Later it appeared without the apostrophe, and today most people think of *bus* as the whole word.

An example of a technical word derived from clipping is the noun *fab,* used in the semiconductor industry to indicate a manufacturing facility for semiconductor wafers. It is probably a clipped form of *fabrication area.* Other examples are *qual* (derived from *qualification*—another technical process in the semiconductor industry), *spec* (from *specification*), and *lab* (from *laboratory*). An interesting phenomenon about clipped words like these is that, even though they don't sound like English words, we treat them just like other words in adding plural markers to them: *fabs, quals, specs,* and *labs.*

Is it important to know the derivations of these clipped forms? Not necessarily—as long as all your readers understand your reference. In the case of industry-specific words like *fab* and *qual,* however, you would probably do better to use their longer forms, *fabrication area* and *wafer qualification,* when writing about them to nonindustry readers. You would surely pause if you heard someone say (as recorded in an interview we read), "We work through regulatory affairs people for day-to-day comms but also meetings and telecons with med and clinical folks."

Back-formations, like clipped forms, are derived by shortening longer words, but back-formations are formed by removing a suffix (or supposed suffix), enabling the new word to serve as a different part of speech. An example of a back-formation is the verb *to donate,* derived from the noun *donation.* Back-formation is a perfectly legitimate and common process in English. Back-formations fill a hole where no single word exists to cover a multiple-word meaning.

Some linguistic "purists" object to new words formed in this manner. Two examples of currently disputed usage are the back-formed verbs *to incent* or *to orientate.* The verb *to incent,* used in sales, is a back-formation derived from the noun *incentive,* and it means "to motivate for money." *To orientate* is a back-formation derived from the noun *orientation.* "OK," the purists might say, "we'll grant you *incent* because it fills a hole (though it still sounds funny to our ears). But *orientate* is unnecessary, because there is already a perfectly good existing verb with the same meaning: *to orient.*"

These purists have a point: invented words are unnecessary if there are already existing one-word synonyms. But what is likely to happen if *orientate* catches on is that it will acquire a specialized sense different from *orient.* And that has already started to happen. Many users today distinguish between *orient,* "to get one's bearings," and *orientate,* "to go through an orientation process."

Blends and Acronyms

Blends, as noted above, are words formed by combining parts (or all) of other words. Like back-formation, blending is a well-established process for coining new words in English. In Chapter 11, "Hyphens," we discussed how words that are often used together (e.g., *book* and *store*) may be joined by hyphens and gradually come to be written as one word, with no space between. This phenomenon is a kind of blending, and many professions—technical or otherwise—have words of this type, which outside that profession are written as separate words. Whole-word blends are especially common in technical industries as brand names or product names, such as *Microsoft* and *LaserWriter*.

The more usual kind of blending, however, is to combine *parts* of words rather than whole words. This usually entails combining the first part of one word with the last part of another. Many now-common words in English are blends of this type: *brunch* (a blend of *breakfast* and *lunch*), *smog* (from *smoke* and *fog*), and *motel* (from *motor hotel*) are several examples. Examples from technical writing include *milspecs* (from *military specifications*) and *hightech* (from *high technology*), both of which also involve clipping. When using blended words from a technical profession, it is important (again) to consider your readers. Will most of them recognize the invented word?

Acronyms are new words invented by combining the initial letters of the name of an object, project, agency, or other entity. Like blends, acronyms are formed by combining parts of several underlying words. Acronyms also resemble clipped forms in that many people no longer know the words underlying them—especially acronyms written in lowercase letters. How many of you know what the letters of *radar, laser,* or *scuba* stand for? Did you even know that they are acronyms?[2]

As with blends (and, indeed, all the words discussed in this section), it's important to consider your audience when deciding which acronyms to include and which to define. Let's consider an earlier citation from a technical document that uses an acronym:

> This Interface Description Document (IDD) provides early control information for the Control Center Design Review.

Notice how the acronym *IDD* is introduced in the first sentence after first listing out the full proper name. This treatment suggests that the writer is

---

[2] *radar* stands for "radio detection and ranging"; *laser* stands for "light amplified by a series of emitted radiations." In the case of *scuba,* we actually know who the inventor was—it was the oceanographer Jacques Cousteau who coined "self-contained underwater breathing apparatus."

teaching this acronym to the reader for later use. However, you shouldn't bother to teach—or even use—such an acronym if you are only going to use it once or twice in a document.

Another way of introducing acronyms suggests that most readers are already familiar with them. In this format, the acronym is used first, followed by the explanation in parentheses:

> DOS (Disk Operating System) is the basic operating system used by most IBM-compatible personal computers.

Sometimes writers assume that some acronyms are so familiar to their readers that they use them without any explanation of the underlying words. Such is the case with *IBM* in the preceding example, and is also demonstrated in the following example from a conference paper:

> In this demonstration, I will simulate bisynchronous, start-stop, and Synchronous Data Link Control (SDLC) device types, as well as communications controllers and CPUs.

Evidently, this writer assumes that all of his readers will recognize *CPU*, so he doesn't bother to write out *central processing unit*, though he *does* explain *SDLC*. This strategy may save space, but it can also backfire: As we mentioned above, documents often reach a legitimately wider audience than the writer initially imagines, so some of the ultimate audience may not be familiar with the unexplained acronym.

Further, the *same* acronym may mean *different* things to different audiences, depending on the context. *PC*, for example, may mean "personal computer" to one audience, "IBM-compatible personal computer" to another audience, "process control" to another audience, and "printed circuit" to still another audience, not to mention "politically correct"! Sometimes context will make the meaning clear, but it is not difficult to conceive of an audience at a technical symposium that would understand *PC* in each of these meanings!

Like jargon, undefined acronyms may also be favored by a writer who wants to gain or show "club membership." If a reader has to ask what the meaning is, then he or she is obviously *not* in the club. Sometimes that is an appropriate use of acronyms—to intentionally exclude those who do not have a "need to know." If that is how you use acronyms, however, make certain that you *really* want to exclude all those audiences.

Two more small points before leaving acronyms: First, although it may not be necessary to know the underlying words behind an acronym, not doing so can sometimes cause amusing redundancies. Returning to the first citation in this section, it is not too hard to imagine people speaking about *IDD documents,* even though the final *D* of the acronym stands for *document!*

And that raises the second point: how to form the plural of an acronym. Let's say in the preceding example that you are not going to be redundant, that you realize that the final *D* of *IDD* stands for *document*. How do you write the plural of the acronym to signify that you are talking about "Interface Description Document*s*"? You will probably find two prevailing ways to signify the plural of an acronym. On the one hand, many handbooks will tell you to simply treat an acronym like any other noun: make it plural by adding an *s* (but a lowercase one) to the end—hence, *IDDs*. In *practice,* however, you may notice that most writers make acronyms plural by adding *'s*—hence, *IDD's*. This practice follows the plural treatment for unusual nouns in English —adding *'s* to avoid confusion with already existing English words or to avoid creating unpronounceable words, as in the following example:

Right: Dot your *i*'s and cross your *t*'s

Wrong: Dot your *is* and cross your *ts*

Our advice is to follow the prevailing practice in your company, division, department, or area.

Word-Class Shifters

A final kind of invented word comes from the tendency of technical writing to creatively shift word classes—that is, to use words of one part of speech (e.g., nouns) as another part of speech (e.g., verbs). In this respect, the phenomenon is not different from back-formations. Unlike back-formations, however, word-class shifters change parts of speech without adding or deleting anything from the word.

Word-class shifters are common in all forms of English and have an honorable history. The most frequent word-class shifts in technical writing are from nouns to verbs and vice versa. We discuss the shift from verbs to nouns in Chapter 16, "Preferring a Verbal Style." In this section, we will limit our discussion to the shift from nouns to verbs.

Perhaps because of the speed with which new nouns enter the language (mirroring the speed of technical innovation), there seems to be a lack of already existing verbs to use in conjunction with those nouns. The solution adopted by many writers is to use those nouns as verbs. A purported guideline in an IBM style manual from the 1970s reads: "Any noun can be verbed." This humorous example demonstrates what it advises, and many of the technical uses of nouns as verbs are equally creative, often employing some of the jargon, clipped nouns, and acronyms that we have discussed in this section. Thus we read:

NOUN	VERB
• *badge* (an identification tag worn by employees for security reasons)	• *to badge* in to a building
• *interface* (the place at which humans and machines meet in a program or product)	• *to interface* with customers
• *qual* (a qualification test for semiconductor wafers)	• *to qual* a batch of wafers
• *IPL* (Initial Program Load)	• *to IPL* the program (note the redundant use of *program*)

When using word-class shifters like these—as with all the other invented words discussed in this section—it's important to consider your audience. Some readers will object to *any* newly coined words, and there's not much you can do about such an audience. Others will object to *some* of these words as jargon, especially if there is an already existing common synonym (like *interact* for *interface*). Still others will be perfectly comfortable with most of these coinages, especially if they are members of the same community of specialists for whom you are writing. As with all vocabulary choices, it's important to balance conciseness with clarity.

Avoiding "Telegraphic" Style

One final kind of conciseness often adopted by writers of technical documents is a style called **telegraphic** style or **"headline"** style. This writing style omits all the "little" words like *a* and *the* in an attempt to save space and to sound more direct, as in the following examples:

> Ease tension on cable at handlebar by loosening lock nut and set screw.
> Mount chain on third sprocket with turn of pedal.
> Adjust tension by three or more turns of stop screw.

While telegraphic style may be appropriate for document headings or for presentation transparencies (where space is at a premium), it is a false economy when applied to technical prose—especially to instructions—because its conciseness is achieved at the expense of flow and reader comprehension.

In terms of flow, telegraphic style often sounds abrupt or terse, forcing the reader to do more work by mentally filling in the omitted words:

> Ease *the* tension on *the* cable at *the* handlebar by loosening *the* lock nut and *the* set screw.

Mount *the* chain on *the* third sprocket with a turn of *the* pedal.

Adjust *the* tension by three or more turns of *the* stop screw.

A more serious problem is the potential for misunderstanding on the part of the reader. Let's consider the first example of telegraphic style cited above:

Ease tension on cable at handlebar by loosening lock nut and set screw.

What part of speech is *set?* It is a word-class shifter, capable of acting as either a noun or a verb. Depending on whether *set* is a noun or a verb, the sentence will have different, mutually exclusive meanings—each of which will result in a different action by the reader:

Ease the tension on the cable at the handlebar by loosening the lock nut

N

and the set screw.

Ease the tension on the cable at the handlebar by loosening the lock nut

V

and set the screw.

Reinserting the "little" word *the* makes the intended meanings clear and removes the possibility for reader misunderstanding.

In Summary

This chapter has examined the impulse to be concise in professional writing by using specialized, technical vocabulary. As we have seen, using a single word in place of several words is not always *clearer.* Sometimes the use of technical vocabulary comes across as being pompous or inflated (as in the use of polysyllabic synonyms derived from a thesaurus). Sometimes it may mystify the reader (as in the case of unfamiliar and unexplained technical jargon or invented words). In the worst cases, it may actually mislead the reader (as with "telegraphic" style). It is important, therefore, to balance the need to be *concise* with the need to be *clear* to the intended audience.

English is a rich language with a tremendous ability to incorporate new words, whether from other languages or from the technical innovation occurring with dizzying speed today. It's exciting to be part of a community of new word users and coiners and to demonstrate your membership in that community by using those new words. Just be careful to be generous in including your readers in that community, too—by either avoiding or explaining any terms they might not understand!

EXERCISE 15-4

Select a document from a technical field you are familiar with. (The document may be one you have written.) Examine the document for occurrences of the following:

- "Thesaurus" writing
- Inappropriate technical jargon or "technobabble"
- Invented words—clipped forms and back-formations; blends and acronyms; word-class shifters
- "Telegraphic" style

Are all of these usages appropriate for the audience of the document? Can you substitute more common words or more appropriate technical vocabulary?

EXERCISE ANSWERS

Exercise 15-1 Answers

Answers will vary with individual students.

Exercise 15-2 Answers

The following proverbs have been translated back into their more well-known forms.

1. An igneous, sedimentary, or conglomerated mass of mineral substances that advances by means of revolving repeatedly on its axis is not apt to accumulate on its surface any leafy bryophytic organisms.

   A rolling stone gathers no moss.

2. It is conceivable that one may take a large, solid-hoofed herbivorous mammal and direct it to a body of hydrogen and oxygen (chemically

combined at the ratio of two molecules of the former to one molecule of the latter), but it does not follow that one can coerce such a mammal to take such material into its oral cavity and pass it down its esophagus.

You can lead a horse to water, but you can't make it drink.

3. A small vertebrate covered with furry appendages, held in the terminal section of one's forelimb, is of equal relative value to two such organisms located in a small herbaceous plant not exceeding 25 feet in height at maturity.

A bird in the hand is worth two in the bush.

4. Pulchritude in the human organism descends no further than the subcutaneous layer of the outer dermis.

Beauty is only skin-deep.

5. It is foolish for one to enumerate the embryonic members of a common group of domesticated fowl until they have been incubated.

Don't count your chickens before they're hatched.

6. Bodies of accumulated liquids whose upper surfaces seem to be in a state of relative tranquillity frequently have currents flowing at great distances below the surface.

Still waters often run deep.

7. A container kept under constant surveillance will not reach a state of extreme heat capable of vaporizing liquids.

A watched pot never boils.

Exercise 15-3 Answers

The underlined words below are the more common synonyms for the words in the left column. A case could be made for almost *all* the words in the left-hand column used in specialized ways.

1. activate   <u>start</u>

2. apprise   <u>inform</u>

3. contingent upon   <u>dependent on</u>

4. deem   <u>think</u>

5. facilitate   <u>help</u>

6. implement   <u>carry out</u>

7. interface (verb)   <u>work</u>

8. initiate   <u>begin</u>

9. termination   <u>end</u>

10. utilization   <u>use</u>

Exercise 15-4 Answers

Answers will vary with individual students' documents.

chapter 16

Preferring a Verbal Style

In the preceding chapter, we joked about the ease with which technical professions could "verb" nouns in order to create verb equivalents for new inventions and processes. In this chapter, we discuss the *opposite* tendency—that is, the tendency of much professional writing to "noun" verbs or adjectives by adding certain suffixes, a process called **nominalization** ("making nounlike").

The impulse behind nominalization seems to be to sound more "impressive" or "professional" since it always results in more words being used to say basically the same thing. But as we saw in the last chapter when we examined the thesaurus school of writing, if you sound like you are trying to impress, that's the impression you will create—that you are *trying* to impress.

Further, the use of too many nouns in professional writing creates a leaden, heavy effect, which we will call a **nominal style.** Frequent use of nominalized verbs and adjectives is one characteristic of a nominal style; heavy use of long strings of nouns (noun compounds) and prepositional phrases is another characteristic. We discuss this latter characteristic in Chapter 17, "Unpacking Noun Compounds." The important point to note here is that a nominal style will slow your writing down. We want to encourage you to use the opposite, leaner style, one that puts the action in the verbs. We call this leaner style a **verbal style.**

This chapter shows you how to create a verbal style by recapturing actions and qualities from nominalizations. The main advice of the chapter is to express actions and qualities as verbs and adjectives, rather than as nouns.

In this chapter, you will learn:

- Why a verbal style is important
- How to identify nominalizations
- How to turn nominalizations back into verbs, thereby eliminating weak "placeholder" verbs
- How to determine which nominalizations play a useful role and which should be changed

The Importance of a Verbal Style

In Chapter 6, "Common Problems with Verbs," we said that verbs are the nuclei of clauses, the centers around which subjects and objects revolve. It is important, therefore, to let the verbs express the action of a clause or a sentence. Otherwise, the verb is a hollow placeholder, an empty word filling the verb's position in the clause, while the real action is being expressed by a noun. Letting the verbs express the action is also a way of being more *concise*. When the verb expresses the action, the sentence is usually shorter and more direct; when the action is expressed in nominal forms, the sentence requires more words (including the empty "placeholder" verb) to express the same meaning.

But, you may ask, aren't verbs *always* the action words in sentences? No. You have already seen in earlier chapters that some sentences do not express an action at all but rather describe a state of affairs. Consider, for example, the following sentence:

Jane is a pilot.

This sentence is an example of a linking verb sentence, a kind of formula that says A = B. There is no action expressed.

It is also possible for sentences to express an action but for that action to be expressed by a noun, rather than by a verb. Consider the following sentence:

My attendance in the class was at the request of my manager.

Initially, this sentence looks similar to the preceding sentence in that the main verb is a form of *to be*. But unlike the preceding sentence, there *is* an action (in fact two of them) expressed here. *Was at the request of* could be paraphrased by *was requested by*:

My attendance in the class was requested by my manager.

But that's a **passive** construction (i.e., the subject is not acting; active and passive constructions are covered in Chapters 18 and 19), so let's make it active:

My manager *requested* my attendance in the class.

So far, so good. Now the subject, *manager,* is doing something. But there's still another action lurking in the sentence—the one contained in *attendance.* If we express that action as a verb, we get the following:

My manager requested that I *attend* the class.

This is a more direct and—not coincidentally—shorter sentence than the one we began with.

The transformation from the two nominalizations of the original sentence to their verb equivalents in the final version nicely illustrates the difference between a nominal style and a verbal style. As we said above, much professional writing uses a nominal style, and that style is a contributing factor to the weightiness (and abstractness) of professional prose. We want to advocate a prose style that is lean and direct. That means *expressing actions and qualities as verbs and adjectives,* rather than as nouns. Notice that the second sentence of this paragraph demonstrates the very qualities of the nominal style that it describes:

[Nominal] style is a contributing factor to the weightiness (and abstractness) of professional prose.

Contributing factor, weightiness, and *abstractness* are all nominal forms of what could be expressed as verbs or adjectives. See how much more direct this sentence is when expressed in a verbal style, with the action centered in the verb and qualities in modifying adjectives:

Nominal style *contributes* to a *weighty* and *abstract* professional prose.

Notice that the verbal-style sentence is shorter than the nominal-style one by four words. (But notice also that we had to change the sentence structure slightly to get to the verbal style.)

Recognizing Nominalizations

How do you recognize nominalizations, the noun forms of verbs and adjectives? Word endings (**suffixes**) are a great help here. The following suffixes usually indicate a nominalized form of a verb:

-ion (and its related forms *-tion* or *-ation*)
-ance (and its related form *-ence*)
-ment

The suffix -*ion* is probably the most common indicator of a nominalized verb. In fact, the word *nominalization* itself contains this suffix!

The suffixes below usually indicate a nominalized form of an adjective:

-*ity*
-*ness*

Words ending in these suffixes are usually nominalized forms of actions or qualities. These nominalized forms refer to "the act of [verb]ing" or "the state or quality of being [adjective]," and their meanings are generally more abstract than the verb or adjective from which they are derived. In the nominalizations that we have already seen in the preceding section, *attendance* means "the act of *attend*ing," *weightiness* means "the quality of being *weighty*," and *abstractness* means "the quality of being *abstract*." You probably sense that these nominalized forms are more abstract than their verb and adjective forms.

Not *all* nouns ending in these suffixes, however, are abstract nominalizations. *Regulation* is an abstract nominalized verb meaning "the act of regulating," but regulation*s* is a quite concrete noun meaning "*things* that regulate." *Management* may be an abstract nominalization meaning "the act of managing," but more typically it is a concrete noun meaning "the *people* who manage."

Further, these suffixes are not the only ones that indicate nominalizations. Many verbs can be nominalized simply by changing the concluding letters—without adding an entire suffix. Thus, *respond* becomes *response*, *pursue* becomes *pursuit*, *defend* becomes *defense*, and so on. Other verbs can become nominalized without any change at all. Examples of these word-class shifters include *claim, need, conduct, import*, and *research*.

Whatever the *form* of a nominalized verb or adjective, the *meaning* of such nominalizations is abstract. It focuses more on the *act* of doing something or the *state* of being something, rather than on the action or quality itself.

EXERCISE 16 - 1

Identify the underlying verbs or adjectives in the following nominalizations. Also state the meaning of each nominalization: Identify the nominalizations that are *not* abstract. (Some of them, like *management* above, have two meanings: an abstract one and a concrete one).

Nominalization	Underlying Verb or Adjective	Meaning of the Nominalization
1. discussion		
2. offense		
3. coordination		
4. violations		
5. appearance		
6. diligence		
7. procurement		
8. measurement		
9. luminosity		
10. readiness		

Gerunds

One additional type of nominalization is so common that it has a special name: gerund. A **gerund** is the noun use of the *-ing* form of a verb (called a participle in Chapter 6, "Common Problems with Verbs"). Gerunds are frequently the names of activities; thus, we get sentences like the following:

Swimming is one of my favorite sports.

That's a perfectly acceptable sentence, and it would be awkward to substitute an infinitive verb for the gerund:

To swim is one of my favorite sports.

However, gerunds are used many times in professional writing to express an activity when the verb form would make the sentence more direct and shorter. Consider the following sentence:

This program is useful in *the teaching of* department procedures to new employees.

In this sentence, *teaching* is a gerund. Expressing it as a verb would allow us to delete two words (*the* and *of*) and would make *department procedures* the direct object of *teaching,* rather than a prepositional phrase modifier of it:

> This program is useful in *teaching* department procedures to new employees.

You might take this revision one step further:

> This program *teaches* department procedures to new employees in a useful way.

Now the sentence expresses its action in the main verb *teaches.* Notice, too, the preferred S-V-O pattern:

> **s**   **v**   **o**
> This program teaches department procedures to new employees in a useful way.

Be on the lookout for gerunds that you can turn back into verbs. You will typically be able to eliminate a few other words in the process.

Eliminating Weak Verbs

One characteristic of **linking-verb** clauses and sentences is that they do not express any action but rather a state of affairs. Professional writing is often characterized by a high proportion of sentences (as high as 30 or 40 percent) with weak linking verbs like *be, seem, appear,* and *become.* A document that is full of such sentences generally has a weighty style that deadens the overall directness of the document.

In the above sections, you have seen that nominalizations often have the same effect. Therefore, it should come as no surprise that nominalizations often occur *together with* linking verbs. Consider, for example, the following sentence:

> Resolution of the conflict is a necessity if we are to continue operating as a team.

This is a linking-verb sentence: the main verb is a form of *to be* (*is*). The subject is *resolution,* a nominalization of the verb *resolve.* The subject complement, *necessity,* is also a nominalized form—either of the adjective *necessary* or the helping verb *need.* Notice what happens when we turn both of those nominalizations back into verbs:

We *need* to *resolve* the conflict if we are to continue operating as a team.

Suddenly there is action in the sentence! And where is the former main verb *is?* It vanished when we rephrased the sentence in a verbal style.

In addition to linking verbs, there are other weak verbs that occur with nominalizations. Like linking verbs, these weak "placeholder" verbs also vanish when the action is recaptured from the nominalized form, as in the following examples:

perform analysis	becomes	*analyze*
conduct measurements	becomes	*measure*
increase motivation	becomes	*motivate*
achieve completion	becomes	*complete*

Identifying weak verbs like these will often help you when you are hunting nominalizations.

EXERCISE 16-2

Underline the weak verbs in the following sentences. Rewrite the sentences with stronger verbs, recapturing the action from nominalizations as necessary.

1. Paul has a work assignment on the UP project.

2. He has demonstrated cooperation with others working on the project.

3. However, Paul shows a lack of programming knowledge.

4. This has been a hindrance to him and the group.

5. The little amount of code that he *has* written is indicative of his lack of efficiency in attaining completion of even elementary programming tasks.

The Uses (and Abuses) of Nominalizations

We're not suggesting that you should always avoid nominalizations. Nominalizations are useful when you want to talk about the action or quality in itself, without ascribing it to a doer or a recipient. For example, you might want to talk about *reciprocity* as an important legal concept without specifying *who* was being *reciprocal* to *whom*. And some nominalizations have become fixed, either in themselves or as parts of larger expressions—words such as *ventilation, oxidation,* and *capital formation.* We *are* suggesting, however, that you be wary of using nominalizations to express the main action in a sentence. What nominalizations usually do is to *suppress,* rather than *express,* the action.

Like the other types of vocabulary discussed in this unit, nominalizations can pose more of a problem initially for readers than for writers. For writers, the nominalization may be transparent because it is used all the time in a work setting. And if you're writing for other workers in the same setting, it may be perfectly acceptable to *perform problem determination procedures,* for example. (If this phrase is used all the time, it may well get turned into an acronym, *PDPs.*) But be careful: readers unfamiliar with these procedures may well find such a phrase opaque or purposely misleading. Why talk about *performing problem determination procedures* when *determining problems* might be clearer (if a more difficult goal to achieve)?

EXERCISE 16-3

In the following sentences, first underline all the nominalized verbs and adjectives. (Be on the lookout especially for *-ing* verbs used as gerunds.) Then decide which ones should be changed, and rewrite the sentences appropriately.

1. There may be problems in the motivating of employees during the implementation of the new manufacturing process.

2. The necessity for the new process came from the unreliability of the current process.

3. Acceptance of the new process was made because of its repeatability of production within given standards.

4. Greater cost savings were one factor in the selection of this process.

5. Defect reduction and an increase in productivity were the other factors.

6. By converting to the new process, minimization of deviation occurs, thus providing more consistency in our products.

7. Uniformity is much better across the lots since implementation of the new process in the test area.

8. Provided that we can secure the approval of higher management, we would like to suggest that the completion of implementation of the new process in all manufacturing areas be by March 15.

EXERCISE 16-4

Rewrite the following letter to make the style more verbal. Underline all the nominalizations in the following document. Change them back into verbs or adjectives as appropriate. Be prepared to defend your choices for those you do *not* think should be changed.

Notice how changing the nominalizations back into verbs and adjectives allows you to eliminate weak verbs, as well.

Dear Madam:

Please accept our apologies for the inconvenience and personal frustration you have experienced as a result of the processing delay of your refund claim.

As you know, we have rules and procedures to follow in the identity determination and refund payment to claimants. Sometimes, these rules that are intended to provide protection for the consumer may seem bureaucratic and unbending.

However, it is extremely important that refund claims be delivered to the proper owners. Identity verification and the provision of proof of purchase are claimant responsibilities.

We would like to continue in the processing of your claim; however, we must again ask you for a provision of proof of former residence at the address in Dallas. Once this address verification is received, our evaluation will be continued.

A lack of response from you within sixty days will be taken as an indication of your lack of interest in the pursuit of your claim, and your file will be closed accordingly.

Your patience and cooperation in this matter are greatly appreciated.

In Summary

This chapter has begun a two-chapter discussion of the problems of the heaviness, wordiness, and inactivity created by a nominal style and has shown you how to avoid those problems by using a lighter, leaner, more action-oriented verbal style.

In this particular chapter, we have examined nominalizations—noun forms of verbs and adjectives. You have seen that recapturing the underlying verbs and adjectives out of nominalizations has several advantages:

- It increases the directness of a sentence by placing the action in the verb.
- It eliminates extra words, including placeholder verbs.

You have learned how to identify nominalizations by looking for words ending in suffixes like *-ion, -ance, -ment, -ity, -ness,* or *-ing* preceded by *the* and followed by *of.* You have also learned to look for other nominalizations that, although not as easily identifiable by particular suffixes, still abstract the action or quality out of verbs and adjectives.

Finally, we have considered those times when nominalizations are appropriate: when you consciously *intend* to talk about a process or abstract quality in and of itself, rather than attributing it to a particular person performing a particular action. As we noted in our discussion of technical jargon in the last chapter, the deciding factor about using nominalizations *must* be how easily your intended audience will understand the nominalized verb or adjective.

EXERCISE ANSWERS

Exercise 16-1 Answers

Underlying verbs and adjectives are filled in, as are the meanings of the nominalizations. "Concrete" nominalizations are identified as such; all the rest are abstract, focusing on the act of performing or the state of being, rather than on the specific action or quality.

Nominalization	Underlying Verb or Adjective	Meaning of the Nominalization
1. discussion	discuss	"the act of discussing"
2. offense	offend	"the act of offending" (abstract) or "an occasion when one has offended" (concrete)

3. coordination	coordinate	"the act of coordinating"
4. violations	violate	"specific instances when someone has violated a rule or law" (concrete, but compare with *violation*, "the act of violating")
5. appearance	appear	"the act of appearing"
6. diligence	diligent	"the state of being diligent"
7. procurement	procure	"the act of procuring"
8. measurement	measure	"the act of measuring" (abstract) or "a particular value derived from measuring" (concrete)
9. luminosity	luminous	"the quality of being luminous"
10. readiness	ready	"the quality of being ready"

Exercise 16-2 Answers

Weak verbs in the original versions have been underlined. Sentences have been rewritten with stronger verbs (in underlined italics) re-captured from nominalizations.

1. Paul <u>has</u> a work assignment on the UP project.

Paul *<u>is assigned to work</u>* on the UP project.

2. He has <u>demonstrated</u> cooperation with others working on the project.

He has *<u>cooperated</u>* with others working on the project.

3. However, Paul <u>shows</u> a lack of programming knowledge.

However, Paul *<u>lacks</u>* programming knowledge.

4. This has <u>been</u> a hindrance to him and the group.

This has *<u>hindered</u>* him and the group.

5. The little amount of code that he *has* written <u>is</u> indicative of his lack of efficiency in <u>attaining</u> completion of even elementary programming tasks.

The little amount of code that he *has* written *<u>indicates</u>* his inefficiency in *<u>completing</u>* even elementary programming tasks.

Exercise 16-3 Answers

Nominalized verbs and adjectives are underlined. Rewritten sentences appear below, with rewritten nominalization in underlined italics.

1. There may be problems in the motivating of employees during the implementation of the new manufacturing process.

There may be problems *motivating* employees while *implementing* the new manufacturing process.

2. The necessity for the new process came from the unreliability of the current process.

A new process was *necessary* because the current process was *unreliable*.

Or, putting the purpose clause up front:

Because the current process was *unreliable,* a new process was *necessary*.

3. Acceptance of the new process was made because of its repeatability of production within given standards.

Repeatability is a useful nominal in discussing production, so both should probably remain unchanged. However, there is no reason to retain acceptance:

The new process was *accepted* because of its repeatability of production within given standards.

4. Greater cost savings were one factor in the selection of this process.

Savings is not really an abstract nominalization, but a specific quantity, so it should remain:

Greater cost savings were one factor in *selecting* this process.

5. Defect reduction and an increase in productivity were the other factors.

Productivity is a useful nominalization, quite common in many industries and businesses, so it remains:

Reducing defects and *increasing* productivity were the other factors.

Or, to make the sentence more parallel to the one preceding it, with adjectives modifying the factors:

<u>Reduced</u> defects and <u>increased</u> productivity were the other factors.

6. By converting to the new process, <u>minimization</u> of <u>deviation</u> occurs, thus providing more <u>consistency</u> in our products.

Deviation is a useful concept in manufacturing, so it remains unchanged in the following revision:

Converting to the new process <u>*minimizes*</u> deviation, thus making our product more <u>*consistent*</u>.

7. <u>Uniformity</u> is much better across the lots since <u>implementation</u> of the new process in the test area.

The lots are more <u>*uniform*</u> since the new process has been <u>*implemented*</u> in the test area.

8. Provided that we can secure the <u>approval</u> of higher management, we would like to suggest that the <u>completion</u> of <u>implementation</u> of the new process in all manufacturing areas be by March 15.

Although it ends in a nominal suffix, management is not a nominalization here because it does not mean "the act of managing" but rather "the people who manage":

If higher management <u>*approves,*</u> we suggest that the new process *be* <u>*completely implemented*</u> in all manufacturing areas by March 15.

Exercise 16-4 Answers

Nominalized verbs and adjectives are underlined.

Dear Madam:

Please accept our <u>apologies</u> for the <u>inconvenience</u> and personal <u>frustration</u> you have experienced as a <u>result</u> of the <u>processing</u> delay of your <u>refund</u> <u>claim</u>.

As you know, we have rules and procedures to follow in the identity determination and refund payment to claimants. Sometimes, these rules that are intended to provide protection for the consumer may seem bureaucratic and unbending.

However, it is extremely important that refund claims be delivered to the proper owners. Identity verification and the provision of proof of purchase are claimant responsibilities.

We would like to continue in the processing of your claim; however, we must again ask you for a provision of proof of former residence at the address in Dallas. Once this address verification is received, our evaluation will be continued.

A lack of response from you within sixty days will be taken as an indication of your lack of interest in the pursuit of your claim, and your file will be closed accordingly.

Your patience and cooperation in this matter are greatly appreciated.

Here is one possible revision using a more verbal style. Note that we have retained some useful nominalizations:

Dear Madam:

We apologize for the inconvenience you have experienced as a result of our delay in processing your claim for a refund.

As you know, we have procedures to follow in determining identity and in paying refunds to claimants. Sometimes, these rules that are intended to protect the consumer may seem bureaucratic and unbending.

However, it is extremely important that we refund claims to the proper owners. Claimants are responsible for verifying identity and providing proof of purchase.

We would like to continue processing your claim; however, we must again ask you to provide proof of your former residence at the address in Dallas. Once we receive this information, we will continue evaluating your claim.

If you do not respond within sixty days, we will close your file accordingly.

We greatly appreciate your patience and cooperation in this matter.

chapter 17

Unpacking Noun Compounds

The last chapter began a discussion of nominal style—the heavy reliance on nouns that gives a leaden, wordy quality to much professional writing while hiding the real action of a clause or sentence. In this chapter, we focus on another characteristic of nominal style—using long **noun compounds**—and show you how to "unpack" them to achieve a more verbal style.

A noun compound is a noun phrase made up of two (or more) nouns, where the initial nouns act as modifiers of the last (head) noun in the phrase. English is full of two-word noun compounds, like *baseball* and *television set* (and you read about some of those in Chapter 11, "Hyphens"). But when three, four, or more nouns stack up on top of each other, it's often difficult to determine which noun is modifying which. Particularly in scientific and technical writing, long noun compounds abound, as the following examples illustrate:

> reentry support booster jets
> approach avoidance mechanism
> night vision navigational direction detector

For noun compounds such as these, intelligibility depends on the background of the reading audience.

In this chapter, you will learn how to:

* Identify which nouns modify which in a noun compound
* Decide when to retain noun compounds and when to rewrite them
* Make your writing style more verbal by unpacking noun compounds in one of two ways: into shorter strings of prepositional phrases, or into verb phrases or full clauses

How Many Nouns in a Row?

Two-noun compounds are common enough in English and present no real problem of comprehension. Like typical noun phrases, where a head noun is modified by several adjectives preceding it, the head of the phrase in a two-noun compound is modified by the noun preceding it. The problem arises, however, when we get two (or more) nouns together modifying a head noun. Then it is often not so clear which noun is modifying which.

Consider the following example:

customer data input

What does this compound mean? It seems to have two different meanings, depending on where we group the middle noun, *data:*

[customer data] input

or

customer [data input]

In the first bracketing, the meaning of the phrase seems to be "input of customer data (that is, input of data *about* the customer) by someone else." The meaning of the second phrase seems to be "data input *by* the customer."

In cases like these, where the relationship among nouns is potentially confusing, readers may have no difficulty understanding the writer's intended meaning. Either the context makes clear what meaning is intended, or the reader's own background knowledge makes the intended meaning clear. In a situation where readers possess sufficient background in a field of specialization, then, readers will have no difficulty understanding long noun compounds common to that field. But do all your intended readers have that knowledge? That is the question to ask in using long noun compounds.

EXERCISE 17-1

Draw square brackets around the nouns (and adjectives) that cluster together in the following noun compounds. Are there any compounds that are ambiguous—that is, ones you could bracket in more than

one way? Be on the watch for redundant nouns that could simply be deleted.

1. problem determination procedures

2. screen display damage

3. installing dealer sessions

4. corporate database integrity maintenance

5. customer skills transfer sessions

6. voice software service support

7. metal contamination reduction

8. Control Program Facility Concept Manual (a book title)

9. strategic application development productivity tool

10. tactical munitions dispenser statistical process control implementation program

---

The answer to the question posed in this section's heading "How Many Nouns in a Row?" is not an actual value like five or six. The likelihood of a reader understanding the noun compound does not depend on an upper limit for the number of nouns but rather on the writer's skill in explaining terms in context or on the reader's own background. And in cases where the meaning is *not* clear, you may have to "unpack" the noun compound in one of the ways discussed in the next section.

Two Ways to Unpack Noun Compounds

The justification behind using noun compounds seems to be that it is more concise to stack nouns *in front of* the head word in the phrase rather than to string them out as a series of "cascaded" prepositional phrases *behind* the head noun. This justification is valid as long as your intended audience will be familiar with the resulting conglomeration of nouns.

But when there is the possibility that your audience will *not* be familiar with the phrases, you will serve them better if you unpack the noun compound in one of two ways: as a string of prepositional phrases following the head noun; or as a verb phrase or full clause, recovering a verb from any nominalizations in the original compound.

Unpacking Noun Compounds into Prepositional Phrases

In the preceding sections, we have already seen examples of noun compounds unpacked into strings of prepositional phrases. The technique for unpacking noun compounds into strings of prepositional phrases is to start with the final noun as the beginning of the phrase and then to list out each preceding noun from the original compound *in reverse order* from its occurrence in that compound, separated by a preposition. It's easier to show this visually:

$$\text{Noun}_1 + \text{Noun}_2 + \text{Head Noun (or } N_1 + N_2 + HN) \rightarrow$$
$$\downarrow$$
$$\text{Head Noun} + \text{Preposition} + \text{Noun}_2 + \text{Preposition} + \text{Noun}_1$$

Now let's demonstrate this formula with some actual noun compounds:

$N_1 + HN \rightarrow HN + Prep + N_1$
drugstore $\rightarrow$ store for drugs

$N_1 + N_2 + HN \rightarrow HN + Prep + N_2 + Prep + N_1$
customer data input $\rightarrow$ input of data about/by the customer

$NP_1 + N_2 + HN \rightarrow$
(corporate database) integrity maintenance $\rightarrow$

$HN + Prep + N_2 + Prep + NP_1$
maintenance of the integrity of the corporate database

In this last example, the reason for writing the formula with a noun phrase (corporate database) instead of just nouns is to keep adjective-noun phrases together. You can also stop unpacking noun compounds at any stage, as illustrated in the unpacking of the dense noun compound below:

strategic application development productivity tool

First, bracket the nouns that go together. Then start rewriting the phrase using prepositions to separate the clusters of phrases.

[strategic application [development]] [productivity tool] $\rightarrow$
[productivity tool] for [strategic application [development]] $\rightarrow$
[productivity tool] for the [development] of [strategic applications] $\rightarrow$
[tool] to increase [productivity] in the [development] of [strategic applications]

It is not always necessary to unpack the original phrase all the way down to the final stage. Sometimes the intermediate versions are sufficiently clear.

Turning Noun Compounds into Verb Phrases or Full Clauses

Another way to unpack noun compounds is to turn them into verb phrases or full clauses by recapturing verbs from any nominalizations in the compounds. Because this strategy results in a more verbal style, this way of unpacking noun compounds is actually preferable to the strategy of stringing out the compound into prepositional phrases, which still results in a nominal-style construction.

Let's consider the last noun compound discussed in the preceding section:

strategic application development productivity tool

There are three nominalizations in the compound: *application, development,* and *productivity.* However, two of them—*application* and *productivity*—are frequently used terms in the computer industry, so that leaves *development* as an abstract nominalization meaning "the act of developing." Using the technique of unpacking the compound into its component noun phrases separated by prepositions gives us the following:

productivity tool for the development of strategic applications

All we have to do now is recover the verb from *development:*

productivity tool for *developing* strategic applications

Notice that this version, as well as using an *-ing* verb, is actually two words *shorter* than the unpacked version we began with.

Consider another example:

problem determination procedures

In Exercise 17-1, you identified *problem determination procedures* as a noun compound, with *problem determination* being the "bracketed" nouns. Using the technique of unpacking noun compounds into a head noun followed by prepositional phrases would yield:

procedures for problem determination

or

procedures for the determination of problems

But *determination* is also a nominalization, so let's recapture the verb out of it:

> procedures for determining problems

If we had begun with a context sentence like the following:

> The customer service representative performed the problem determination procedures.

we could now rewrite it as:

> The customer service representative performed the procedures for determining problems.

But *performed the procedure for determining* is really a wordy way of saying *determined,* so we could "elevate" *determined* to be the main verb of the clause:

> The customer service representative determined the problems.

This time, unpacking the noun compound yields a complete clause.

So you now have two strategies to use in unpacking noun compounds when those compounds may cause confusion to your readers: the first strategy is to string the compound out into nouns or noun phrases separated by prepositions; the second strategy is to turn the compound into verb phrases (or full clauses) by recovering nominalized verbs and adjectives. Now it's time to practice these strategies in an exercise.

EXERCISE 17-2

In Exercise 17-1, you practiced bracketing the following noun compounds. Now you are given context sentences for each compound. Rewrite any potentially confusing ones, using one or both of the two strategies discussed in this section.

1. Excessive brightness may cause screen display damage.
2. All of the already-shipped computers will be upgraded through installing dealer sessions.
3. One of your main tasks as new manager of MIS (Management Information Systems) is corporate database integrity maintenance.

4. One of the best methods for teaching new software is through customer skills transfer sessions, letting experienced customers teach new customers.

5. Voice software service support for the new telecommunications line has been suspended until the new version is released.

6. With the new grid array package, a 35 percent metal contamination reduction can be achieved.

7. The new Control Program Facility Concept Manual lists many helpful hints and ideas, but I prefer the old CPFC manual.

8. This new strategic application development productivity tool reduces our product development cycle time by 20 percent.

9. The Defense Department has contracted our Quality Assurance department to create a tactical munitions dispenser statistical process control implementation program.

In Summary

This chapter concludes our discussion of nominal style—the use of nominalizations and noun compounds and, to a lesser extent, long strings of prepositional phrases—which creates a heavy quality in much professional writing. In this chapter, we have focused on unpacking long noun compounds of more than two nouns in length, especially where the relationship of the modifying nouns is potentially ambiguous to your readers.

You have seen two ways to make ambiguous noun compounds clearer: first, by stringing together the modifying nouns (or noun phrases) with prepositions; second, by turning them into verb phrases or full clauses with recovered nominalized verbs or adjectives. This second strategy has the advantage of using a more verbal style—that is, a style where the action is in the verb—and therefore requires fewer words to express the same meaning.

Putting It All Together

This exercise asks you to pull together your learning from Chapters 13–17. First, read through the following excerpt from the first page of an operating manual for a computer terminal. Then rewrite the

excerpt to make it more user-friendly. Pay special attention to the following:

- **Consistency of vocabulary**
- **Technical terms and jargon**
- **Noun forms of verbs**
- **Noun compounds**

You might wish to *identify* problems in these areas before *rewriting* them. You might also find it easier to read through for *one type* of construction at a time. For example, go through once and circle all synonyms; then underline all technical terms and jargon; finally, bracket noun forms of verbs and noun compounds.

1.0   INSTALLATION AND INTRODUCTION

The DTA-5A should be positioned on a steady surface and at a comfortable user access level. A three-inch minimum clearance space must be provided at the rear of the DTA-5A to provide ease of access to the power switch and brightness control. Care should be taken that magazines or other paraphernalia do not fall behind the terminal and impede ventilation. The line cord should then be connected to a grounded power source.

The DTA-5A power switch is located on the rear unit panel. After a one-minute warm-up period, the monitor should display a blinking block cursor in the upper-left screen corner. This position will be referred to as the HOME or HOME-UP position throughout this manual. If the cursor does not appear in the home position of an otherwise clear screen, power down the terminal and power up again. If the cursor still does not appear, refer to Section 8 of this manual.

Adjust the brightness control, on the rear, for comfortable viewing while maintaining a black background. Excessive brightness will cause premature phosphor degradation or burning not covered under warranty.

EXERCISE ANSWERS

Exercise 17-1 Answers

Nouns and adjectives that cluster together have been bracketed in the following noun compounds. Where possible, redundant nouns have been eliminated. Several of the examples contain alternative bracketing (to indicate ambiguous relationships among the modifiers).

1. [problem determination] procedures

2. [screen display] damage

   or just

   screen damage

3. [installing dealer] sessions

   or

   installing [dealer sessions]

   although that seems an unlikely reading

4. [corporate[database integrity]] maintenance

   or

   [corporate database] [integrity maintenance]

   but either seems to mean the same thing

5. This one seems truly ambiguous. It could mean either:

   [customer skills] [transfer sessions]

   or

   [customer [skills transfer]] sessions

   depending on whether the *skills* are those involved in *relating to* customers or skills of the customer.

6. This is also ambiguous, and *service* is redundant. The remaining three-word compound could either mean:

   [voice software] support

   that is, support *for* voice software, or

   voice [software support]

that is, software support delivered *by* voice over the telephone, as opposed to *print* software support.

7. Another ambiguous one that could mean either:

metal [contamination reduction]

that is, a reduction of contaminants *in* metal or

[metal contamination] reduction

that is, a reduction of *metallic* contaminants (in some other substance).

8. [[Control Program]Facility] [Concept Manual]

or

[Control Program] [[Facility Concept] Manual]

The problem here is what to do with *Facility:* does it cluster with *Control Program* or with *Concept?*

9. [[strategic application]development] [productivity tool]

or

[strategic[application development]] [productivity tool]

At issue here is the scope of *strategic:* is it modifying *application* or *application tool?*

10. [[tactical munitions]dispenser] [statistical[process control]] [implementation program]

or

[tactical[munitions dispenser]] [statistical[process control] [implementation program]

Similarly at issue in this example is the scope of the initial adjective *tactical.* What's *tactical,* the *munitions* or the *munitions dispenser?*

Exercise 17-2 Answers

Potentially confusing noun compounds have been rewritten and italicized in the versions following each original sentence.

1. Excessive brightness may cause screen display damage.

Excessive brightness may *damage* the screen.

2. All of the already-shipped computers will be upgraded through installing dealer sessions.

All of the already-shipped computers will be upgraded through sessions
at installing dealers' locations.

3. One of your main tasks as new manager of MIS (Management Information Systems) is corporate database integrity maintenance.

One of your main tasks as new manager of MIS (Management Information Systems) is *to maintain the integrity of the* corporate database.

4. One of the best methods for teaching new software is through customer
skills transfer sessions, letting experienced customers teach new customers.

One of the best methods for teaching new software is *to hold sessions
where customers teach other customers.*

5. Voice software service support for the new telecommunications line has
been suspended until the new version is released.

Support for the voice software for the new telecommunications line has
been suspended until the new version is released.

6. With the new grid array package, a 35 percent metal contamination
reduction can be achieved.

The new grid array package *can reduce metal contamination by 35 percent.*
This version assumes that metal contamination *is unambiguous to your readers.*

7. The new Control Program Facility Concept Manual lists many helpful
hints and ideas, but I prefer the old CPFC manual.
Book title can't be changed.

8. This new strategic application development productivity tool reduces our
product development cycle time by 20 percent.

This new *productivity tool for developing strategic applications* reduces
our product development cycle time by 20 percent.

9. The Defense Department has contracted our Quality Assurance department to create a tactical munitions dispenser statistical process control
implementation program.

The Defense Department has contracted our Quality Assurance department to create a *program to implement* statistical process control *for* tactical munitions dispensers.

Putting It All Together Answer

Synonyms are circled. Technical terms and jargon are underlined. Noun compounds and noun forms of verbs are bracketed.

1.0   [INSTALLATION] AND [INTRODUCTION]

The (DTA-5A) should be <u>positioned</u> on a steady <u>surface</u> and at a [comfortable <u>user access</u> level]. [A <u>three-inch minimum clearance space</u>] must be provided at the (rear) of the (DTA-5A) to provide [ease of access] to the [power switch] and [brightness control]. Care should be taken that <u>magazines</u> or other <u>paraphernalia</u> do not fall (behind) the [terminal] and impede [ventilation]. The [line cord] should then be connected to a <u>grounded</u> [power source].

The (DTA-5A) [power switch] is located on the (rear) (unit) panel. After a <u>one-minute</u> [warm-up period], the (monitor) should display a blinking [block cursor] in the (upper-left) screen (corner). (This <u>position</u>) will be referred to as the [HOME or HOME-UP position] throughout this (manual). If the (cursor) does not appear in the [home position] of an otherwise clear (screen), power down the (terminal) and <u>power up</u> again. If the (cursor) still does not appear, refer to Section 8 of this (manual).

Adjust the [brightness control], on the (rear) for comfortable viewing while maintaining a black background. Excessive [brightness] will cause <u>premature</u> [phosphor degradation] or (burning) not covered under <u>warranty</u>.

Below is a "cleaned-up" version of the instructions, rewritten in a more user-friendly way.

1.0   INSTALLING THE DTA-5A

The DTA-5A should be placed on a steady surface and at a comfortable height. At least three inches of space should be left at the rear of the terminal for easy access to the POWER SWITCH and BRIGHTNESS CONTROL. Care should be taken not to let magazines or other material fall behind the terminal: they will block ventilation. The power cord should be connected to a grounded electrical outlet.

The DTA-5A POWER SWITCH is located on the rear of the terminal. After warming up for a minute, the terminal should display a blinking cursor in the upper-left corner of the screen (the "home" position). If the cursor does not appear in the home position, flip the POWER SWITCH off and back on. If the cursor still does not appear, refer to Section 8 of this manual.

Adjust the BRIGHTNESS CONTROL, on the rear, for comfortable viewing while maintaining a black background. Excessive brightness will cause burning not covered under your warranty.

"Professional writing is appropriately *active* and *personal,* rather than passive and impersonal."

Unit Five encourages you to prefer a style that is active and personal. Chapters 18, "Recognizing Active and Passive Voice," and 19, "When to Prefer the Passive Voice," help you understand and make intelligent choices about using active and passive voice structures. Such control is important. More than any other stylistic choice, the choice of voice determines whether your prose style is lively (active) or removed (passive). The active voice centers on actions and actors, answering explicitly "Who does what to whom?" The passive voice focuses on receivers of actions, answering the questions "What was done?" or "What happened?" Generally, a passive style doesn't read as easily and sometimes actually obscures important information about who is acting in what ways.

Chapters 18 and 19 will require some concentration and some logical application of the grammar you already know or have picked up in earlier chapters. The nice thing about active/passive voice is that the distinction is perfectly logical and learnable. You can always recognize an active sentence because the grammatical subject is the actor, doing what the verb describes. When the subject is the actor, there are certain other recognizable traits to the active sentence. Once you can distinguish between active and passive voice, you can exert powerful control over stylistic choices with the goal of making your writing clear, coherent, and effective.

Many people were taught to use passive voice structures in order to avoid using personal pronouns like *I* or *we*. We would suggest that the writing situation determines what role you can effectively create in your writing to represent you—the author—and to represent your readers. Choosing a more active, personal style can be appropriate and welcomed in many writing situations. Chapter 20, "Projecting

248

Personality," brings together a wide range of features that constitute voice or personal style in writing. It looks at what role you assume as the writer in a text and what role you give your reader. If you enjoy experimenting with a playful, or formal, or elaborate style, you will enjoy the discussion and exercises in this chapter.

chapter 18

Recognizing Active and Passive Voice

In This Chapter

Knowing when to choose active or passive verb constructions goes right to the heart of developing a strong, vigorous writing style. Passive constructions sap energy from prose, leaving it bloated and flatulent. Active constructions allow your readers to see exactly who is doing what to whom. If you cultivate an active style, you are more likely to be understood, and others are more likely to perceive you as someone who is confident, articulate, and decisive.

In this chapter, you will learn:

• How to recognize the four features that differentiate active from passive voice
• How to change passive sentences into active ones
• How to avoid confusing passive sentences with past tense or linking verb sentences

Identifying Active and Passive Voice

"Who's zoomin' who?" Aretha Franklin asks in her song. We usually want our readers to know exactly who is doing what to whom—we want to be as straightforward as possible about just what is going on. For this reason, good writers prefer **active** over **passive** constructions. Consider the following:

ACTIVE: The manager fired the new employee.

PASSIVE: The new employee was fired by the manager.

In active sentences, the grammatical subject is the actor with regard to the action—in the above example, the one who is doing the firing. In passive sentences, the subject is not doing anything but rather is being

250

acted upon. In the first sample sentence, the new employee is not doing anything; he or she is being acted upon. In the second sentence, the new employee is the grammatical subject, though not the actor. The real actor—the manager—is moved to a less prominent spot in the sentence, buried within a prepositional phrase.

EXERCISE 18-1

Each of the following sentences is passive, where the subject is not the doer of the action. Find the actor and make the actor the subject by turning the passive sentence into an active sentence.

1. The construction delays were investigated by the contractor.

2. Several reasons for missing the deadline were discovered by him.

3. The tile was delivered to the wrong site by the freight company.

4. The roof installation was held up by unrelenting rain.

5. The ceiling fixtures were backordered by Acme Lighting.

6. Everything had been delayed by events beyond the control of the contractor.

Features That Distinguish Active from Passive

Compare these two sentences:

The human factors lab tested the new workstation design.
The new workstation design was tested by the human factors lab.

The first example is active; the second is passive. In each version, we have the same basic information. The difference is in the *ordering* of that information. How we decide to order information has much to do with what we want to emphasize. The same information has a different emphasis when arranged in a different order. (We will have more to say about sentence emphasis in Chapter 21, "Managing Sentence Emphasis.")

In the active version, the subject of the sentence—what the sentence is about—is *the human factors lab.* In this sentence, the grammatical subject is also the **actor,** the one doing the acting (in this case, the one doing the testing). But in the passive version, the subject of the sentence is *the new work station design,* which is not doing the testing but is being tested. This is the essential difference between active and passive sentences: In active sentences, the grammatical subject is also the actor; in passive sentences, the grammatical subject is the **receiver** of the action.

This sentence exemplifies several other differences that typically distinguish active from passive. In the passive version, the actor is moved to a prepositional phrase beginning with *by*. Notice that the prepositional phrase containing the actor could be deleted, and we would still have a complete sentence:

The new workstation design was tested.

We no longer know who did the testing, only that it was done (by someone).

The verb phrase in the passive version is different, too. Instead of the single, active verb *tested,* we have a verb phrase with a form of *to be* (*was*) and the *-en* or *-ed* (past participle) form of the main verb (*tested*).

All passive sentences share four features that can help you identify them:

1. The subject is not the actor—the doer—of the action.
2. The actor is often contained in a prepositional phrase beginning with *by,* or the actor is deleted.
3. The verb phrase contains some form of the verb *to be* acting as a helping verb.
4. The main verb takes the past participle *-en* or *-ed* form.

Use these features to help you in completing the next exercise. Remember that it is not enough for just *one* of these features to be present; there must be *several* of them.

EXERCISE 18-2

Identify which of the following clauses or sentences are active and which are passive. First, locate the action of the clause: what is happening or has happened? Then, circle the actor. To identify the actor, ask yourself, "Who or what is doing the action?" If the actor is the subject of the clause, the clause is active. If the actor is contained in a prepositional *by* phrase or not present, you have a passive clause.

Rewrite the passive clauses as active. (You may have to recreate an actor subject when you do.)

1. George solved the problem of production delays on the new system.

2. The problem of production delays was solved.

3. For the first time, our second-quarter earnings have surpassed those of the first quarter.

4. The time delay switch malfunctions every time.

5. As usual, the cut-sheet paper feeder was jammed by the new letterhead.

6. Mercury Oil in Ft. Worth has been looking for co-op students to work as lab assistants on its synfuels project.

7. Certain students were not considered for the positions because their applications were not received before the cutoff date.

8. The top location for new chip production facilities is New Mexico.

9. Management decided to transfer certain design and product development functions to the Cleveland site, but the production lines will not be affected by the decision.

10. A software virus was discovered by the systems analyst.

Avoiding Confusion between Active and Passive

It is easy to get confused in trying to identify passive constructions. You need to distinguish passive constructions from past tense. *All* verb phrases, active or passive, carry some indication of tense—whether the action took place in the past, present, or future. People sometimes confuse the past participle form of the verb (signaled by an *-ed* or *-en* ending on the verb) that occurs in passive constructions with the past-tense form of the verb (also often signaled by *-ed*). Consider the difference between the following sentences:

> Proper identification *was required* in order to enter the site.
>
> The security officer *required* proper identification from Paul in order for him to enter the site.

The first verb is both passive and in the past tense; the second verb is only in the past tense. Notice in the second example that the security officer is the one who is requiring proper identification, so the construction is active voice. One way to distinguish past participles from past-tense verbs is to remember that the past participle *always* needs a helping verb when it is the main verb form; a past-tense verb can stand on its own.

Passive doesn't mean past tense; passive sentences can be past, present, or future tense. Here the passive sentence from the preceding example is rewritten in three different tenses (past, present, and future):

Proper identification *was required* in order to enter the site.

Proper identification *is required* in order to enter the site.

Proper identification *will be required* in order to enter the site.

Finally, just because a sentence has some form of the verb *to be*, it is not necessarily passive. Sentence 8 in Exercise 18-2, for example, is *neither* passive nor active:

The top location for new chip production facilities is New Mexico.

It is a linking verb sentence. As you will recall from Chapter 4, "Parts of Sentences and Parts of Speech," linking verbs do not express action; they simply link the subject with the subject complement. Without some kind of action expressed in the verb, sentences can be neither active nor passive.

Thus, to recognize passives, you need to do more than simply spy an *-ed* form of a verb or a form of the verb *to be*. You need to determine "Who is doing what to whom?" and then decide if the one performing the doing is the subject of the sentence. The four characteristics of passive constructions identified previously work together; at least three will be present in each instance of the passive voice.

EXERCISE 18-3

Look closely at the following examples. Which are passive constructions?

1. Several IRS auditors are examining the books because of discrepancies in the year-end figures.

2. As long ago as September, they had requested complete billing logs from all of our data-entry clerks.

3. Unfortunately, the records from several clerks remained incomplete for the period of November 15 to November 30.

4. Nobody believes there was any intentional wrongdoing.

5. However, we will need to revise the way we do things.

6. The comptroller's office, which is ultimately responsible for maintaining complete records, will have revised its procedures by the time our audit is complete.

If you said that none of these sentences is passive, you were correct— move to the front of the class.

EXERCISE 18-4

Underline the passive verb phrases in the following memo.

TO: J. V. McIntyre

FROM: A. F. Laming

SUBJECT: HCIP replies needed on Venus packages

DATE: 5-17-96

Per IPSSI 14-056, Hardware Change Implementation Plan (HCIP) replies are required back within five working days of receipt. If more time is needed, a written notification with the date the reply will arrive is required. The reply is to be given to us at the Venus Change Control Center.

Listed on the attached page are HCIP replies currently needed from Procurement. All of them have exceeded their five-day due date. The deadline has been extended and replies will be accepted until 06-15-96.

Either a completed reply or a memo stating when the replies will be completed is needed from your group as soon as possible on these items.

In Summary

You can learn to distinguish active from passive sentences so that you are able to prefer active to passive and able to change from one to another. Asking "Who is doing what to whom?" is a good way to find out if the underlying sentence structure is active. If the grammatical subject is doing the action, the sentence is active.

You will notice several features of passive sentences that appear together: The grammatical subject is not the actor; the actor is in a *by* phrase or deleted, and the verb is an *-ed* or *-en* participle form with a form of *to be*. We won't pretend that it is easy to understand and use the distinction between passive and active; we have seen too many writing teachers who are confused about the differences! But we will say that, with a little effort, you can understand and use the difference to take control of your style.

Chapter 19, "When to Prefer the Passive Voice" is really a continuation of this one, offering more practice at distinguishing passive from active and more reasons for choosing one or the other. We recommend working through these two chapters a couple of times if you really want to remember the difference between active and passive and use that knowledge to good advantage.

EXERCISE ANSWERS

Exercise 18-1 Answers

Below are the active versions of the passive original sentences.

1. The contractor investigated the construction delays.

2. He discovered several reasons for missing the deadline.

3. The freight company delivered the tile to the wrong site.

4. Unrelenting rain held up the roof installation.

5. Acme Lighting backordered the ceiling fixtures.

6. Events beyond the control of the contractor had delayed everything.

Exercise 18-2 Answers

The following clauses or sentences are identified as either active or passive. The passive clauses are rewritten to be active. (The actor in each sentence is circled.)

1. George solved the problem of production delays on the new system. (active)

2. The problem of production delays was solved. (passive)

   George [or someone] solved the problem of production delays.

3. For the first time, our second-quarter earnings have surpassed those of the first quarter. (active)

4. The time delay switch malfunctions every time. (active)

5. As usual, the cut-sheet paper feeder was jammed by the new letterhead. (passive)

   As usual, the new letterhead jammed the cut-sheet paper feeder.

6. Mercury Oil in Ft. Worth has been looking for co-op students to work as lab assistants on its synfuels project. (active)

7. Certain students were not considered for the positions because their applications were not received before the cutoff date. (Both clauses are passive.)

   They [Mercury Oil or someone] did not consider certain students for the positions because they did not receive the students' applications before the cutoff date.

8. The top location for new chip production facilities is in New Mexico. (This is a linking-verb sentence and thus neither active nor passive.)

9. Management decided to transfer certain design and product development functions to the Cleveland site, but the production lines will not be affected by the decision. (The first clause is active; the second clause is passive.)

   . . . but the decision will not affect the production lines.

10. A software virus was discovered by the systems analyst. (passive)

    The systems analyst discovered a software virus.

Exercise 18-3 Answers

None of the clauses is passive.

Exercise 18-4 Answers

The passive verb phrases are underlined in the following memo.

TO: J. V. McIntyre

FROM: A. F. Laming

SUBJECT: HCIP replies <u>needed</u> on Venus packages (The *to be* form
            of the verb is omitted in the abbreviated style of this
            subject line.)

DATE: 5-17-96

Per IPSSI 14-056, Hardware Change Implementation Plan (HCIP)
replies <u>are required</u> back within five working days of receipt. If more
time <u>is needed,</u> a written notification with the date the reply will
arrive <u>is required.</u> The reply <u>is to be given</u> to us at the Venus Change
Control Center.

<u>Listed</u> on the attached page <u>are</u> HCIP replies currently <u>needed</u>
from Procurement. All of them have exceeded their five-day due
date. The deadline <u>has been extended</u> and replies<u> will be accepted</u>
until 06-15-96.

Either a completed reply or a memo stating when the replies <u>will</u>
<u>be completed</u> <u>is needed</u> from your group as soon as possible on
these items.

chapter 19

When to Prefer the Passive Voice

The previous chapter discussed how to recognize passive and active voice and why you should generally prefer active voice in your writing. In this chapter, you will learn how to make informed choices between passive voice and active voice. You will learn:

- How choosing passive or active voice can help you avoid assigning responsibility
- How passive voice can help you focus on what happened, rather than on who did what
- How passive and active constructions can help you control the flow of information from one sentence to the next in a paragraph
- How passive and active constructions can help you strategically identify participant roles in a paragraph

There are good reasons for preferring active voice. The active voice makes it clear just who is doing what to whom. The active voice places the doer of the action in the subject position; it makes the subject the actor. Schematically, active sentences look like this:

GRAMMAR:	subject	verb	object
ROLE:	actor	action	receiver

When grammatical subjects line up with actors and verbs line up with actions, readers have an easier time understanding and remembering the important information in a sentence. Experiments with matched passages of text show that active passages take less time to read than passive. When tested on recall, readers also remember more facts with greater accuracy when the information is presented in active voice. These are strong arguments for preferring the active voice.

Passive voice often leads to confusion, as in the following installation instructions:

The EGR card should be installed in Slot 4.

Do you know from the sentence whether the card *should already have been installed* or whether this sentence is telling us to *install the card now?* In such cases, active voice is preferable for its clarity:

Install the EGR card in Slot 4.

Now the meaning of the sentence (if, indeed, it is an instruction) is clear.

Active sentences make best use of the expected S-V-O pattern of English sentences. They allow you to communicate efficiently with the greatest chance that your information will be accurately understood and remembered. They take fewer words and read more directly. All things being equal, you should prefer the active voice.

Preferring the Passive

As soon as we suggest that you learn to recognize and prefer the active voice, we need to acknowledge that there are situations in which passive is preferable. In this section, we suggest situations where you might choose to use passive over active structures. As you read, see if you can think of other such situations.

Using Passive to Avoid Assigning Responsibility

Sometimes a writer simply does not want to say who did something. Using the passive voice lets a writer get by without assigning responsibility:

Overtime and holiday pay for all nonsalaried employees will be reduced from double-time to time-and-a-half.

It has been reported that certain employees have been the victims of sexual harassment.

Using the passive voice in such instances lets the writer avoid saying who is responsible by deleting the actor from the sentence. (Of course, readers of such sentences will be wondering who the actor is: "Who decided to reduce overtime pay?" "Who reported sexual harassment?")

Sometimes, of course, you don't *know* who did something, and in these circumstances passive is a natural choice:

My car radio was stolen last night.

However, even in cases like this one, there is also an active version that avoids assigning responsibility—one that uses an indefinite pronoun for a subject:

Someone stole my car radio last night.

Using Passives to Focus on What Happened

Often there is nothing underhanded about not saying who or what is doing the action. Sometimes a writer simply wants to focus on the *what* of a sentence and not the *who*. For example, it is traditional in scientific writing to use the passive as a way of focusing attention on what happened, not on who did it:

It was found that corticosteroids reduced inflammation associated with arthritis.

Viscosity was increased until the gauges indicated a pressure of two pounds per square inch within the cylinder.

Here, the researcher may simply decide that it makes sense to focus on the results and procedures, not on the person doing the research. It would be pointless to write *I found,* or *The experimenter found,* or *I increased the viscosity.* Passive structures allow a writer to focus on important information instead of on who did something.

Even scientists, however, know there are times to prefer active over passive. The best style guides, and the instructions to authors for very prestigious scientific journals, urge authors to use active structures when possible and even to use *I* or *we* when appropriate, as in the following examples:

We decided to test the hypothesis that reading time would be significantly increased when interline spacing was reduced to less than 2 mm.

We have adjusted the data to account for our observation that atmospheric contaminants entered our "clean" room and left a thin film on the surface of the bearings.

In instances such as these, the active, personal constructions are clearly preferable, since what is being reported are instances of personal judgment. The active constructions appropriately highlight the researcher's role as a thinking, guiding presence.

Using Passives to Manage the Flow of Information

Deliberately choosing between active and passive structures gives you a tool for managing the flow of information in your prose. Everyone wants to cultivate a smooth style, one that moves easily and logically from point to point, leading the reader gently along toward appropriate conclusions. How sentences begin and end has much to do with achieving this smooth, flowing prose. Systematically choosing passives, which allows a writer to move to the front of a sentence what would otherwise be toward the end, can sometimes contribute to smooth linkage.

For example, suppose a new product has completed the development cycle and you are writing an internal progress report. You might write a paragraph that looks like this:

> The final phases of development for the new workstation have been completed. The design of the workstation has been tested by the human factors lab. The software for the workstation has been beta-tested at three sites and thoroughly debugged. The documentation has gone through three levels of edit and has passed user testing under lab conditions. The initial marketing plans have been redefined using prototype workstations and extensive surveying to update the original strategy.

Each sentence in this passage is passive. The first introduces the topic of the paragraph: *the first phases of development have been completed.* Each successive sentence then introduces some aspect of the final phases of development—design testing, software debugging, documentation editing, and redefining the marketing plans. It makes good sense here to use the passive to maintain continuity from sentence to sentence. Passives keep the reader's attention focused on the phases of development in this process description. This is, after all, a report on development. Decisions about the focus of the paragraph dictate the use of passive voice.

In other situations, you might use a combination of passive and active constructions to maintain focus on the topic of a paragraph. For example, let's say that you were writing an announcement about a new workstation, the development of which was the topic of the previous example:

> Acme Products this week announces the release of their new workstation, the DTA-5A. The DTA-5A incorporates the latest in workstation technology and has been thoroughly tested under the most rigorous conditions.

Notice that the second sentence mixes both an active verb (*incorporates*) and a passive verb (*has been tested*) in referring to the DTA-5A. This is because the DTA-5A is the subject of both actions, even though it is the receiver rather than the doer of the second action. To maintain focus on the

DTA-5A, we have to mix active and passive constructions. Compare this sentence to one in which both actions are rendered in the active voice:

> The DTA-5A incorporates the latest in workstation technology, and Acme Products has thoroughly tested it under the most rigorous conditions.

Now the sentence focus seems to tug in two different directions: one direction focusing on the workstation, the other focusing on Acme Products.

This practice of mixing passives and actives within the same paragraph—or even within the same sentence—may contradict another of those shadowy prohibitions from your school days about not mixing passive and actives, but notice that we are doing so *purposefully*, rather than haphazardly. A slavish adherence to the same voice (active or passive) within the same sentence can result in awkward, unfocused sentences.

Using Passive and Active Voice Strategically

Sometimes active and passive can be systematically varied to encourage clear understanding. Suppose you are describing how to make a withdrawal from an automatic teller. You might write as follows:

> Enter the amount you wish to withdraw. Your account will be checked to see that you have sufficient funds. If your account does have sufficient funds, you will be prompted to confirm that the amount you have requested is correct. Press "YES" or "NO." If you press "YES," the transaction will be completed and the money will be issued from the top-left slot. If you press "NO," you will be prompted to enter the correct amount. When you have finished your transaction, press "DONE." Your card will be returned through the middle slot and a receipt will be issued.

In this passage, active structures are used to show what *you* need to do, while passive structures are used to show what is done by the *teller machine*. Shifting between passive and active in such passages gives the writer a fine tool to guide a reader through a process.

EXERCISE 19 - 1

In this exercise, all of the sentences in each set contain passive structures. Examine each set and determine if you could improve the sentences by changing one or more of the structures to active. Be prepared to defend your choices of passive or active constructions based on the uses of passive discussed in this chapter.

1. Most decisions about new office computing systems are made these days by the in-house computer hobbyist. Consequently, new systems are often chosen because this hacker wants the latest, greatest equipment. Other people in the office are often baffled by having to continually learn new systems. The overall productivity of the office is reduced by the constant changes in software and hardware.

2. A new sales territory will be created for Sarah Givens, our recently hired graduate from the University of Arizona. Possible clients in the southwest quadrant will be identified by each of the current sales reps. Existing accounts in this quadrant will be taken over by Sarah on October 1.

3. It was reported by Engineering that the new laminates are not performing as expected. Specifically, the top layer is being worn away by friction between the sheathing and the base plate. A new top-layer compound containing epoxies will be tested and, if successful, substituted for the current styrenes.

4. The bid was submitted by Falcon Designs after the closing date. We were caught by this late submission. The deadline could not be changed unless the whole bidding process were reopened. Then the whole project would be set back three weeks by reopening the bidding.

5. Some important papers were lost during the personnel review process. Several letters of reprimand that had been placed in George Slater's file by his manager could not be found. Copies were provided, however, from the manager's backup files.

6. A review of the key design criteria should be completed before our next meeting. Additionally, the timetable with key project milestones should be revised and updated to reflect the decisions made at the July 23 meeting.

7. The banquet was highlighted by the presentation of awards. Ann Jaspers was presented an award by the president for her redesign of

the office automation system. Fred Duke was given recognition by his work group for his efforts to coordinate the new just-in-time parts inventory system.

EXERCISE 19-2

Following is a "cleaned-up" version of the DTA-5A instructions analyzed at the end of Unit Four. Read through the instructions, this time being aware of the distribution of passive constructions. (Underline these constructions to help you see any patterns of occurrence.) Is there a good reason for the use of the passive in each occurrence? If not, try turning the construction into an active one.

1.0   INSTALLING THE DTA-5A

The DTA-5A should be placed on a steady surface and at a comfortable height. At least three inches of space should be left at the rear of the terminal for easy access to the Power Switch and Brightness Control. Care should be taken not to let magazines or other material fall behind the terminal: they will block ventilation. The power cord should be connected to a grounded electrical outlet.

The DTA-5A Power Switch is located on the rear of the terminal. After warming up for a minute, the terminal should display a blinking cursor in the upper-left position of the screen (the "home" position). If the cursor does not appear in the home position, flip the Power Switch off and back on. If the cursor still does not appear, refer to Section 8 of this manual.

Adjust the Brightness Control, on the rear, for comfortable viewing while maintaining a black background. Excessive brightness will cause burning not covered under your warranty.

In Summary

From the examples we have chosen in this chapter, it should be clear that we would argue that you need to make decisions about when to use the passive. Prefer the active, but be aware that passive structures are a resource to be exploited. We are not saying you should avoid passives at all costs. Decisions to use passives should be based on your writing situation: the particular relations of you, your readers, and your topic.

Unfortunately, many writers do not consciously choose to use passive constructions but do so by default. For many writers, passive sounds normal, objective, and desirable. All things being equal, these writers will choose to write in the passive because that is what sounds most managerial, most educated, or most formal.

It is not easy to change writing habits, especially ones like the preference for passive constructions. Strong institutional pressures force many writers to continue using inflated, bureaucratic-sounding language, and passives are the quickest route to creating such language. So when we urge you to cultivate an active style, we know it is not easy.

You will be surprised, however, if you do adopt an active style—surprised at the gains in directness, clarity, force, and vigor. Active sentences, as every professional writer knows, are a real key to a strong style.

EXERCISE ANSWERS

Exercise 19-1 Answers

Below are some sample revisions of the paragraphs, along with the logic for the revisions. Depending on the focus one intended, other revisions would be equally possible.

1. Most decisions about new office computing systems are made these days by the in-house computer hobbyist. Consequently, new systems are often chosen because this hacker wants the latest, greatest equipment. Other people in the office are often baffled by having to continually learn new systems. The overall productivity of the office is reduced by the constant changes in software and hardware.

The paragraph is about the changes in office computing systems, so the passive constructions in the first two sentences are justified. The subject constructions—most decisions about new office computing systems and new systems—help to maintain a focus on new systems rather than people. It might be worth making the last two sentences focus on the systems as well, so a revised paragraph might keep the first two sentences in passive voice and cast the last two in active voice:

Most decisions about new office computing systems are made these days by the in-house computer hobbyist. Consequently, new systems are often chosen because this hacker wants the latest, greatest equipment. *Continually having to learn new systems* often baffles other people in the office. *These constant changes in software and hardware* reduce the overall productivity of the office.

2. A new sales territory will be created for Sarah Givens, our recently hired graduate from the University of Arizona. Possible clients in the southwest quadrant will be identified by each of the current sales reps. Existing accounts in this quadrant will be taken over by Sarah on October 1.

If the focus is supposed to be on the new sales territory, no changes are necessary. If, however, the focus is supposed to be on Sarah and the existing reps, the passage should be reordered and rewritten as follows:

A new sales territory will be created for Sarah Givens, our recently hired graduate from the University of Arizona. *Sarah will take over existing accounts in the southwest quadrant on October 1. Current reps should identify possible clients in this quadrant for Sarah to contact.*

3. It was reported by Engineering that the new laminates are not performing as expected. Specifically, the top layer is being worn away by friction between the sheathing and the base plate. A new top-layer compound containing epoxies will be tested and, if successful, substituted for the current styrenes.

The focus here is appropriately on laminates. The only unnecessary passive is the first one:

Engineering reported that the new laminates are not performing as expected. Specifically, the top layer is being worn away by friction between the sheathing and the base plate. A new top-layer compound containing epoxies will be tested and, if successful, substituted for the current styrenes.

4. The bid was submitted by Falcon Designs after the closing date. We were caught by this late submission. The deadline could not be changed unless the whole bidding process were reopened. Then the whole project would be set back three weeks by reopening the bidding.

If the focus of the paragraph is supposed to be on our response to the late submission, then most of it could be rewritten in active voice:

Falcon Designs submitted their bid after the closing date. This late submission caught us by surprise. We could not change the deadline unless we reopened the whole bidding process. Reopening the bidding like this would set the whole project back by three weeks.

5. Some important papers were lost during the personnel review process. Several letters of reprimand that had been placed in George Slater's file by his manager could not be found. Copies were provided, however, from the manager's backup files.

The focus of the paragraph seems to be on what happened to the papers, so the passive voice is warranted throughout.

6. A review of the key design criteria should be completed before our next meeting. Additionally, the timetable with key project milestones should be revised and updated to reflect the decisions made at the July 23 meeting.

Here it seems important to specify who is going to do what. In the revision below, the focus is on an understood you:

Please review the key design criteria before our next meeting. Additionally, please revise the timetable with key project milestones and update it to reflect the decisions made at the July 23 meeting.

7. The banquet was highlighted by the presentation of awards. Ann Jaspers was presented an award by the president for her redesign of the office automation system. Fred Duke was given recognition by his work group for his efforts to coordinate the new just-in-time parts inventory system.

If the focus of the paragraph is supposed to be on the highlight of the banquet—the presentation of awards—then the passives are justified since they put the recipients in subject position.

Exercise 19-2 Answers

Passive constructions are underlined in the following version. Passive voice does not seem to be used consistently for any purpose in the passage: most of the initial instructions are passive, but all the later ones are active.

1.0   INSTALLING THE DTA-5A

The DTA-5A should be placed on a steady surface and at a comfortable height. At least three inches of space should be left at the rear of the terminal for easy access to the Power Switch and Brightness Control. Care should be taken not to let magazines or other material fall behind the terminal: they will block ventilation. The power cord should be connected to a grounded electrical outlet.

The DTA-5A Power Switch is located on the rear of the terminal. After warming up for a minute, the terminal should display a blinking cursor in the upper-left position of the screen (the "home" position). If the cursor does not appear in the home position, flip the Power Switch off and back on. If the cursor still does not appear, refer to Section 8 of this manual.

Adjust the Brightness Control, on the rear, for comfortable viewing while maintaining a black background. Excessive brightness will cause burning not covered under your warranty.

Below is a "cleaned up" version of the instructions, with all of the instructions represented in active voice and in numbered steps:

1.0   Installing the DTA-5A

1. Place the DTA-5A on a steady surface and at a comfortable height. Leave at least three inches at the rear of the terminal for easy to access to the POWER SWITCH and BRIGHTNESS CONTROL. Be careful not to let magazines or other material fall behind the terminal: they will block ventilation.

2. Connect the power cord to a grounded electrical outlet.

3. The DTA-5A POWER SWITCH is located on the rear of the terminal. Flip the switch up to the "on" position.

4. After a minute, the terminal should display a blinking cursor in the upper-left position of the screen (the "home" position). If the cursor does not appear in the home position, flip the POWER SWITCH off and back on. If the cursor still does not appear, refer to Section 8 of this manual.

5. Adjust the BRIGHTNESS CONTROL, on the rear, for comfortable viewing while maintaining a black background.

CAUTION: Excess brightness will cause burning not covered under your warranty.

chapter 20

Projecting
Personality

This chapter focuses on ways in which to project a personal presence in your writing. Generally, you want to work toward a style that is active and personal. Focusing on people doing things helps your writing to be understood, allows your readers to view you sympathetically, and encourages your readers toward action.

In the discussion of the Communication Triangle in Chapter 1, "Writing on the Job," we made a point that is worth repeating here:

> Every time you write, you establish some sort of relationship between yourself and your audience. You try to get them to do things for you, or you do the things they have asked you to do, or you do things together. As a writer, you can assume a role of either asking or telling someone to do something, of either cajoling someone into cooperation or threatening them with undesirable consequences. In other words, you don't simply send messages about the world when you write—you impose a relationship on the receiver of the message.

You can never totally control the effects your language has on other people. Once you write something, others pick it up and interpret it according to the different ways they think about the world and according to the highly individual ways they read meaning into language. But you *can* be sensitive to the nuances of language and predict the likely effects your writing will have on your audience. You can at least think about the writer/reader relationship, the base of the Communication Triangle, and choose a style that is most likely to establish the relationship that you hope will be most productive.

When you finish this chapter, you should be prepared to exercise control over four dimensions of personality in writing:

- How to control levels of formality, or overall tone
- How to choose appropriate discourse roles for writer and reader
- How to create a playful style
- How to use touches of elegance

It would be inappropriate for us to make too great a claim about the potential impact of this chapter. On the one hand, because you have been using the language all your life, you already know at some level the topics of this chapter. If you speak English as a second language, you will have a sense for how writers and readers are projected into a text in your native language, but you will need to work to control the ways similar meanings are conveyed in English. Thus, we are not teaching you from scratch but helping you to recall and consider in a new light what you already know.

On the other hand, these matters of voice, persona, and personality are so delicate and so various that writers must continually strive to use them effectively. These are not discrete, objective topics to learn in one reading but aspects of style that you must pay attention to over time, with the goal of growing increasingly comfortable with your level of control.

Levels of Formality

Writers must always consider what is an appropriate level of formality. Speakers do the same, almost unconsciously. You would not talk the same way to your spouse as you would to your boss, and you would not talk the same way to a close team member as you would to a new hire. You adjust your word choice, grammar, and style to the occasion, with an emphasis on choosing appropriate language for a given situation. What is appropriate language in a given situation is influenced by such factors as how close you are to your audience, how seriously you view the business at hand, and how pressured you are by time constraints. The best speakers and writers are sensitive to such situational constraints and are constantly adapting their tone, perhaps even unconsciously, to the various situations in which they find themselves.

You might imagine levels of formality arranged along a continuum, from close, intimate, informal language at one end to highly formal, almost frozen language at the other[1] (see Figure 20.1). At the intimate

---

[1] Loosely adapted from the highly readable and enjoyable work on conversation styles by Martin Joos, *The Five Clocks*.

Figure 20.1 *Levels of Formality*

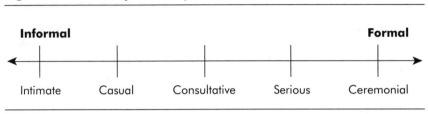

end of the scale—the language appropriate to lovers or close friends—language is highly coded, with many meanings unspoken or conveyed with special, insider language (*Okey-dokey, pumpkin*). Moving toward the casual speech of friends and coworkers, you would find informal sentences, slang, jargon, or other insider language, and frequent reliance on shared jokes or certain ways of talking about those outside the close circle.

In the consultative range would be common forms of business language, what you might mean if you said someone conducted himself or herself in a *businesslike manner*. The language is more explicit: there are likely to be more formal words and phrases used, and the language is likely to be somewhat neutral in tone, suitable for the ordinary conduct of business affairs. In writing, certain informal style features tend to disappear toward the right end of the continuum: contractions, words that sound more like spoken English than written, and perhaps direct address through *you* constructions. You expect a consultative tone when you enter a business establishment, when you talk with someone for the first time, or when you interact with other professionals.

Moving toward the more serious levels of formality, as when someone speaks to a judge in a traffic court or discusses with a doctor a patient's condition, the language becomes highly serious, and the participants maintain a rigorous decorum. There is not likely to be any joking around, and all traces of slang and insider language are absent. The sentences become longer and more formally structured.

At the far end of the continuum, language becomes stiff and frozen. This is the ceremonial language of sermons or prepared speeches. It is frequently rehearsed, and, if delivered orally, it is often read from a detailed script or written copy. An example of this level is the language of weddings or funerals, toasts or dedications, when the words and sentences are likely to be highly formulaic and ritualistic. Frequently, the language contains archaic words and elaborate, poetic structures.

Figure 20.2 *Formality of Written Documents*

Informal				Formal
Personal Letters, Notes	Memos, E-mail, Sales Letters, Tutorials	Manuals, Progress Reports, Quarterly Reports	Formal Reports, Procedures, Business Plans, Proposals	Audits, Mil-Specs, Legal Briefs, Incident Reports

A continuum of formality for different *written* documents might look roughly like Figure 20.2. Most documents, of course, are not pure. An annual report, for example, will mix the consultative tone of the CEO's letter to shareholders with the more formal, ceremonial language of the independent auditor's report. But the diagram does offer a way to think about variations in language and how situations influence appropriate choices.

Choosing Appropriate Language

Our discussion here has been intentionally loose, using the term *language* to include both *speaking* and *writing*. Both speaking and writing can usefully be thought of as ranging along the continuum from informal to formal. The overall tone or voice that is projected when someone speaks or writes is influenced by many factors working together: word choice, pronouns, slang, reference patterns, joking or humorous asides, elaborate or simply constructed phrases and sentences. There is no simple recommendation to be made here beyond the general encouragement that you should be aware of levels of formality and adapt your language accordingly.

Textbooks on writing from twenty or thirty years ago would offer cut-and-dried advice about the need for formal writing in business settings: avoid contractions; don't use *you;* use a formal vocabulary; don't begin sentences with *and* or *but;* keep sentences to an average of sixteen to twenty words; have six to eight sentences per paragraph. It is fair to say, however, that business practice is evolving in the direction of informality. What would once have been considered too informal in business settings—in both writing and speaking—is now considered appropriate. Taste is evolving, rules (or preferences) relaxing, and a friendly, informal style is emerging as the norm.

Even though what is considered appropriate is evolving toward informality, you still need a sensitive ear with regard to style. It is easy to give offense by coming off as too personal, too informal, or too risqué. Status hierarchies, even in reengineered corporations, still exist, and those who are too informal across ranks do so at some risk of censure. Inappropriate humor, offensive slang, and other breaches of decorum do not often earn points in the modern office, especially since most work environments now have a mix of women and men from various ethnic groups and sociocultural backgrounds.

Choosing appropriate language is something like a game in which the rules are not always stable or well-defined, and the outcomes are highly unpredictable. In such a game, it is best to stay alert, exercise some caution about engaging in risky verbal behavior, and take some pleasure in watching the way others play the game.

Discourse Roles

Discourse roles refer to the ways in which you choose to refer to yourself, to your reader, and to others through the choice of pronouns. To use this book as an example, we try to consistently refer to ourselves, the writers, as *we*. We have chosen the first person, plural form because there really are two of us collaborating on these chapters. We have also chosen to give the book a somewhat direct, informal appeal by referring to you, the reader, as *you*. We directly address you, asking you to consider some distinction or to work some exercise. If we want you to consider a general example, we will write in the third person about *writers* and what *they* generally do.

Pronoun choices help you set an inclusive, personal relation between *us* and *you* as opposed to *them*. Alternately, pronoun choices that avoid first- and second-person pronouns allow you to maintain the appearance of an objective or neutral stance and to keep the focus on the topic rather than on the participants. (In Chapters 18 and 19, we mentioned that one of the functions of passive voice was to help writers maintain this "objective" stance through avoiding personal pronouns.) In choosing and using pronouns, you need to make conscious choices about how to represent the interpersonal relations in the text. The use of first person could have been avoided in this book (through just this kind of passive sentence with a deleted agent; notice the sentence we just wrote doesn't say who would be avoiding the use of first person, just that *It could be avoided [by someone]*). And we didn't have to choose to use *you*, either. We could have written about *writers* or *employees* and left it up to you to place yourself in the described role.

Direct address, in which the reader is addressed directly by the writer, is a powerful form of involvement. In tutorial documentation, for example, a writer will write many action-oriented sentences in imperative constructions:

> Place the printer on a solid surface, away from direct sources of heat and sunlight.

The subject *you* is understood in such direct address constructions, and such sentences bring along with them a whole set of circumstances of reader engagement in directed action (taking directions to set up a printer in this example). You saw such use of direct address in Exercise 19-2 in the last chapter.

Beyond pronouns, there are several other constructions that signal the relation of writer to reader. Some constructions involve the reader in imaginative ways, by asking the reader to *imagine* something or to *consider, estimate, question, agree,* or *disagree.* Many words have a human component and require at least an imaginative act of reasoning or emotional involvement in the text.

Some sentence modifiers refer indirectly to a reader's thoughtful engagement with the text, as the following example illustrates:

> Obviously, the new procedures have upset routines and can be expected to disrupt productivity for at least a few weeks.

In this example, the word *obviously* involves the reader in a reasoning process, one that is expected by the writer to have shared results: the observation should be *obvious* to both writer and reader. The verb construction plays into the same line of reasoning: because the passive *can be expected* has no stated actor, everyone involved, writer and reader included, can expect to see a disruption in productivity. There is a whole class of words that engages readers in such reasoning processes: *without a doubt, clearly, ethically speaking, surely, honestly.* While readers are always engaged in figuring out what the writer intends and whether the writer is to be trusted, some words play directly to issues of credibility and consent.

Consistency is the principle that guides choices among first, second, and third person, singular and plural. Once you make a decision about how to represent yourself and your audience, you can't shift inappropriately from one representation to another. You invite your readers to enter into the text by adopting a defined role. Thoughtful analysis of how to refer to your readers and yourself can help your writing project an appropriate personal style.

EXERCISE 20-1

Evaluate the level of formality in word choice and sentence construction and the choices of discourse roles in the following passage. Does the writer make appropriate choices?

It pays to become a registered user.

With most products that you buy, you have little reason to send in the registration card. With software, however, you need to know when new versions become available. We can tell you about new versions only if you send in the registration card. Tear out the postage-paid card at the front of this manual and drop it in the mail today.

You'll be glad you did because:

- Our Technical Support group will sign you up for free, unlimited support for as long as you use our software. There's no expiration on support, so send in your card and start your free support now.

- You'll get advance notification of new versions and products, before public announcements.

- We will offer you significant discounts on new versions of TaxPac and other new products.

- You'll be eligible to be a beta tester for new TaxPac versions or other new products. Beta testers start using new versions before we release that product for sale. They give us great advice about how new features should work and they help us fine-tune the product.

- From time to time, we are able to arrange special discounts on software products from leading software companies. We can make these discounts available to you only if we have your name and address as a registered TaxPac user.

With all these benefits, it's smart to send in your registration card. There's truly no reason not to.

Playfulness

Even in the most serious of situations, an appropriate style can be delivered with a light touch: of playfulness, humor, or deft, interesting choices of words and phrasing. Good writers are never ponderous; they know what it means to take some pleasure in choosing apt words and making telling associations of meaning and sound. This is to say, quite simply, that all language is poetic. Good writing pleases the ear.

Language makes part of its meaning through stylistic choices: surprising juxtapositions of words, the use of metaphors or other figures of speech, a playful switching of levels of formality in word choice, or creative and intricate phrasing. A fine writer or speaker is entertaining in part because of the element of unpredictability: the audience is not quite sure what is coming next, but they know it will be interesting to the mind and ear.

You can cultivate an element of playfulness in your style that will make your writing a pleasure both to write and to be read. A first step in cultivating a light style is to hear your own voice. Listen to your words as you read them aloud or, better yet, have someone read a passage of your writing back to you. Notice where your sentences flow smoothly and where you or your reader has trouble reading with the right phrasing. You might need to lighten up a little or to untangle and divide long, involved sentences, or to begin fewer constructions with *that* or *which* (constructions that usually lead to a heavy style).

A light, playful style always begins with verbs. An active style relies on lively verbs to surprise, to wow, to tweak, to delight. Along with lively verbs, a playful style relies on particularity: getting just the right word, the specific detail, in the right place. A light style never pastes prepackaged phrases together to make sentences. Words are carefully and sometimes playfully chosen, one by one, to create new phrasings and new sentences.

If you can hear your own voice in your writing, that is usually a good sign. If your writing is dull, deadly boring, if it sounds like some committee of bureaucrats wrote it, then our advice is to lighten up. You don't want to sound as though you studied at the Thesaurus School of Writing. You want to find your own words and be present, as yourself, in your writing.

EXERCISE 20-2

This exercise is best done with someone else or with the class. There are no right or wrong answers. Words can be heavy or light, depending on the subtle sound associations we make. Which of the following words strike you as heavy or ponderous? What substitutions might you make? Which might lend a touch of playfulness to your writing? What situations might call for one term or another?

paradigm	specificity	prioritization
aplomb	beastly	frisky
panoply	a bunch	modular
blotto	initialization	fuzzy
spontaneity	bamboozled	anterior
utilization	eke	interface
functional	specification	screwed up

EXERCISE 20-3

What sources of playfulness do you see in the following passage? This is marketing language from Voyager's catalog of CD-ROM products (the CD being advertised is _For All Mankind_ by Al Reinert, available from Voyager, One Bridge Street, Irvington, NY). Can you use similar kinds of playfulness in your writing at work or are these kinds of stylistic effects only appropriate to a marketing situation?

The twenty-four astronauts who traveled to the moon between 1968 and 1972 were, in Al Reinert's words, "the first extraterrestrial humans." This is the story of their voyage to another world, captured on their film (NASA outfitted them all with 16 mm cameras) and in their own words.

It will knock your socks off. The footage is spectacular. Like tourists, the astronauts reflexively reached for their cameras when something surprising or simply beautiful floated into view, which was about every five minutes. The first glimpse of what astronaut Harrison Schmitt called the "beautifully, brilliantly illuminated blue marble that we call the earth" was only the first shot to make us swallow hard.

Reinert's movie is "pure reality"; he realized that the stuff of myth requires no embellishment. (Thank heavens Spielberg or Disney didn't get there first.) From 238,000 miles up, God-squad moments and timeworn phrases—"one small step for man," "man must explore," "mankind's greatest adventure"—are not clichés but the intimate thoughts of humble, eloquent men exquisitely aware of their own vulnerability and extraordinary privilege. There's plenty of clowning around, too—dancing on the moon, weightless ham-sandwich making. The contract between human antics and the vastness of space had us constantly reaching for reality checks, only to remember what was happening.

Describing himself as more an archaeologist than a filmmaker, Reinert spent ten years conducting eighty hours of interviews and dealing with a warehouse full of NASA film. From blastoff to splash-down, *For All Mankind* is a composite of all the Apollo missions combined, the grandest human undertaking in history.

Elegance

Beyond a plain style is a playful style; beyond playful, elegant. More formal occasions call for a touch of elegance. The Greeks talked about three styles: low, middle, and high. A high style cultivates graceful expression. It takes pleasure in lingering over wording and phrasing, offering choices that can be appreciated for their refinement.

There are some old tricks that writers have taught themselves for creating a high style. One is to pay attention to how words sound. Language always brings sound with it. Even silent readers voice the sounds of the passages they are reading: they subvocalize, moving their vocal cords as they read to themselves. Good writers are alert to the poetics of sound and rhythm in prose.

Another way to achieve elegance is through structural means, rather than simply word choice. A traditional sentence structure that carefully controls rhythm is the periodic sentence. In a **periodic sentence,** the beginning of the sentence is loaded, and closure is delayed. In the following examples, notice how the tension builds and builds, before a quick, emphatic ending:

> Without a will, that critical document that makes it clear to all the exact intentions of the deceased, with only the frequently contradictory words of closely involved and interested family members, the courts take control.

> Has it never occurred to you, never crossed your mind during idle moments as you sat contemplating your fate, that one day you, too, unable to control your own fate, unable to make decisions about conduct of your affairs, might find yourself at the mercy of a hospital staff?

These sentences delay closure while adding on a series of qualifications. The opposite of periodic sentences are sentences that move quickly to establish a subject-verb-object base and tack the long, modifying phrases to the end of the sentence. Such sentences can be called **loose** or **cumulative:**

> The department established a new document center, staffed by new hires, with the task of editing, producing, and coordinating all technical publications produced throughout the organization.

> The document center is structured as a profit center, with charge-back billing, a graduated fee structure based on level of edit, and local control over work scheduling and processing.

As writers develop styles that move from utilitarian toward elegant, variation is key. Accomplished stylists use a full range of patterns and develop interesting and complex textures in their prose. Sometimes the prose structures are intentionally artistic, as in certain prose figures that go by names like *chiasmus, asyndeton,* and *polysyndeton.*

Chiasmus is the reversing of the grammatical pattern from the first clause or phrase to the second, as in Kennedy's famous example, "Ask not what your country can do for you, but what you can do for your country." A more prosaic example is, "If we don't look out for our business partners' interests, they can hardly be expected to look out for ours."

Asyndeton is the intentional omission of connecting words, such as conjunctions and prepositions, as in "I came, I saw, I conquered." It conveys a sense of spare economy and a sense of things unsaid, "This project seems to be characterized by delays: back-orders from our suppliers, slippage on our milestones, inconsistency in management commitment."

Polysyndeton involves connecting a series of grammatical phrases or clauses with repeated conjunctions, as in the first book of Genesis: "And God said, 'Let there be a firmament in the midst of the waters, and let it separate the waters from the waters.' And God made the firmament and separated the waters from the waters which were above the firmament. And it was so. And God called the firmament Heaven. And there was evening and there was morning, a second day." Here, the structural device lends dignity and portentousness to the passage. In other contexts, a series of conjunctions can create a sense that things are piling up: "And they doubled their order and the shipper waited too long to get back to us and the warehouse was calling every hour and the whole thing started to look like a mess."

These three stylistic devices are present in much elegant writing. There are many more. Though only academic rhetoricians would know the names of these patterns now, they were once much studied and practiced by school children as they developed control over style. You can elevate your own style by noticing and using particular grammatical structures that have a special appeal to your ear.

Good stylists also frequently turn to language that plays with meaning in intentionally metaphoric ways. **Metaphors** are words used in figurative senses, where something is described as something else. The moon is a *ghostly galleon* or a *benevolent old man*. The computer presents a *desktop*, with *windows*, and a *cursor* that *scrolls*. Language is thoroughly metaphoric, and good stylists (and technical writers) use metaphor to explain complex ideas and to help readers visualize meanings. Sometimes writers—especially in advertising copy—play with ambiguity, where two meanings surface for a single phrase. Sometimes writers allow a term for a part to stand for the whole, as when *White House* stands for the executive branch of the government or when *bottom line* stands for profits and losses of an entire company.

We can only suggest here some of the richness in the language for creating stylistic playfulness and elegance. Good stylists cultivate their repertoire, notice how other writers do things, develop their ear for a fine phrase, and are always interested in creating varied textures in their prose.

EXERCISE 20-4

Elegant, or at least clever, phrasing can be found in much popular journalism. Here is a passage from a newsstand periodical that demonstrates clever word choice, use of metaphor, and a penchant for unusually active verbs. Read the passage for its style. Note the surprises in word choice. Circle the metaphors that stand out. Underline active verbs. Try to determine where the rhythm comes from.

Of course, many new management ideas are yesterday's theories warmed over and disguised under a sauce of new buzzwords. Others are mere fads, feel-good illusions peddled by false prophets who convince managers that their solutions make large-scale change easy. . . . If much of what the gurus offer in their endless rounds of seminar-giving, speechifying, and scribbling is dross, there's real gold out there, too. A few of these new oracles of modern management are having a profound impact on some of the nation's biggest companies. . . . They generally agree that time can be squeezed out of every job; that self managed teams throw more challenge and meaning into employment, and that companies sorely need to create networks of relationships with customers, suppliers, and competitors to gain greater competitive advantage. . . . The new gurus aren't all proselytizing from the same text, but they do have several tenets in common. Nearly all these preachers shun incremental change. They urge managers to think in radical terms, dramatically overhauling entire operations at a stroke. ("Management's New Gurus," *Business Week,* August 31, 1992, pp. 44–52.)

In Summary

Projecting personality through your writing style is much like projecting personality while you speak. You gauge the situation, the audience, and your purposes, and you speak in a language that is, ideally, both comfortable and appropriate to the occasion. With people you know and like, you generally relax into a more informal voice; with strangers, important people, or members of certain professions, you probably maintain a more formal voice.

It is not just one or two identifiable features that project personality, though some elements of the grammatical system are implicated more than others. Pronouns, naturally, involve you in decisions about personality, because you must decide one way or the other to be present in the text (as *I* or *we*) or to write from a more objective stance without self reference. Similarly, you need to decide how to construe your reader, whether directly through the second-person pronoun *you* or indirectly through third-person constructions. In reality, however, all the choices you make—of words, phrasing, or sentence types—work together to project a personal or an impersonal voice. Everyone recognizes occasions when language is inappropriate, offensive, false, or otherwise out of tune with the situation.

Like speaking, writing is fundamentally a creative act. You take on roles, project different personalities in different situations, and engage in certain creative interaction with your audience. If you can do so with some sense of play, and occasionally with elegance, you will project a style that is pleasurable both to write and to read.

Putting It All Together

Reexamine the following memo from Exercise 18-4. Your task in this exercise is to rewrite it in different ways, using active and passive voice *strategically* to distinguish actions performed by the writer and the reader. Also be aware of the references to the writer and the reader that you use. Will you use personal pronouns at all? Will you use *only* personal pronouns? Or will you use a mix of personal pronouns and third-person references?

TO: J. V. McIntyre

FROM: A. F. Laming

SUBJECT: HCIP replies needed on Venus packages

DATE: 5-17-96

Per IPSSI 14-056, Hardware Change Implementation Plan (HCIP) replies are required back within five working days of receipt. If more time is needed, a written notification with the date the reply will arrive is required. The reply is to be given to us at the Venus Change Control Center.

Listed on the attached page are HCIP replies currently needed from Procurement. All of them have exceeded their five-day due date. The deadline has been extended and replies will be accepted until 6-15-96.

Either a completed reply or a memo stating when the replies will be completed is needed from your group as soon as possible on these items.

In a classroom setting, three different groups might each produce one of the following revisions of the original version: The original version uses passive voice for the actions of *both* the writer and the reader.

READER	WRITER	
	ACTIVE	PASSIVE
ACTIVE	Revision 1	Revision 2
PASSIVE	Revision 3	Original

E X E R C I S E   A N S W E R S

Exercise 20-1 Answers

This passage has a highly interactive style, with frequent use of second person and a friendly, casual, and informal voice. The writer uses you *constructions consistently to refer to the reader, while using* we *and* our *to refer to the company. Most of the sentences have personal pronouns as subjects and active verbs. The style is active and personal, not passive and impersonal. There is an alternation set up between* us *and* you *that gives the passage a rhythm.*

Other elements that contribute to the informal, friendly style include contractions (you'll, there's, it's) and informal vocabulary that feels more appropriate to speaking than to writing (it pays, drop it in the mail, so send in your card, great advice). Several phrases appeal to a reader who is smart and opportunistic (you need to know, they give us great advice, it's smart to send in your card).

Exercise 20-2 Answers

Answers will vary.

Exercise 20-3 Answers

This passage uses a range of devices to create a playful, light touch:

- *slang phrases* (knock your socks off, thank heavens, clowning around, reality checks)
- *opposites* (blastoff/splashdown, humble/eloquent, reality/myth, archaeologist/filmmaker)
- *particularity* (weightless ham sandwiches, 238,000 miles up)
- *figures of speech* (beautifully, brilliantly illuminated blue marble that we call the earth)
- *balanced phrases with lofty language* (eloquent men exquisitely aware of their own vulnerability and extraordinary privilege)

Such language can be used in subtle ways in business documents, though not to the obvious extent it is used here. Writing a business letter or trip report in such language would surprise and amuse most of your readers, who would consider such language inappropriate or excessive. There are, however, many restrained ways in which you can give your prose a light touch that will make your style expressive and interesting but not excessive.

Exercise 20-4 Answers

Metaphors are circled. Active verbs are underlined. The rhythm in the passage comes from sentence variety: some long (3, 5), some short and direct (7). Some of the sentences structures are cumulative, with modifiers loosely stacked at the end of the sentence (2, 5). A periodic structure uses an opening dependent clause (3). While the passage feels informal and personal, there is no use of first- or second-person pronouns.

(1) Of course, many new management ideas are yesterday's theories warmed over and disguised under a (sauce) of new buzzwords.

(2) Others are mere fads, feel-good illusions (peddled) by false (prophets) who <u>convince</u> managers that their solutions <u>make</u> large-scale change easy. . . . (3) If much of what the (gurus) <u>offer</u> in their endless rounds of seminar-giving, speechifying, and scribbling is (dross,) there's real (gold) out there, too. (4) A few of these new (oracles) of modern management are having a profound impact on some of the nation's biggest companies. . . . (5) They generally <u>agree</u> that time can be (squeezed) out of every job; that self managed teams (throw) more challenge and meaning into employment, and that companies sorely <u>need</u> to create (networks) of relationships with customers, suppliers, and competitors to gain greater competitive advantage. . . . (6) The new (gurus) aren't all (proselytizing) from the same text, but they do have several tenets in common. (7) Nearly all these (preachers) <u>shun</u> incremental change. (8) They <u>urge</u> managers to think in radical terms, dramatically overhauling entire operations at a (stroke.) ("Management's New Gurus," *Business Week,* August 31, 1992, pp. 44–52.)

Putting It All Together Answers

The Revision 1 strategy phrases *everything* actively—actions that the writer and the reader each perform. The result is fairly direct, but the use of personal pronouns *we* and *you* softens the directness.

TO: J. V. McIntyre

FROM: A. F. Laming

SUBJECT: HCIP replies needed on Venus packages

DATE: 5-17-96

IPSSI 14-056 requires that groups return Hardware Change Implementation Plan (HCIP) replies within five working days of receipt. If a
group needs more time, it must submit written notification to us at the
Venus Change Control Center of the date the reply will arrive.

On the attached page, we have listed HCIP replies we currently
need from Procurement. All of them have exceeded their five-day due
date. However, we have extended the deadline to 6-15-96.

As soon as possible, we need either the completed HCIP replies or
a memo stating when you will complete the replies.

Thank you.

*How would this revision be different if the writer had used I instead of we?
What if the writer had used only third-person references (the Venus Change
Control Center and Procurement) instead of using personal pronouns?*

*The Revision 2 strategy uses active voice for everything the memo reader
must do, while keeping the passive voice for actions performed by the writer.
This strategy might increase the weightiness of the requirements; it would
certainly make the memo less friendly:*

TO: J. V. McIntyre

FROM: A. F. Laming

SUBJECT: HCIP replies needed on Venus packages

DATE: 5-17-96

Per IPSSI 14-056, Hardware Change Implementation Plan (HCIP)
replies are required back within five working days of receipt. If a
group needs more time, written notification is required with the date

the reply will arrive. You must send the reply to us at the Venus Change Control Center.

Listed on the attached page are HCIP replies currently needed from Procurement. All of them have exceeded their five-day due date. The deadline has been extended and replies will be accepted until 6-15-96.

Either a completed reply or a memo stating when you will complete the replies is needed as soon as possible on these items.

Again note the use of the personal pronoun you. *What would the effect be of avoiding personal pronouns and substituting third-person references to the reader?*

The Revision 3 strategy is just the opposite of Revision 2: here everything the reader must do is phrased passively, while everything the writer does is active. This strategy has the effect of "softening" the memo by stating the required actions of the addressee more indirectly. But if you were the reader, would the required response be clear to you? (Again, what difference would it make if all the personal pronouns were replaced with third-person references?)

TO: J. V. McIntyre

FROM: A. F. Laming

SUBJECT: HCIP replies needed on Venus packages

DATE: 5-17-96

IPSSI 14-056 requires that Hardware Change Implementation Plan (HCIP) replies be returned to us at the Venus Change Control Center within five working days of receipt. If more time is needed, we require written notification of the date the reply will be sent.

On the attached page are HCIP replies currently needed from Procurement. The five-day due date has been exceeded by all of them. However, we have extended the deadline and will accept replies until 6-15-96.

As soon as possible, we need either a completed reply from your group or a memo stating when the replies on these items will be completed.

You have now seen four versions of this memo (the original plus the three revisions). Which version works best? Does your answer depend on the circumstances surrounding the memo and the relations between the writer and reader?

"Professional writing *emphasizes* what is important— and downplays what is *not.*"

Not only does professional writing use *correct* sentence structures, it also uses *effective* ones. This unit comes full circle to Unit Two, where we discussed grammatically correct structures. Here we discuss structures that emphasize or downplay information appropriately. You will notice a number of the same topics from Unit Two coming up here, as well as topics from the succeeding units: the need to keep the main subject close to the main verb, using the right punctuation to emphasize (or downplay) information, and choosing mainly active and verbal sentence structures but occasionally using passive or nominal ones for an intended effect.

The principle for good writing presented in this unit returns to the two possible relations between grammatical units (words, phrases, clauses, and sentences): subordination and coordination. Chapter 21, "Managing Sentence Emphasis," is about subordinating lesser information at the beginning of a sentence in order to emphasize the main point at the end of a sentence. Chapter 22, "Parallel Structure," is about coordinating information of equal importance. As you will see, this coordination can take place at several grammatical levels. Chapter 23, "Maintaining Flow from Sentence to Sentence," picks up a melody from Chapter 21 and turns it into a theme: picking up the topic from the end of the previous sentence and starting the next sentence with it. Chapter 24, "Defining a Professional Look," discusses *visual* structures that emphasize or downplay information. Finally, Chapter 25, "Conclusion: The Marks of a Professional Style," provides a concluding summary of the principles and practices encouraged throughout this book.

The choices you make as a writer about coordinating or subordinating information all act to "shade" the meaning of your sentences, sometimes subtly, sometimes not. As with all aspects of style in professional writing, the most effective choices are often the ones least noticed—or noted with pleasure—by your reader.

chapter 21

Managing Sentence Emphasis

This chapter returns to the basic grammatical structures—phrases, clauses, and sentences—set out in Unit Two. Here, we discuss how to manage those structures in order to create **sentence emphasis,** the quality achieved by placing your important information in important structures and positions in a sentence.

There are two steps to achieving sentence emphasis. The first step is to express your main point in an important grammatical structure (in an independent clause, for example). The second step is to put that structure in a position of speech emphasis (at the end of the sentence, for example). Of course, you can't highlight some information without also downplaying other information. Downplaying information means putting less important grammatical structures (dependent clauses and phrases, for instance) in less emphatic positions in the sentence or clause (away from the beginning or end).

Highlighting and downplaying are complementary sides of emphasis: you can't do one without doing the other. The basic principle here is this: Make your sentence structure match your meaning.

In this chapter, you will learn to do this in the following ways:

- By choosing grammatical structures that highlight and downplay information appropriately
- By assigning those structures to positions of greater and lesser speech emphasis within the clause and sentence

Not only does managing sentence emphasis make your main point stand out, it also creates variety in your writing style. Effective style is a balance between rhythm and variation: Too much of the same rhythm (for example, the same sentence construction) is boring; too much variation is confusing and choppy. Finding a balance between the two will be a key focus of this entire unit.

Emphasis in Grammatical Structures

In Chapter 4, "Parts of Sentences and Parts of Speech," we concluded with a hierarchy of grammatical structures arranged from simplest structures (words) to most complex structures (sentences). Because independent clauses can stand by themselves as simple sentences, we might distinguish them from dependent clauses by placing them further up the hierarchy. We then end up with the hierarchy of grammatical importance shown in Figure 21.1.

The point of reintroducing the grammatical hierarchy here is simple: To create structural emphasis for your main idea, put the main idea in the independent clause of the sentence. To downplay supporting ideas, put them in dependent clauses or, to really downplay them, reduce them from clauses to phrases or words.

You may remember from school calling the independent clause the *main clause* and the dependent clause the *subordinate clause* (perhaps without distinguishing different dependent clauses as either subordinate or relative). These alternate terms parallel the distinction we are making here: main ideas in the main clause, subordinate ideas in the subordinate clause.

You already know how to recognize and create independent clauses. Here we will look at some ways to reduce independent clauses to dependent clauses, phrases, and even words.

Figure 21.1 *Modified Hierarchy of Grammatical Structures*

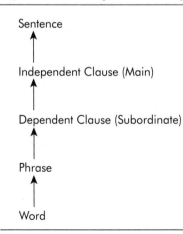

Sentence

Independent Clause (Main)

Dependent Clause (Subordinate)

Phrase

Word

From Independent to Dependent Clauses

Consider the following paragraph. Each sentence is simple—that is, it contains only one, independent clause:

> (1) National Technical Support for DataStar has been withdrawn by Apex Computer effective July 1, 1996. (2) The local Customer Center will continue to offer support for DataStar for the indefinite future. (3) Problems may still exist with DataStar. (4) Any problems will have full local Customer Center support.

Each sentence in the paragraph is grammatically correct, but no one would say that the paragraph is particularly *effective*. The repeated structure of single-clause sentences is, at best, monotonous.

What does the main point of the paragraph seem to be? It is probably the point expressed in the second sentence: that customers of Apex's DataStar product will still have local support for the product even though national support has been withdrawn. How can we emphasize that point? By putting the other information into less important, dependent clauses. One approach to downplaying the other sentences is to turn the first independent clauses into a subordinate clause, one that begins with a subordinating conjunction like *although, because, since, when,* or *if.*

> (1) *Although* National Technical Support for DataStar has been withdrawn by Apex Computer effective July 1, 1996, (2) the local Customer Center will continue to offer support for DataStar for the indefinite future.

The resulting complex sentence now emphasizes the continued support for the indefinite future.

Does it make a difference to the meaning of the sentence whether you subordinate one sentence or the other? Indeed it does. Consider what happens if you subordinate the second sentence:

> (1) National Technical Support for DataStar has been withdrawn by Apex Computer effective July 1, 1996, (2) *although* the local Customer Center will continue to offer support for DataStar for the indefinite future.

What does the main point of the sentence seem to be now? Do you catch the shift in emphasis to the national support having been withdrawn? The continued support now seems almost an afterthought or a begrudging commitment.

The second way to reduce an independent clause to a dependent one is by turning it into a relative clause beginning with a relative pronoun like *that, which, who, what,* or *when.* Look at the third and fourth sentences:

(3) Problems may still exist with DataStar. (4) Any problems will have full local Customer Center support.

Which of these sentences do you wish to emphasize? Probably the one that assures DataStar customers of continued local support. So you can turn the third sentence into a relative clause beginning with *that* and incorporate it into the fourth sentence:

(4 and 3) Any problems *that may still exist with DataStar* will have full local Customer Center support.

Here, the emphasis is solidly on Customer Center support. Again, the emphasis is crucially affected by whether you subordinate one clause or the other. If you make the fourth sentence into a dependent, relative clause, the sentence has a different emphasis:

(3 and 4) Problems—*which will have full local Customer Center support*—may still exist with DataStar.

What is the emphasis now?

Your ear will probably tell you which kind of dependent clause to use when you want to downplay information from an independent clause. Sometimes subordinate clauses work best; other times relative clauses do.

EXERCISE 21-1

Consider the following two independent clauses:

coal power is cheaper than solar power
solar power is cleaner than coal power

1. Write a sentence in which you turn the first clause into a subordinate one, joining it to the second, independent clause.

2. Now write a sentence in which you turn the second clause into a subordinate one joined to the first independent clause. What is the difference in emphasis between the two sentences you have written?

3. Next write a third sentence in which you turn the first clause into a relative clause modifying *solar power* in the second clause. What changes in the wording of the comparison do you have to make?

4. Finally, write a fourth sentence in which you turn the first clause into a relative clause modifying *coal power* in the second clause. (Notice that you did not have to change the wording of the second clause this time.) Which sentence is stronger: the third sentence or the fourth? Notice which sentence ends with the independent clause.

Reducing Clauses to Phrases and Words

In downplaying information structurally, you don't have to maintain it in a full clause (albeit a dependent one). Instead, you can reduce the information to a noun phrase, a verb phrase, or sometimes a prepositional phrase. We will demonstrate these "structural reductions" with some examples below.

Consider the following complex sentence, in which the first clause is subordinated to the second:

Although he was unhappy with his team's decision, James continued to put forth his best effort to help them succeed.

It is possible to reduce the subordinate clause even further, to a modifying phrase:

Although ~~he was~~ unhappy with his team's decision, James continued to put forth his best effort to help them succeed.

Consider a different version of this sentence, one with a relative cause instead of a subordinate one:

> James, who was unhappy with his team's decision, nevertheless put forth his best effort to help them succeed.

You can also reduce information in the relative clause to a modifying phrase.

> James, ~~who was~~ unhappy with his team's decision, nevertheless put forth his best effort to help them succeed.

Following the principle in Chapter 7, "Placing Modifiers Effectively," about keeping subjects and verbs as close together as possible, you might want to move the modifying phrase to precede the independent clause:

> Unhappy with his team's decision, James nevertheless put forth his best effort to help them succeed.

(As you will see later in this chapter, there is another reason to move the modifying phrase up front for emphasis.)

It is not necessary to go through the grammatical hierarchy one step at a time, reducing independent clauses to dependent ones, dependent clause to phrases, phrases to words. Sometimes you can jump directly from a complete sentence down to a phrase:

> The cursor will appear at the upper-left corner of the screen. (Throughout this manual, we will refer to this position as the HOME position.)

In this example, you can reduce the second sentence directly to a parenthetical noun phrase modifying *corner* in the first sentence:

> The cursor will appear at the upper-left corner of the screen (the HOME position).

Sometimes you can even reduce an independent clause to a word! In the following example, the first clause can be reduced to a single word:

> I hope that this explanation will suffice.
> Hopefully, this explanation will suffice.

(Some purists would object to this construction, arguing that the adverbial modifier *hopefully* dangles because there is no verb for it to modify. They would prefer a construction such as *It is to be hoped that*...or *I am hopeful that*...or *Hopefully, I will offer an explanation that*.... In reality, no reader interprets the adverb *hopefully* as modifying the verb *suffice*. It is acting here as a sentence adverb indicating the attitude of the speaker of the sentence.)

In reducing information structurally, then, you have many choices: dependent clause, phrase, or word. The more you reduce it, the less important it becomes—and the more the remaining information is highlighted.

Speech Emphasis

After placing the important information in an important grammatical structure, the second step in achieving sentence emphasis is to place that grammatical structure in a position of **speech emphasis.** What are these positions of speech emphasis? Generally, they are the beginning and ending of the structure. In the next three sections, we consider these positions of emphasis within the clause and within the sentence.

Emphatic Positions within the Clause

In Chapter 4, "Parts of Sentences and Parts of Speech," you learned about the basic subject-predicate construction of a clause. The subject identifies a topic, while the predicate makes some comment about that topic. Where is the new information in a clause? Presumably, in the comment we make about the topic. There is an interesting phenomenon in speech that corresponds to the placement of new information in the predicate. Read the following sentence out loud:

The new engineer identified a flaw in the design.

Where is your voice the loudest? If you are like most readers, you placed greater speech emphasis on *a fláw in the desígn.* (We use the rising accent [´] to indicate primary stress.) Was there any place else where your voice was loud? You probably also placed some (though not as much) speech emphasis on *the new enginèer.* (We use the falling accent [`] to indicate secondary stress.)

What happens if we flip the order of elements in the sentence? Try reading the following revision out loud:

A flaw in the design was discovered by the new engineer.

You probably stressed the same elements, but this time your voice was probably louder on *the new enginéer* than on *a flàw in the design.* This reversal in the stressed elements means that it is the *positions* occupied by the information, rather than the information itself, that cause the stress.

Now try reading the following clauses out loud:

The new engineer is very talented.

Her name is Jane.

Jane is a graduate of MIT.

Again, if you are like most readers, you probably put some stress on the beginning of each clause, but your voice was loudest at the end.

We can sum up this discussion by noting that there are *two* positions of speech emphasis in a simple subject-predicate clause: the beginning and the end. The beginning of the clause—usually the subject—announces the topic; it receives secondary stress. However, the end of the clause—whether that is a direct object, a subject complement, a verb phrase, or a prepositional phrase—receives the primary stress, so that is where the new information (presumably the main point of the clause) should go. This phenomenon is sometimes called *end weight,* and you may have encountered advice in other writing courses to "end strong." Now you know why.

Emphatic Positions for In-Clause Modifiers

Thus far, we have looked at clauses with simple subject-predicate constructions. But as we have seen throughout this book, real language often contains more complicated clause structures, with many modifiers in different positions within the clause. Where are the positions of speech emphasis in these structures?

The primary stress still falls at the end of the clause. Consider a revised version of one of the example sentences from above:

The engineer discovered a flaw in the design of the new workstation.

In this revised version, *enginèer, flàw,* and *desìgn* all get secondary stress, but the primary stress falls at the very end of the sentence, on *wórkstation.*

If the final modifier is *too* long, however, the intended point of the clause may be lost because the main grammatical element of the predicate (the direct object, subject complement, or simple predicate) may no longer be in the most prominent, final position of the clause but instead buried somewhere in the middle (as in the sentence you just read). Consider the following example:

The engineer discovered a flaw in the design of the new workstation after receiving several complaints from customers.

In this version, the primary stress falls on *cústomers.* If that is the intended point of the writer, well and good. But if the main point is that *the engineer discovered a flâw,* that point is lost. The speech emphasis is out of synch with the structural emphasis. How do we recover the emphasis on the *flâw?* In Chapter 7, "Placing Modifiers Effectively," you learned that modifiers of time, purpose, and condition should be placed up front in a clause whenever possible. Part of the rationale for doing this was to put modifiers as close as possible to what they modified. In those cases, the modifiers were actually modifying the whole clause, so we placed them up front.

Now we can talk about a second reason for "fronting" those modifiers: Doing so allows the primary speech emphasis of the clause to fall on the primary grammatical element at the end of the clause. It also creates a second primary emphasis up front at the end of the modifier because the comma separating the modifier from the main clause gives the speaker (or reader) a chance to stop and breathe. Here is a revised version of the preceding example sentence:

> After receiving several complaints from customers, the engineer discovered a flaw in the design of the new workstation.

Now there are two words with primary stress: *cústomers* and *wórkstation.* These two words fall at the end of the two grammatical structures—a participial verb phrase and a clause—separated by a comma. The comma provides a breathing space, allowing each structure to have a position of primary stress at the end. Further, the revised sentence also makes sense in terms of the time order of events and so carries a natural logic that makes it easy to read and interpret.

So now we can state a revised characterization of primary stress: The primary stress in a simple clause falls at the end of the clause. If there are any "fronted" elements in the clause, they also receive primary stress at the end of the fronted element.

Before closing this section, it is worth noting that, in addition to fronting modifiers for additional stress, English has some structural patterns for reorganizing the usual subject-predicate elements of a simple clause into a linking-verb construction in order to put the emphasized element into end position. Below is the original clause from the beginning of this section, together with various versions that emphasize different elements at the end of the clause:

> The engineer identified a flaw in the design.
>
> The one who discovered a flaw in the design was the engineer.
>
> What the engineer did was to discover a flaw in the design.
>
> What the engineer discovered was a flaw in the design.

Thus, there are a number of structural ways to put the main point in the position of primary speech emphasis at the end of a clause or a clause modifier, even if they are not the "normal" subject-predicate constructions.

Emphatic Positions within the Sentence

In the section on structural emphasis, we commented on the shift in emphasis created by downplaying different independent clauses in a sentence. In particular, we commented on the difference in emphasis between the following two versions of the same clauses:

Version 1
(1) Although National Technical Support for DataStar has been withdrawn by Apex Computer effective July 1, 1996, (2) the local Customer Center will continue to offer support for DataStar for the indefinite future.

Version 2
(1) National Technical Support for DataStar has been withdrawn by Apex Computer effective July 1, 1996, (2) although the local Customer Center will continue to offer support for DataStar for the indefinite future.

Version 1 has structural emphasis on the second clause. In Version 2, the structural emphasis is on the first clause. Doesn't Version 1 seem to be a little stronger, a little more *emphatic?* This is because the **structural emphasis** coincides with its *speech* emphasis: that is, the information in the independent clause (the structural emphasis) is *also* at the end of the sentence (the position of speech emphasis).

In Version 2, on the other hand, the two systems of emphasis are not working together: the information in the independent clause ends in the middle of the sentence, while the position of speech emphasis at the end of the sentence is occupied by the phrase *for the indefinite future.* The sentence would probably work better if the order of clauses were reversed, with the dependent clause first. And indeed this seems to be the case, as shown in the following revision:

Version 2a
(2) Although the local Customer Center will continue to offer support for DataStar for the indefinite future, (1) National Technical Support has been withdrawn by Apex Computer effective July 1, 1996.

Doesn't this version seem stronger than Version 2? The stronger emphasis of Version 2a points to the need to end strong, with the independent clause at the end of the sentence, as in Version 1 (assuming, of course, that this is the emphasis you want).

This *dependent clause, independent clause* pattern has long been known to be a strong sentence structure. In classical rhetoric, this pattern was called a periodic sentence, because the main point is delayed until the end, close to the period. The opposite pattern (*independent clause dependent clause*—note the lack of a comma between the clauses) is called a loose sentence pattern because the point of the sentence is made first, in the independent clause, and then "loosened" by the succeeding dependent clause.

In a way, our discussion of emphatic positions in sentences simply continues our discussion of emphatic positions in clauses: As in clauses, the position of primary emphasis in a sentence is at the end of the sentence. Not only do we want to put modifying phrases up front in clauses, but we also want to put modifying, dependent clauses and phrases at the front of sentences.

EXERCISE 21-2

This exercise is similar to Exercise 21-1, in which you were asked to downplay different independent clauses in various ways and to consider the differences in structural emphasis. Here, you are asked in addition to rearrange the clauses to create periodic and loose constructions and to consider the differences in speech emphasis. Consider the following two independent clauses:

Morse Code Tester cannot send Morse code signals

Morse Code Tester is useful in testing your comprehension of Morse code dots and dashes

1. Write a sentence in which you turn the first clause into a subordinate one but maintain the same clause order as above. What kind of construction have you created with the subordinate clause first—a periodic or a loose one?

2. Now reverse the order of clauses. What kind of construction do you
   have now? Where is the *structural* emphasis in the sentence? Where is
   the *speech* emphasis? Which version of the sentence seems stronger—
   Version 1 or 2?

3. Now write a new sentence using the original clause order above and
   turn the *second* clause into a relative clause modifying *Morse Code Tester*
   in the first clause.

4. Finally, reverse the sentence by making it passive. (It should now begin
   with *Morse code signals.*) Notice where the relative clause occurs now.
   Which version of the sentence ends with the independent clause? Which
   version seems stronger—Version 3 or 4? Which version is the periodic
   construction?

EXERCISE 21-3

**Decide which information in the following paragraph you wish to em-
phasize. Underline the clauses where that information occurs. Then
reduce the other independent clauses to dependent clauses, phrases,
or words. Be aware of the order of clauses and modifying elements in
your resulting sentences:**

(1) You want to print many similar documents. (2) You can use
DataStar to produce customized versions of form letters. (3) You enter
the form letter text in a master file. (4) The text will remain the same

for all the letters. (5) You supply the name of a data file. (6) The data file contains specific names, addresses, etc. (7) The master file contains marked places. (8) DataStar inserts specific names, addresses, etc. in these marked places. (9) DataStar reaches the end of the data file. (10) DataStar stops producing the letters.

Emphatic Positions within Larger Units of Discourse

Much has been said in this chapter about positions of emphasis in sentences. If you pay attention to beginnings and endings of your sentences and make sure that you place important information in these positions of emphasis, your writing will be easier to follow.

You can extend this same thinking about emphasis to paragraphs and larger units of discourse. In paragraphs, place orienting information that states the topic of a paragraph at the beginning of the paragraph in a topic sentence. Such a sentence orients your reader and controls what follows in the paragraph. It also helps your reader skim longer documents by reading the first sentence of each paragraph to see what you are writing about and where you are going with it. You do not need to define *topic sentence* too specifically; you can think in whatever terms are most comfortable for you: starting with a leading generalization, core generalization, main message, summary statement, or, simply, the point.

Also pay close attention to what you put in the final (emphatic) position for new information in a paragraph: the last sentence. Place the most important information in the final slot of the paragraph: a summary of the problem you identify or your argument about a recommended course of action. Think of the last sentence in a paragraph or section as the concluding sentence, the one sentence that really pulls the argument together.

Get in the habit of playing the first sentence off the last one in each paragraph. These positions of emphasis are critical junctures where you state the case and make your point.

You can take this line of thinking up one more level. The positions of emphasis in whole documents are the beginning and the end. Make sure your position is clearly stated in both positions, so the reader can read either the first paragraph or the last and know what your point is and what action you are seeking. If you are delivering a key message in a document, make sure the reader knows it at the beginning and is reminded at the end. Try not to bury your important information in the middle of paragraphs or in the middle of long documents. Your point is certain to be lost on many readers unless it occupies the positions of emphasis.

In Summary

This chapter has looked at the two systems that work to create sentence emphasis: grammatical structure and speech emphasis. In the hierarchy of grammatical structures, more important information should be placed in more important grammatical structures, such as independent clauses. In the system of speech emphasis, important information should come at the ends of grammatical units—whether phrases, clauses, or sentences—where the primary stress occurs.

The strongest emphasis is created when the two systems coincide, when writers put information in important grammatical structures and in strong positions at the ends of clauses and sentences.

EXERCISE ANSWERS

Exercise 21-1 Answers

Here are some possible responses to the exercise working with the following sentences:

coal power is cheaper than solar power
solar power is cleaner than coal power

1. Write a sentence in which you turn the first clause into a subordinate one, joining it to the second, independent clause.

Although coal power is cheaper than solar power, solar power is cleaner.

2. Now write a sentence in which you turn the second clause into a subordinate one, joined to the first independent clause. What is the difference in emphasis between the two sentences you have written?

Coal power is cheaper than solar power although solar power is cleaner.

This sentence seems weaker than the first one. The order with the dependent clause first seems to work better.

3. Next write a third sentence in which you turn the first clause into a rela-tive clause modifying *solar power* in the second clause. What changes in the wording of the comparison do you have to make?

Solar power, which is more expensive than coal power, is cleaner.

In order to modify solar power *with the information contained in the first clause, you have to reorder the comparison to focus on solar power being more expensive, rather than coal power being cheaper.*

4. Finally, write a fourth sentence in which you turn the first clause into a relative clause modifying *coal power* in the second clause. (Notice that you did not have to change the wording of the second clause this time.) Which sentence is stronger: the third sentence or the fourth? Notice which sentence ends with the independent clause.

Solar power is cleaner than coal power, which is cheaper.

Sentence 3 seems stronger; it also ends with the independent clause.

Exercise 21-2 Answers

Here are some possible responses to the exercise working with the following sentences:

Morse Code Tester cannot send Morse code signals
Morse Code Tester is useful in testing your comprehension of Morse code dots and dashes

1. Write a sentence in which you turn the first clause into a subordinate one but maintain the same clause order as above. What kind of con-struction have you created with the subordinate clause first—a periodic or a loose one?

Although Morse Code Tester cannot send Morse code signals, it is use-ful in testing your comprehension of Morse code dots and dashes.

This is a periodic construction.

2. Now reverse the order of clauses. What kind of construction do you have now? Where is the *structural* emphasis in the sentence? Where is the *speech* emphasis? Which version of the sentence seems stronger—Version 1 or 2?

Morse Code Tester is useful in testing your comprehension of Morse code dots and dashes although it cannot send Morse code signals.

This is now a loose construction. The structural emphasis is in the first clause, but the speech emphasis on the end of the first clause becomes secondary to the primary emphasis on signals because there is no "breathing space" in the middle of the sentence. Version 1—the periodic construction—seems stronger.

3. Now write a second sentence in which you turn the second clause into a relative clause modifying *Morse Code Tester* in the first clause.

Morse Code Tester, which is useful in testing your comprehension of Morse code dots and dashes, cannot send Morse code signals.

4. Finally, reverse the sentence by making it passive. (It should now begin with *Morse code signals.* . . .) Notice where the relative clause occurs now. Which version of the sentence ends with the independent clause? Which version seems stronger—Version 3 or 4? Which version is the periodic construction?

Morse code signals cannot be sent by Morse Code Tester, which is useful in testing your comprehension of Morse code dots and dashes.

Version 3 ends with the independent clause and seems stronger. (It is also the periodic construction.) The relative clause at the end of Version 4 seems to unravel the sentence, dissolving the main point in the independent clause.

Exercise 21-3 Answers

If we assume that the purpose of this paragraph is to emphasize what DataStar can do for a potential customer, we would probably emphasize those sentences in which *you* (the customer) and *DataStar*

are the actors. Here is one possible revision, with changes from the original italicized.

(1) *When* you want to print many similar documents, (2) you can use DataStar to produce customized versions of form letters. (3) *In a master file,* you enter the form letter text (4) *that* will remain the same for all the letters.

(We changed the position of the modifier in a master file *in order to clearly make* form letter text *the subject of the relative clause that follows.)*

(5) You supply the name of a data file (6) *that* contains specific names, addresses, etc. (8) DataStar inserts specific names, addresses, etc. from the data file into the marked places (7) *that are* contained in the master file.

(We changed the order and voice in order to make marked places *the subject of the relative clause.)*

(9) *When* DataStar reaches the end of the data file, (10) *it* stops producing the letters.

Now here is a "clean" version of the paragraph:

When you want to print many similar documents, you can use DataStar to produce customized versions of form letters. In a master file, you enter the form letter text that will remain the same for all the letters. You supply the name of a data file that contains specific names, addresses, etc. DataStar inserts specific names, addresses, etc. from the data file into the marked places that are contained in the master file. When DataStar reaches the end of the data file, it stops producing the letters.

chapter 22

Parallel Structure

In the preceding chapter, you learned how to use sentence structure to show the relationship between more important information and less important information. Specifically, you learned to place important information at the end of the main clause. Doing so allows you to match the most important information (the point of the sentence) with the position of greatest sentence emphasis. You also saw how less important information can be downplayed by keeping it away from the end of the sentence, and placed in subordinate grammatical positions, such as modifiers in phrases and dependent clauses.

This chapter poses a different challenge. Suppose you have two pieces of information that are essentially equal in importance. How do you show this equality? The answer is to use **parallel structure**—that is, to put ideas of equal or parallel importance in parallel grammatical form. This chapter is concerned with **coordinate phrasing,** in which two or more pieces of information of equal importance are treated equally. There is only one learning objective in this chapter, but it is a powerful stylistic principle: Put parallel ideas in parallel grammatical form.

The power of this principle derives from its wide applicability. It works equally well for coordinate phrases, clauses, whole sentences, and even entire documents.

Coordinate versus Subordinate

In one way, language structure is very simple: ideas, phrases, sentences, paragraphs, and so on can be either subordinate or coordinate. If part of a sentence or part of a report is subordinate, it is of less importance, lower on the hierarchy. If an element is coordinate, it is of equal rank with some other element on the hierarchy. Every outline and every organizational chart expresses the two relations shown in Figure 22.1. All such diagrams show the same two sorts of relations—subordinate, when an element is at a lower position, and coordinate, when an element is at the same level as some other element.

Let's look at how the principle of coordination works at each level of language construction through parallel structure.

Parallel Phrases

Effective writers and speakers use parallel phrases to lend elegance to their sentences through balance and rhythm, as in the following examples:

> A year or so later another article appeared, reporting Harlow's astonishing discovery that all of the little monkeys on which he had earlier experimented had turned out to be incurably psychotic. Not a single monkey could mate, not a single monkey could play, not a single monkey could in fact become anything more than the twisted half-creatures that Harlow's new discovery had made of them.
>
> —Wayne C. Booth

> Most commonly we come to books with blurred and divided minds, asking of fiction that it shall be true, of poetry that it shall be false, of biography that it shall be flattering, of history that it shall enforce our own prejudices.
>
> —Virginia Woolf

Figure 22.1 *Simple Branching Structure*

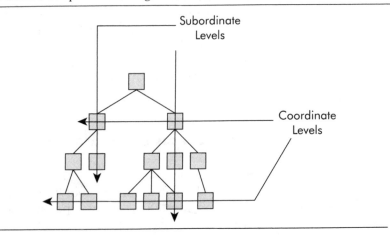

But how about little faults, little pains, little worries. The cosmic ulcer comes not from great concerns, but from little irritations....A man is destroyed by the duck nibblings of nagging, small bills, telephones (wrong number), athlete's foot, ragweed, the common cold, boredom.

—John Steinbeck

Examine each of these examples for grammatical structures that are repeated from phrase to phrase. In at least one of the sentences in each example, a strict parallel structure announces the coordinate status of the information. The sentences read smoothly, easily, and effortlessly. When the phrases come at the end of the sentence *and* exhibit a strict parallelism, the effect is particularly strong. Such sentences close gracefully, with the emphatic information underscored by the parallel structure.

All of the three examples reflect a literary prose style—a high style of writing appropriate to learned authors. But the principle of parallel structure can be applied as easily to normal, everyday writing on the job.

When coordinate ideas are expressed in grammatical forms that are *not* parallel, the effect can be jarring:

WRONG: Our difficulties with the supplier can be cleared up by shipping all orders with at least two weeks lead time, if we can look ahead and predict our cyclical needs, and maintenance of a small on-hand inventory.

Each of the three corrective actions (*by shipping, if we can look ahead,* and *maintenance*) is expressed in a different grammatical form, though they could *and should* be expressed in parallel structure. After all, each occupies a coordinate slot in the idea hierarchy of the sentence since each offers a solution to the difficulties. Rewritten in parallel form, the sentence reads much better, as in the following two possibilities:

Our difficulties with the supplier can be cleared up by shipping all orders with at least two weeks lead time, by looking ahead to predict our cyclical needs, and by maintaining a small, on-hand inventory.

Our difficulties with the supplier can be cleared up if we ship all orders with at least two weeks lead time, if we look ahead to predict our cyclical needs, and if we maintain a small, on-hand inventory.

The gain here is both in style and in clarity.

EXERCISE 22-1

The following sentences have coordinate phrases that could be better expressed in parallel form. Rewrite the sentences appropriately. If you have trouble rewriting the sentences, you might try to decide what items are being coordinated. You might also try to reformat the sentence to show the intended parallelism. The first sentence has been corrected and reformatted as an example.

1. He likes delegating responsibility on important projects, but also to be informed if something goes wrong.

   He likes {delegating responsibility on important projects, but also
      {being informed if something goes wrong.

2. Through the course, I've become familiar with the different manuals, the terminology, and who to go to for help.

3. Mary is taking a night class in spreadsheet accounting at the company and has been attending the weekend college to study labor relations.

4. She praised him not because his work was excellent but he finished on time.

5. Sam has been working to establish a better arbitration system for manager/employee disputes, to begin a new program for employee training, and developing ways to encourage early retirement.

6. The documentation seminar stressed having a sure sense of the user's tasks, the importance of clearly identified actions, and that some check on learning is usually necessary.

7. Excessive brightness can cause burning or the phosphor element to prematurely degrade. This is not covered under warranty.

Parallel Structure with Lists

Parallel structure is particularly important when information is broken out in lists. The list structure can really help a reader distinguish parallel elements of whatever sort:

- Steps in a process
- Parts of a mechanism
- Objectives for a committee

In this last sentence, each listed element is a parallel phrase—a head noun followed by a prepositional phrase. A second example uses somewhat more complicated phrasing but demonstrates a similar parallel structure in its list:

> We have established three milestones for the Laser Project:
> 1. To complete the prototype development with all synchronous components in place by August 16
> 2. To test the prototype design and operation under simulated climatic conditions by November 30
> 3. To redesign the prototype for demonstration to our client on January 10

In this example, each milestone is phrased around a *to* form of the verb (the infinitive form), followed by an object construction with some modification, and completed with a target date. It is not important here to know the grammatical terms for the parallel structures. You can still hear and see the strict parallel form that contributes to the list's clarity. Coupled with its visual structure, the parallel list highlights for the reader the three stages of the project.

In the preceding two examples, each item in the list (whether bulleted or numbered) began with a capital letter. However, no item ended with a period (not even the last item in each list). This is a recent convention of punctuating vertical lists. People have pointed out that a period at the end of the list is redundant, since the clear line of space before the beginning of the next sentence or paragraph on the next line clearly indicates the end. Current practice of most organizations is to use a period to end a vertical list when *each* item ends with a period—that is, when each item is a complete sentence. The following example demonstrates this punctuation convention; notice how each of the four steps in the process is a complete imperative sentence:

> To install the printer board, first remove the case from the PC in the following manner:
> 1. Unplug the computer.
> 2. Remove the five screws from the back panel.
> 3. Lift the back of the metal cover.
> 4. Slide the metal cover back and off the computer.

$$\blacksquare\!\!-\!\!-\!\!-\!\!-\boxed{\textbf{E X E R C I S E \quad 2 2 - 2}}\!\!-\!\!-\!\!-\!\!\blacksquare$$

Rewrite the following list[1] so that each item is in parallel grammatical form. You might wish first to identify the type of grammatical structure of each bullet in order to choose the best structure suggested by the lead-in sentence to the list.

An effective document database will have the following characteristics:

- It will use declarative formatting so that text and graphics can be reused.

- Text and graphics will be written in screen-size modules so they can be assembled later into documents.

- text modules that are easily accessible throughout an organization

- making documents available for concurrent tasks

- Users can print customized documents on demand.

- using mass storage devices

- Data integrity is safeguarded.

Parallel Structure with Sentences in Paragraphs

Parallel structure is most commonly discussed in the context of phrases within sentences, but it can be a powerful organizing principle when extended beyond the sentence to show how two or more sentences, or whole sections of writing, are coordinate. Within a paragraph, beginning each sentence with a coordinate structure allows a writer to make several consecutive points while maintaining the reader's focus on their close relationship, as the following example illustrates:

Surely the [Writers' War] Board knows what democracy is. It is the don't in "Don't shove." It is the hole in the stuffed shirt through which the sawdust slowly trickles; it is a dent in the high hat. Democracy is the recurrent suspicion that more than half of the people are right more than half of the time. It is the feeling of privacy in the voting

[1] List adapted from Geoffrey James, *Document Databases*. New York: Van Nostrand Reinhold, 1985.

booths, the feeling of communion in the libraries, the feeling of vitality everywhere. Democracy is the score at the beginning of the ninth inning. It is an idea which hasn't been disproved yet, a song the words of which have not gone bad. It's the mustard on the hot dog and the cream in the rationed coffee. Democracy is a request coming from the War Board, in the middle of a morning in the middle of a war, wanting to know what democracy is.

—E. B. White

In this example, the writer uses a string of propositions, carrying the same subject construction from one sentence to the next (*democracy* or *it*). The use of parallel subject phrases allows the reader to notice easily the coordinate status of each of the propositions. The structure carries the reader along from one parallel proposition to the next. Before you leave this example, notice, too, the parallel phrases within sentences that establish rhythm and make the writing flow.

Finally, notice that E. B. White is a crafty stylist who knows that setting up expectations for parallel structure and then slightly changing the structure is effective in avoiding monotony: *It is the feeling of privacy in the voting booths, the feeling of communion in the libraries, the feeling of vitality everywhere.* The final *everywhere* changes the parallel structure from a series of prepositional phrases beginning with *in*. This change lets White play with parallel phrasing without losing the ability to surprise the reader. (We highly recommend White's famous book, *Elements of Style*, coauthored with William Strunk, Jr.)

Here is another example, with a somewhat different texture, in which parallel structure works, sometimes at the beginnings of related sentences, sometimes within the predications:

The recent illumination of linguistic abilities has revolutionary implications for our understanding of language and its role in human affairs, and for our view of humanity itself. Most educated people already have opinions about language. They know that it is man's most important cultural invention, the quintessential example of his capacity to use symbols, and a biologically unprecedented event irrevocably separating him from other animals. They know that language pervades thought, with different languages causing their speakers to construe reality in different ways. They know that children learn to talk from role models and caregivers. They know that grammatical sophistication used to be nurtured in the schools, but sagging educational standards and the debasements of popular culture have led to a frightening decline in the ability of the average person to construct a grammatical sentence. They also know that English is a zany, logic-defying tongue, in which one drives on a parkway and parks in a driveway, plays at a recital and recites at a play. . . . In the pages that follow, I will try to convince you that every one of these common opinions is wrong!

— Steven Pinker, *The Language Instinct*

Changing the paragraph's layout might help you see the parallel structures:

The recent illumination of linguistic abilities has revolutionary implications
> for our understanding of language and its role in human affairs, and
> for our view of humanity itself.

Most educated people already have opinions about language.
They know that it is
> man's most important cultural invention,
> the quintessential example of his capacity to use symbols, and
> a biologically unprecedented event irrevocably separating him from other animals.

They know
> that language pervades thought, with different languages causing their speakers to construe reality in different ways.

They know
> that children learn to talk from role models and caregivers.

They know
> that grammatical sophistication used to be nurtured in the schools, but sagging educational standards and the debasements of popular culture have led to a frightening decline in the ability of the average person to construct a grammatical sentence.

They also know
> that English is a zany, logic-defying tongue, in which one
>> drives on a parkway and parks in a driveway,
>> plays at a recital and recites at a play. . . .

In the pages that follow, I will try to convince you that every one of these common opinions is wrong!

Parallel Structures beyond the Paragraph

A similar attention to parallel structure can signal the coordinate relation of one paragraph to the next or of one section of a report to the next. For example, a string of paragraphs might each lead off with a topic sentence that carries the same form as the other topic sentences in the series of paragraphs:

Our first objective must be to cut unprofitable operations.
Xxxxxxxxxx xxxx xxxx xxxxxxxxxxxxxxxxxxx xxxxxxxxxx xxxxxxxxxxxxx
xxxxxxxxxx xxx xxxxxxxxxxxxx xxxx.

Our second objective must be to consolidate management functions. Xxxxxx xxxxxxxxxxx xxx xxxxx xxxxxxxxxx x xxxxxxxxxx xx
xxxxxxxxxxxxxxxxx xxxxxxxxxxxxxxxx xxxxxxxxxx xxxxxxx xx.

Our third objective must be to eliminate cost overruns during
production. Xxxx xxxx xxxxxxxxxxxxxx xxxxxx xx x xxxxxxxx xxx xxxxxx
xxxxxx xxxxxxxxxxxxxxxx xxxxxx xxxxxxxxxxx.

Such parallel topic sentences from paragraph to paragraph can keep a reader
on track, helping him or her to see and hear the hierarchical organization of
the report.

A second example shows how an initial paragraph can set up the structure for a section of a report, with a parallel construction cueing each element in the structure:

There are two sorts of graphics editing programs: pixel-oriented
and object-oriented. Xxxx xxxxxx xxxxxx xxxx xxxx xxxxxxxx xxx.

With a pixel-oriented graphics editor, the artist edits dots on a
screen. Xxxxxx xxxx xxxxxxx xxxx xxxx xxx xxx x xxx xxx xxxx xx xxxxxx
xxxxx xxxx xxxx xx x x xxxxxx xxxx xxx.

With an object-oriented graphics editor, the artist edits whole
shapes. Xxxx xxxxx xxxx xxxx xxxx xxx xxx x xxxxxxx xxx xxxxxxx xxxxxx
xxx xx xxxx xxx x xxx x xxxxxx xxx x xxxxxx xxxxxxxxxxx.

Even with intervening paragraphs, this stylistic device of the repeated
prepositional phrase (*With a pixel, With an object*) can remind the writer
of the structure that he or she is committed to and cue the reader on the
relation of part to part.

EXERCISE 22-3

**Use each of the following sentences as a model for a sentence of
your own, substituting your own information. Keep the grammatical
pattern but fill in different information in each slot.**

1. By reporting a man's political strengths, they made him a front runner; by

mentioning his weaknesses and liabilities, they cut him down. (Timothy

Crouse)

2. That handicap does not hurt them because, if they have a nose for news, they do not need a tongue or ears; they bring more to the events they cover than they take away from them. (Robert Darnton)

3. A mass of Latin words falls upon the facts like soft snow, blurring the outlines and covering up the details. (George Orwell)

4. The expected chaos and panic did not materialize, however, because a group of paranoid schizophrenics, once released from their cells, immediately took charge of the evacuation, organized it, and carried it out quickly and efficiently. (Hendrik Hertzberg and David McClelland)

5. At the 330-volt level, the learner refuses not only to touch the shock plate but also to provide any answers. (Stanley Milgram)

6. If a certain line of experiments runs nowhere, it is omitted from the final report. If an inspired guess turns out to be correct, it is *not* reported as an inspired guess. (Isaac Asimov)

7. Rusty hoops on swaying poles represented the permanent recreational equipment, although bats and balls could be borrowed from the P.E. teacher if the borrower was qualified and if the diamond wasn't occupied. (Maya Angelou)

EXERCISE 22-4

Imagine that what follows are your notes from an internal meeting to discuss progress on a contract with a new client, ARCO Industries. Rewrite the notes as minutes, using parallel form where useful.

Mary reported on discussions with ARCO about extending the contract beyond the two-year commitment we originally discussed. They like the idea because it allows them to plan for the long term. They also want us to consider a lease arrangement on the cultivating equipment. They figure it might save costs in the long run. One other thing: can we commit to supplying them with nitrogen fertilizer on a demand basis? They would like a guaranteed supply, even if they call on short notice.

From our perspective, Bill mentioned the need for some changes in billing. As proposed, the lag time before payment will be about sixty-five days. He'd like to see it around thirty-five. He also pointed out that we need to revise the section of the contract that stipulates penalties for failure to deliver on time. A two-day grace period would solve the problem and not interfere with ARCO's schedule. The only other change he thought necessary was updating the projections on seed production to reflect the increased capacity of our third new greenhouse.

In Summary

The objective of this chapter has been to show you how to put parallel ideas into parallel grammatical form. You have seen how parallel structure operates between phrases within prose paragraphs, between items within a list, between sentences within paragraphs, and even between paragraphs within whole documents.

Parallelism is a powerful tool for reducing the processing time a reader takes to understand your message. Parallelism signals to the reader that certain things are *semantically* similar because they are expressed in a way that is *stylistically* similar.

Controlling coordination (showing which elements are similar) and subordination (showing which elements are less important than others) is an effective way of achieving effective emphasis for your message. In the next chapter, you will read about another means of achieving emphasis: controlling the *flow* of information from sentence to sentence.

EXERCISE ANSWERS

Exercise 22-1 Answers

There are many ways the sentences could be rewritten. Here is one way for each.

1. He likes delegating responsibility on important projects, but also to be informed if something goes wrong.

He likes *to delegate* responsibility on important projects, but *he* also *likes* to be informed if something goes wrong.

2. Through the course, I've become familiar with the different manuals, the terminology, and who to go to for help.

Through the course, I've become familiar with the different manuals, *with* the terminology, and *with the sources* of help.

3. Mary is taking a night class in spreadsheet accounting at the company and has been attending the weekend college to study labor relations.

Mary is taking a night class in spreadsheet accounting at the company and *a* weekend *class in* labor relations *at* the college.

4. She praised him not because his work was excellent but he finished on time.

She praised him not because his work was excellent but *because his work was* finished on time.

5. Sam has been working to establish a better arbitration system for manager/employee disputes, to begin a new program for employee training, and developing ways to encourage early retirement.

Sam has been working to establish a better arbitration system for manager/employee disputes, to begin a new program for employee training, and *to develop* ways to encourage early retirement.

6. The documentation seminar stressed having a sure sense of the user's tasks, the importance of clearly identified actions, and that some check on learning is usually necessary.

The documentation seminar stressed *the need for* having a sure sense of the user's tasks, *for* clearly identifying actions, and *for checking* on *the user's* learning.

7. Excessive brightness can cause burning or the phosphor element to prematurely degrade. This is not covered under warranty.

Excessive brightness can cause burning or premature degrad*ing of* the phosphor element. *Neither of* these is covered under warranty.

Exercise 22-2 Answers

There are many possible revisions of the items in this list. One possibility is to turn each item into a simple sentence consisting of one passive, independent clause.

An effective document database will have the following characteristics:

- Declarative formatting will be used.
- Text and graphics will be written in screen-size modules.
- Text modules will be easily accessible throughout an organization.
- Documents will be available for concurrent tasks.
- Users will be allowed to print customized documents on demand.
- Mass storage devices will be used.
- Data integrity will be safeguarded.

Another possibility is to turn each item into a verb phrase completing the lead-in word will. *(Note the difference in punctuation.)*

An effective document database will:

- Use declarative formatting
- Write text and graphics in screen-size modules
- Make text modules easily accessible throughout an organization
- Make documents available for concurrent tasks
- Allow users to print customized documents on demand
- Use mass storage devices
- Safeguard data integrity

Exercise 22-3 Answers

Answers will vary.

Exercise 22-4 Answers

Here is one possible revision for the first paragraph that brings the three ARCO requests into parallel structure. (Deletions are crossed through; additions are italicized.)

Mary reported on discussions with ARCO about extending the contract *with them* beyond the two-year commitment we originally discussed. ARCO likes the idea because it allows them to plan for the long term. They *would like* ~~also want us to consider~~ a *long-term* lease arrangement on the cultivating equipment. ~~They figure it might~~ *in order to save costs in the long run. They would also like our commitment to* supply~~ing~~ them with nitrogen fertilizer on a demand basis. *Finally, they would like* a guaranteed supply, even if they call on short notice.

The second paragraph might benefit from more radical revision. The parallel structures line up each action on the bullets, followed by comments where needed:

Bill recommended several changes involving our contract with ARCO:

- Limit the payment period to thirty-five days. Under ARCO's proposed terms, the lag time before payment would be about sixty-five days.

- Insert a two-day grace period in the section of the contract that stipulates penalties for failure to deliver on time. A two-day grace period would solve the problem and would not interfere with ARCO's schedule.

- Update the projections on seed production to reflect the increased capacity of our third new greenhouse.

chapter 23

Maintaining Flow from Sentence to Sentence

Many of the qualities of good writing pertain to the structure and style of individual sentences. However, as you have just seen in Chapter 22, "Parallel Structure," another quality of good writing is the connection *between* sentences. In the last chapter, we looked at putting elements of parallel importance in parallel structure. The effect of this parallelism is to make a text—especially lists—flow more smoothly, without interruption. In this chapter, we also examine flow, but this time, the flow of topics from sentence to sentence.

The term **coherence** is used to describe the characteristic of documents that seem to flow smoothly from beginning to end. Writing is coherent if it maintains focus on the same topic within a paragraph (or group of paragraphs) and then gracefully passes the focus on to a new topic.

In this chapter, we will talk about two ways of maintaining focus on the same topic within a paragraph:

- Repeating the same grammatical subject for each sentence within a paragraph
- "Chaining" the topic focus from the end of one sentence to the beginning of the next

We will call the first way of maintaining focus **head-to-head;** the second way, **tail-to-head.**

Head-to-Head Focus

One way to make writing flow is by repeating the same subject from sentence to sentence within a paragraph. An example of this *head-to-head* connection can be seen in the following pair of sentences:

LS is a small but useful program that does just one thing. It lets you list on your screen the contents of a directory or disk.

The subject of the first sentence is *LS.* The subject of the second sentence is the pronoun *it,* which refers back to *LS.* The topic of these two sentences is the program *LS;* the repetition of *LS* (or a substituted pronoun) from sentence to sentence maintains focus on that topic.

We can graphically represent the head-to-head focus in the above example in the following way:

$$\text{Subject}_1 \quad V_{linking} \quad \text{Object}_2$$
$$\text{LS} \qquad\quad \text{is} \qquad\quad \text{a program} \ldots$$
$$\downarrow$$
$$\text{Subject}_1 \quad V \qquad \text{Object}_{3 \text{ (clause)}}$$
$$\text{It} \qquad\quad \text{lets} \qquad \text{you list on your screen} \ldots$$

(The subscript numbers designate the *things* referred to, not the subject or object number. Thus *LS* and *it* are both designated by subscript 1 because they refer to the same thing.)

It would be possible to continue this scheme by making *LS* the subject of succeeding sentences within the paragraph. Thus, the next sentence might read as follows:

The program produces a UNIX-like directory listing that is more customizable than that produced by the **dir** command in DOS.

The graphic representation for the resulting paragraph would look like this:

$$\text{Subject}_1 \quad V_{linking} \quad \text{Object}_2$$
$$\text{LS} \qquad\quad \text{is} \qquad\quad \text{a program} \ldots$$
$$\downarrow$$
$$\text{Subject}_1 \quad V \qquad \text{Object}_{3 \text{ (clause)}}$$
$$\text{It} \qquad\quad \text{lets} \qquad \text{you list on your screen} \ldots$$
$$\downarrow$$
$$\text{Subject}_1 \qquad\qquad V \quad \text{Object}_4$$
$$\text{The program} \quad \text{produces a UNIX-like directory} \ldots$$

And the text of the complete paragraph would read like this:

> *LS* is a small but useful program that does just one thing: *It* lets you list on your screen the contents of a directory or disk. *The program* produces a UNIX-like directory listing that is more customizable than that produced by the **dir** command in DOS.

You could add sentences to this paragraph, keeping the same subject, although a *long* paragraph with this head-to-head chaining might get monotonous.

EXERCISE 23-1

Try writing a sentence to complete each of the following paragraphs. Maintain the focus on the topic by repeating the grammatical subject in some form (e.g., repetition or pronouns or synonyms) in each new sentence. Compare your completed sentences for the different paragraphs with those of your classmates.

1. Writing on the job often takes longer than most people would like. Planning is tough because of constant interruptions from coworkers and the telephone.

2. Nowadays, most home buyers are opting for fixed-rate mortgages rather than variable-rate ones. These buyers can get fixed interest rates of 6 to 7 percent interest, depending on the size of their loan.

3. There are many advantages of becoming computer literate. One advantage is being able to use home finance programs that keep track of all your accounts, write checks, predict your cash flow, and even pay bills.

Tail-to-Head Focus

Another way to maintain coherence within a paragraph is by "chaining" the topic from the end of one sentence to the beginning of the next sentence. In this *tail-to-head* focus, the end of one sentence (often, but not always, the object) is picked up at the beginning (often, but not always, the subject) of the next sentence.

Topic chaining from tail-to-head is common in stories. Consider the opening of a typical fairy tale:

> Once upon a time, there was a faraway *kingdom*. In the *kingdom* there lived a *prince*. The *prince* was very unhappy because he didn't have a bride.

The first sentence ends with *kingdom;* the second sentence begins with the prepositional phrase *in the kingdom.* The second sentence ends with *prince;* the third sentence begins with *prince* as the subject.

An example of tail-to-head connection in professional writing can be seen in the following pair of sentences, which continue the paragraph on the *LS* program:

> LS lists on your screen *the contents of a directory or disk. These contents* may be listed in various ways.

In this example, the subject of the second sentence (*these contents*) picks up the head word of the object phrase of the previous sentence (*the contents of a directory or disk*).

Graphically, the topic chaining between the two sentences would look something like this:

Subject₁-V-Object₂

$$\downarrow$$

Subject₂-V-Object₃

A continuing sentence using tail-to-head focus might look something like the following:

> *One way* is by alphabetical order.

The chained topic of the paragraph moves from *contents* to *various ways.* Graphically, the resulting paragraph of three sentences looks like this:

Subject$_1$-V-Object$_2$

$\downarrow$

Subject$_2$-V-Object$_3$

$\downarrow$

Subject$_3$-V-Object$_4$

And the complete paragraph reads as follows:

> LS lists on your screen *the contents* of a directory or disk. *These contents* may be listed in various *ways. One way* is by alphabetical order.

EXERCISE 23-2

In the following paragraph, draw brackets around each head and underline each tail (whether a direct object, a subject complement, an object of a preposition, or a simple predicate). Then draw arrows connecting head-to-head and tail-to-head. Identify the type of focus as either head-to-head or tail-to-head.

(1) The ceramic cards used in the training course are produced by Tulsa Micro-Electronics. (2) The cards are produced in layers. (3) The average number of layers is nineteen. (4) Each layer is baked in an oven and fired in a furnace. (5) This process is long but relatively simple. (6) It has three basic steps: print, dry, and bake. (7) These steps are repeated over and over until the board is complete.

Focus in Professional Writing

In actual professional documents, very few paragraphs are linked solely by head-to-head focus or solely by tail-to-head focus; more often, professional paragraphs use a mixture of the two (or are without focus altogether). The most frequent pattern in an effective document is for the topic of the paragraph to be introduced at the end of the first sentence, the position of speech emphasis. Then that topic becomes the grammatical subject for the remainder of the sentences in the paragraph.

Graphically, this pattern may be represented as follows:

$$Subject_1\text{-V-}Object_2$$

$$\downarrow$$

$$Subject_2\text{-V-}Object_3$$

$$\downarrow$$

$$Subject_2\text{-V-}Object_{4,\,\ldots}$$

This pattern is demonstrated in the following paragraph, which draws together some of the sample sentences seen above:

> The LS program lists on your screen *the contents* of a directory or disk. *These contents* may be listed in alphabetical order. *They* may also be listed according to the time the individual files were created or last modified.

The topic of this paragraph is *the contents of the disk.* It would be possible to refocus the paragraph on *what you can do with LS* by changing the subjects of the sentences following the first one:

> With the LS program, *you* can list on your screen the contents of a directory or disk. *You* can list these contents in alphabetical order. *You* can also list them according to the time the individual files were created or last modified.

Now the sentences in the paragraph are tied together by head-to-head connections.

Focus, Sentence Emphasis, and Voice

Maintaining focus on a topic in a paragraph has a lot to do with emphasis, discussed in Chapter 21, "Managing Sentence Emphasis." In that chapter you learned about two ways to achieve sentence emphasis: structural emphasis, in which the most important information is expressed in the most important kind of grammatical structures (independent clauses), and speech emphasis, in which the most important information occurs in one of the two positions of voice stress in a sentence: the very end (for primary stress) or the very beginning (for secondary stress).

The two ways of maintaining topic focus discussed in this chapter take advantage of the systems of structural and speech emphasis: The topic of a paragraph is usually introduced as new information at the end of an independent clause at the end of the first sentence (the position of primary voice stress). This topic is then chained to the head of the next sentence through a tail-to-head connection. Thereafter, the topic occupies the position of secondary voice stress at the head of each sentence, while new information is offered about the topic at the end of each succeeding sentence. So, when you rewrite a paragraph to sharpen the focus, what you are also doing is placing the focus information in structurally and verbally prominent parts of the sentence.

Maintaining focus also has a lot to do with choosing active or passive voice. As you read in Chapter 19, "When to Prefer the Passive Voice," one reason to prefer passive—or even to *mix* active and passive voice constructions—is to maintain a consistent focus. You saw this pattern demonstrated in an example paragraph in the preceding section. Main-clause verbs are italicized:

> The LS program *lists* on your screen the contents of a directory or disk. These contents *may be listed* in alphabetical order. They *may also be listed* according to the time the individual files were created or last modified.

Notice that the first sentence is in the active voice: *The LS program* **lists**. . . . It introduces the topic of the paragraph, *the contents of a directory or disk,* in the tail of the sentence. The second and third sentences pick up this topic as the head of each sentence. Notice that each sentence is in the passive voice: *These contents* **may be listed**. . . . and *They* **may also be listed**. . . . The shift to passive voice is necessary to maintain focus on the topic. (Be careful, however, not to assume that *all* such shifts to passive voice are necessary. You need to examine each occurrence of passive voice to determine if it is appropriate.)

As you progress into more sophisticated editing—where you are concerned more with **appropriateness** than with **correctness**—you will find that features of effective writing tend to work together, in much the same way that features of ineffective writing do. Here we have discussed the interconnections between focus, emphasis, and voice. You will also find connections between nominal style and passive voice. Writers frequently use both in an attempt to sound impressive and to avoid personal references. Fixing problems of nominal style will often lead you into fixing problems of passive voice at the same time. These interconnections should give you some appreciation for how systematic language truly is.

EXERCISE 23-3

The principle of coherence says to use head-to-head or tail-to-head links to maintain focus on the same topic. In the following paragraph, draw brackets around the head of each sentence; underline the tail in each. Then draw arrows connecting head-to-head and tail-to-head. Do you see why the paragraph doesn't flow? (Notice also how the passive constructions and nominalized verb forms contribute to the lack of flow.)

Rewrite the paragraph to improve links between sentences. Try rewriting passives and nominals, too.

(1) New installation options are provided by PS/CICS 1.3.1. (2) Reduction of I/O activity and exploitation of MVS/XA are allowed by these options. (3) However, an increase in CPU usage is likely to be caused by selection of these options. (4) These options should only be used by sites with additional CPU capacity available.

EXERCISE 23-4

Examine a recent piece of your writing for focus. Identify heads and tails of sentences within each paragraph and draw lines connecting them, as possible. Do you find any places where you can improve the focus?

In Summary

In this chapter, we have looked at two ways to maintain flow from sentence to sentence within a paragraph: head-to-head focus, which repeats the same subject from sentence to sentence; and tail-to-head focus, which picks up the end of one sentence as the beginning of the next. We have noted that the focus in paragraphs in many well-written documents is a combination of these two, with the paragraph topic being introduced as the tail of the first sentence and that tail becoming the head of succeeding sentences within the paragraph.

We have also noted the interconnections among focus, emphasis, and voice, pointing out the ways in which one reinforces the others.

Being aware not only of the ways of maintaining focus but also of the interconnections in language when you edit will allow you to consciously control the flow of information between sentences and to focus on the topic that *you* choose.

EXERCISE ANSWERS

Exercise 23-1 Answers

Answers will vary with individual students. Below are some possible answers.

1. Writing on the job often takes longer than most people would like. Planning is tough because of constant interruptions from coworkers and the telephone. *And drafting a document seems like a never-ending job of creating and polishing individual sentences.*

2. Nowadays, most home buyers are opting for fixed-rate mortgages rather than variable-rate ones. These buyers can get fixed interest rates of 6 to 7 percent interest, depending on the size of their loan. *Ten years ago, most people were going for variable-rate mortgages, which were then running three to four points below the 10.5 percent fixed rates of the time.*

3. There are many advantages of becoming computer literate. One advantage is being able to use home finance programs that keep track of all your accounts, write checks, predict your cash flow, and even pay bills. *Another advantage is being able to log on to the Internet, an incredible source of often free information about almost any topic you can imagine.*

Exercise 23-2 Answers

In the following paragraph, heads are bracketed; tails (whether direct objects, subject complements, objects of prepositions, or simple predicates) are underlined. Arrows have been drawn to connect head-to-head and tail-to-head. The dashed arrow between sentence 3 and sentence 4 indicates a "weak" link between *number of layers* at the head of sentence 3 and *Each layer* at the head of sentence 4.

1. [The ceramic cards] used in the training course are produced by <u>Tulsa Micro-Electronics</u>.
   HEAD-TO-HEAD

2. [The cards] are produced in <u>layers</u>.
   TAIL-TO-HEAD

3. [The average number of layers] is <u>nineteen</u>.
   HEAD-TO-HEAD

4. [Each layer] is <u>baked in an oven and fired in a furnace</u>.
   TAIL-TO-HEAD

5. [This process] is <u>long</u> but relatively <u>simple</u>.
   HEAD-TO-HEAD

6. [It] has three basic <u>steps</u>: print, dry, and bake.
   TAIL-TO-HEAD

7a. [These steps] are repeated over and over

7b. until the [card] is <u>complete</u>.

Exercise 23-3 Answers

In the following marked-up version of the original, heads are bracketed; tails are underlined.

1. [New installation options] are provided by <u>PS/CICS 1.3.1</u>.
2. [Reduction of I/O activity] and [exploitation of MVS/XA] are allowed by <u>these options</u>.
3. However, an [increase in CPU usage] is likely to be caused by <u>selection of these options</u>.
4. [These options] should only be used by <u>sites</u> with additional CPU capacity available.

The dashed arrow between the last two sentences indicates a "weak" link between selection of these options at the tail of sentence 3 and These options at the head of sentence 4.

One possible revision focuses on the product itself:

WHAT PS/CICS 1.3.1 DOES

PS/CICS 1.3.1 provides new installation options that reduce I/O activity and exploit MVS/XA. However, these options can also increase CPU usage. Therefore, they should only be used by installations with additional CPU capacity.

Another revision focuses on the user:

WHAT YOU CAN DO WITH PS/CICS 1.3.1

PS/CICS 1.3.1 provides new installation options that allow you to reduce I/O activity and to exploit MVS/XA. However, these options can also increase CPU usage. Therefore, you should only use them if your installation has additional CPU capacity.

Mark the subjects and objects in these two versions to check for coherence.

Exercise 23-4 Answers

Answers will vary.

chapter 24

Defining a Professional Look

Most working professionals are awash in documents, with reports and correspondence piled high. Documents compete for attention, and if they don't look inviting, important, and readable, they will be tossed aside. You can help your busy readers (and create a better chance of your document doing what it is intended to do) by paying attention not just to what a document says but to how it looks, too.

Few people have the time to read documents word for word, from beginning to end. Most readers skim documents, looking for clues to purpose, audience, action, and important details. You can help your busy readers by designing documents that display their meanings and make it easy for readers to size them up quickly to determine an efficient reading strategy.

This chapter discusses several principles of effective document design:

- Using white space actively to signal meaning
- Showing the structure of a document with headings and divisions
- Visually emphasizing or downplaying information
- Including important identifying information on each page of a document
- Choosing appropriate type styles
- Working with a style sheet to control formatting

The concerns of this chapter go well beyond grammar and correctness as they move toward developing an effective and appropriate visual style. In this area, you can think creatively, as a graphic designer might. Ultimately, well-designed documents contribute to the smooth working of your organization and to the delight of your readers.

Use Active White Space

Much of a page is filled not with lines of type but with space. The ink-to-space ratio of particular documents varies widely, of course, with some really dense-looking texts, like encyclopedias, approaching perhaps 80–90 percent coverage of the page with lines of type. Many designers would argue that a more readable page would only be about 40–50 percent text. Open texts, with white space spread meaningfully around a page, invite readers into the text. They say to the reader, "This isn't so hard or so dense. Reading it should be easy because the writer took the time to organize it and to display it effectively."

The text in the book you are reading takes up about 60 percent of each page. To get this open look, we have generous margins. When examples are introduced, they are indented from the left margin. This use of white space actively shows the change in function from one kind of text to another (subheading to body paragraphs to examples and exercises).

We also use white space to open up the page by including space before and after each heading. Paragraph breaks come frequently, with most paragraphs being no longer than six or seven sentences. Although less obvious to the eye, there is also a little extra space between each line within paragraphs. A printer would call this *leading* (pronounced "ledding") after the slugs of lead of variable width that would separate each line in a tray of set type.

A visually inviting style can result from several uses of white space:

- Ample margins and short lines, with extra leading between lines
- Blocks of print indented off the left margin with headings outdented
- Short paragraphs, with space breaks between paragraphs
- Bulleted or numbered list structures where appropriate

We tried to be consistently generous with the white space, so the book would invite you to read it, so you could have the feeling of making good progress, and so there would be plenty of room to make notes in the margin. As the circus barker was fond of saying, "If you don't get 'em in the tent, they ain't gonna see the show." It is hard enough to get people interested in grammar, so we wanted the appearance of this grammar textbook to be inviting and appealing.

The style described above is a very robust design with many variations. We decided to use first-line indents on each paragraph. You might choose differently. If you are going to use space breaks between paragraphs, you do not need first-line indents to show the start of each new paragraph. (With typewriters, it was traditional to indent the first line of each paragraph a full half-inch. With the more modern look of type produced by word processors and laser printers, less indentation often looks just fine.) Some designers play with huge first-line indents of $1^1/_2$ to 3 inches or more. And some highly designed texts use a lot more white space between lines of text or reserve a full third of the page for the left margin.

There are many variables to play with in striking a balance between ink and white space, and there are no simple rules to follow, except that nobody wants to read a page that looks dense. Use white space actively as you design your pages. Imagine readers looking at your document and considering whether it is worth reading. Consider how you can control and expedite the reading process by using white space in creative ways.

Choose Appropriate Justification

One other variable that affects the look of a page is **justification** (sometimes called *alignment*). Word processors offer several options for justification. With left justification, the left margin of a block of text is regular, but the ends of lines are allowed to break on the right margin wherever the words happen to end. There is some evidence that readers use the ragged line lengths to keep their place in the text as their eyes track from line to line. This is most important when lines or paragraphs are long and fonts are small.

In contrast, text can be set for full justification, with squared-off sides on both the left and right margins (as in this book). A good word processor evenly distributes microspaces between the words to force out the leftover space that would appear on the right with left-justified text. Full justification is useful for multicolumned text because it gives a sharp, typeset look to newsletters and brochures. But full justification with narrow columns demands careful use of hyphenation, especially in technical or scientific texts with lots of long words. Otherwise, the long words cause gaps when they are forced to the next line. You have probably noticed the "rivers" of white space that can run down a page when the microspaces happen to line up vertically. With most business documents, you should prefer left justification to full justification.

There are three other special sorts of justification that are occasionally useful: centered, right justified, and decimal aligned. Centered text is useful for headings, lists, and when you are creating special kinds of texts like announcements or invitations. Right justification is useful when you want text to line up against a setting on the right margin, as with page numbers in tables of contents, some headings, or the sender's address at the top of a letter. Decimal alignment is useful for columns of figures that need to be aligned by their decimal points. All the kinds of justification (or alignment) can be called into play to design data tables (see Figure 24.1).

Figure 24.1 *Special Types of Text Justification*

CENTERED TITLES ON FIRST TWO ROWS		
LEFT JUSTIFIED	DECIMAL ALIGNED	RIGHT JUSTIFIED
Trial 1m	4.33	605
Trial 2a	13.27	1903
Trial 3c	123.45	3567

E X E R C I S E   2 4 - 1

Describe the differences in layout and use of white space in the following. Identify situations in which each of the following layouts might be appropriate.

Vendor Specifications for T-131 PC Links
October 1996

The following specifications apply to all vendors submitting contract bids to supply T-131 PC Links to Vanguard Life Support Systems, Inc.

Tolerance Limits

1. A range of .02mm to .03mm is acceptable variance in overall dimensions.

2. Insertion clearance must not exceed .005mm.

3. No more than 2 devices per batch of 1,000 may be outside the dimensional limits.

Temperature and Moisture Limits

1. Electronic components must have a 99.5% reliability over a range of temperatures from −10 to 40 degrees centigrade.

2. Moisture content of board may not exceed .03 percent.

1

This is set in 7-point type, which is at the lower bounds of readability for most people. You might find it in a phone book or an encyclopedia, and the book designer would be sure to choose a font that would be legible at such small size. The kind of paper the type was printed on would be important, too, since some softer papers tend to bleed, with the pressed type getting fuzzy along the edges of the characters as the paper soaks up the ink. Of course, when type is lined up in columns for a reference/lookup function, the designer chooses a font with size and leading that makes sense for the particular purpose the text serves. Looking up a phone number is not the same as reading a set of installation instructions.

Sometimes people pursue a false sense of economy by squeezing lots of text onto a page. They might be trying to save paper or stay within a page limit, and so they reduce the width of margins, or go down a point or two below the recommended font size, or find ways to squeeze white space from between lines. Most such manipulations do damage to the text. Writers would be better off looking at the text and its redundancies. Most writers can eliminate a lot of verbiage by careful editing. Copy fitting can help, too. Sometimes single words wrap at the ends of paragraphs and a careful writer can figure out how to save a whole line of type by doing a little rewriting.

For comfortable reading, text should be printed in a 10-, 11-, or 12-point font on normal leading (which adds an extra point or two of space between each line). Ample margins and space breaks between paragraphs aid readability, as does the use of coated stock, that is, paper that has a bit of clay coating on its surface, giving it some hardness and sheen.

Competitive Analysis   Page 37

New Features

Several new features have been added to the current version
2.51 in the upgrade to 3.0:

- A text box can be sized and moved like a graphic object.
- Objects can be layered: text over text or graphics on text.
- Drag-and-drop applies to words, paragraphs, and graphic items.
- Menubars can be customized to display user-defined features.

Initial Marketing Strategy

Microzone expects to gain market share on the basis of
coupon incentives in computer magazines and on the basis of
ads touting the new features. They should be on track for a
December release and there may be significant added sales
because of high annual Christmas sales of PCs. An expected
share is 14–17%, provided they release the new version
without any significant problems. Any snags could do serious
damage to the project share.

Microzone currently has some 8–9% market share and they
expect close to 90% of current users will use the coupons to
upgrade, since they have priced the upgrade attractively at
$79 for registered users. Users will have a window to upgrade
at that price, probably from December to March. It has been
18 months since the last full number upgrade, so users will
probably go for the special deal.

Competitive Strategy

We need to anticipate the market response to this new
release in our advertising by mounting our own sales
incentive through a program of side-by-side feature
comparison.

A ROBUST QUARTER

Third quarter results are in and

everyone on the Street knows now

that we have exceeded their most rosy

predictions. Our customer base rose

37%, with new long distance markets

opening in Houston, Kansas City, and

Philadelphia. Our operating income is

up 24% and earnings per share rose

30% over last year. Our merger with

ATC Communication positions us

immediately as the sixth largest long

distance provider and gives us critical

mass in a competitive industry.

Show the Structure with Headings and Divisions

Get in the habit of looking at your documents at arm's length to see if
the structure is immediately clear. Can you see the logical divisions of
the text? Is it clear when a subsection is introduced? Can you tell what
goes with what?

White space, as we have just discussed, is one element that lets you
break a text into meaningful subsections. A reader uses the space breaks
between pages, sections, paragraphs, sentences, lists, and visuals to see
a text's structure and components. Use white space actively, with larger

breaks between major divisions (as between sections of a report) and smaller breaks between lower-level divisions (as between paragraphs).

Of immediate help to a reader is the use of white space with headings that break the text into labeled subsections. Even a one-page letter can benefit from headings that direct the reader's attention to important information and tell the reader how to read the page.

The space breaks in the memo in Figure 24.2 show the division into three clearly separated sections. Each section has a different function. The reader can see at a glance why the memo is coming his or her way, what the background is to the memo, and what he or she is expected to do.

The memo has a clean block format with no paragraph indents but with space breaks between paragraphs. Larger breaks come before each heading and smaller space breaks after each heading, so the white space says, "The heading goes with what follows, not with what came before."

Figure 24.2 *The Use of Headings to Break Up Text*

FOLKESTONE INVESTORS

To: Harold Jaspers, Auditor
From: Sally Jenkins, Business V.P.
Date: October 19, 19xx
Subj: **Discrepancies in Earnings Reports**

Purpose
I am writing to ask you to re-audit the earnings figures for the 4th quarter, looking carefully at the figures on depreciation on our Boise and Cheyenne operations.

Background
I noticed some discrepancies in our most recent earnings report, distributed internally last week. I thought we were going to an accelerated schedule on the new equipment, but it appears that the current figures are based on the older, seven-year method. That will drive down our earnings statement and cause some rumbling from the board.

Recommended Action
Please re-recalculate the earnings figures for July-September, paying particular attention to depreciation against earnings calculations. I need you to get back to me before Tuesday, 3 November when these figures have to be forwarded for inclusion in our quarterly report.

Thanks.

Tabbing the entries in the memo header (to, from, date, subject) allows them to line up vertically. Making the subject line boldface allows the clearly stated subject to stand out.

In longer documents, section headings (and sometimes subsection headings) are absolutely critical. In addition to showing the structure of your text to your reader, they can help you while writing. Headings should derive naturally from the logical structure of the text, and as you decide what the subsections of your text are, you will find or create a logical structure. Headings can help you notice when information is out of place, when a sequence is illogical, or when you have information that doesn't seem to fit anywhere in your document structure.

Good headings should often go beyond labels like *Part 3* or *Background*. The more specific and focused they can be, the better, as in the following examples:

Qualified Vendors for the A-3 Injection Molding System

Recommendations for Banquet Caterers

Target Profile for Cartilage Protective Agent (CPA)

When a text centers on actions or procedures, verb phrases often make the best headings:

Connecting the Power Supply

Configuring the Software Switches

Hooking Up Your Printer

When a text answers questions or performs as a reference, questions serve as good headings:

How Do I Qualify for a Loan?

Where Are the Best Interest Rates?

How Can I Choose the Best Lender?

What Are Points?

Readers find such question headings natural and easy to use (as long as the following paragraph provides the answer). Which style of heading you choose, of course, depends on what kind of text you have and whether your reader will expect some predictable heading structure or whether it is up to you to design your own. In general, the best headings are those based on actions specifically related to your text.

Headings follow certain principles of precedence:

- **Boldface** is more important than *italics,* which is more important than plain text.
- Centered is more important than left justified.
- Larger type is more important than smaller.
- ALL CAPS is more important than SMALL CAPS, which is more important than Initial Letter Caps.
- Headings with more white space setting them off are more important than those with less white space.
- Headings and text on the left margin (or outdented into the left margin) are more important than those indented from the left margin.

You can see some of these principles at work in this book.

For simple documents, a single level of heading is sufficient to break the text into sections. For more complex texts, two or three levels can be useful, as long as readers can easily distinguish among the levels. Most readers lose track of their place in hierarchies of more than three levels. In complex texts, decimal numbering systems with the headings can be helpful for indexing and cross-referencing. The trade-off, however, is that many readers have trouble with complicated numbering systems. (Is 3.2.12 before or after 3.11.6?)

Whatever type of headings you choose, remember that their function is to show the reader the structure of the text and to cue him or her on where to find certain kinds of information. Make sure the headings stand out by using some combination of white space, bolded or specially formatted type, and larger type than the body text.

EXERCISE 24-2

1. In the sample memo from Folkestone Investors, could the headings be improved? Should they be made more specific?

2. How would you characterize the headings in this book? Describe them both in terms of their content and format.

Emphasize or Downplay Information Visually

Like punctuation, typeface lets you emphasize or downplay information. The conventions described above that help distinguish levels of headings apply equally well to text:

- **Boldface** makes a word, phrase, or heading stand out from the plain text surrounding it. It is a strong and useful device for saying, "This is important." In this book, we use boldface for headings and for words that are defined in the glossary.
- *Italics* is much less forceful than bold in making text stand out. Italic letters use less ink and thus appear lighter than surrounding plain text. Italic text is useful for helping readers distinguish a word or phrase being defined, for identifying titles of publications, or for conveying a sense that words are spoken or written by hand. Like bold, italics should not be used for extended text.
- Underlining can call attention to words or phrases, but it is being used less all the time. Many computer printers do not handle underlining well. Traditionally, underlining was a way of telling human printers to set text in italics, but now nearly everyone has italics as a choice of type style.

These typographic styles work together with white space and placement of information in a document to determine which information is prominent and which is not. Bulleting a list of key findings can make their importance obvious and can help a reader see exactly what is being claimed. A conclusion that is presented at the beginning of a document enjoys more prominence than one buried in the middle of a document. A message that is bulleted, surrounded by white space, and set in italics is sure to be noticed. A recommendation presented as a single-sentence paragraph at the end of a document under the heading *Recommended Action* or *Action Item* is likely to be noticed and viewed as important to act upon.

Similarly, information that is not important can be downplayed by representing it in paragraphs in plain text. A page header or footer (discussed below) can be printed at the extreme margins of the page in smaller type than the body text, so the reader can consult the header or footer when useful but is not automatically drawn to the header or footer when first looking at the page. Some scientific journals set sections in smaller type if those sections are seen as less important or are less likely to attract reader attention (like methods sections or appendices to a scientific article) than those sections that many readers are expected to read (like the introduction and conclusion).

A general principle of emphasis is that first and last positions are of greater importance than middle positions. (We discussed this principle in terms of emphatic places for sentence information in Chapter 21, "Managing Sentence Emphasis.") Important sentences should come first and last in the overall report, in each section, and in each paragraph. The first and last principle even applies to each sentence, where the beginning establishes the topic and focus and the end delivers the new information.

Many writers exploit the natural importance of first position by creating executive summaries, by presenting findings or conclusions first, or by highlighting key messages up front. They then subordinate background information, details of process, and supporting arguments and data by placing them in the middle sections of the report or middle positions of individual paragraphs. Many documents can be vastly improved simply by pulling important information (messages, conclusions, recommendations) out of the middle of sections or paragraphs and giving them the prominent position they deserve.

Devices for emphasizing or downplaying information should be used with consistency and restraint. It is confusing to use bold or italics for several different purposes in a text, just as it is to change type styles arbitrarily. A report that consists of bulleted list after bulleted list soon loses its effect. A page that is full of boldface sentences and phrases loses focus. Word processors and laser printers offer writers many tools for creating emphasis and visual interest in a document. The professional writer knows how to find a balance between what is possible and what is effective. Too much emphasis in a text means no emphasis at all.

Include Identifying Information

The professional look and usefulness of many documents can be improved by placing important identifying information in headers and footers. A **header** is information printed in the margin area at the top of each page; a **footer** appears at the bottom area of each page. Headers and footers can contain some combination of two or more of the following: a page number, a date, a full title or short title of the document, a section or chapter title, file information for locating the electronic version of a document, or a copyright notice. It is important to distinguish between a head*er,* which repeats information at the top of each page, from a head*ing,* which breaks a document into sections and cues the reader to the specific content of each section.

Especially in longer documents, headers and footers can help readers to find information and to keep pages, sections, documents, and appendices intact and in order. A date can help readers know whether they are looking at the most recent version of a document—which can be especially useful in complex documents that go through repeated revisions and updating. Some word processors allow the insertion of a date stamp, rather than the actual date, so that the date on the document reflects whatever day the file is printed, rather than the date the file was written. A footer that contains file name and directory information can help people track down the original file for updating or archive purposes. Increasingly, computer drives tend to contain so many files in so many directories that it is very difficult to find a file without knowing its name or location.

Sometimes it is helpful to maintain information in headers or footers while a document is in development, but to delete some of the tracking information before the final document is printed. Frequently, authors omit the header/footer or provide different header/footer information on the first page of a document. For printed books and brochures, headers and footers and margins can be set differently for even- and odd-numbered pages. This makes it possible, for example, to have plenty of room for the binding and to place page numbers on outside corners where they are most visible and useful, rather than in the binding.

Choose Appropriate Type Styles

Word processors and laser printers enable individuals to use type in ways that only print shops could handle ten years ago. Your choices of type determine whether a document looks serious or playful, readable or forbidding.

Our choice of type **font** (or type style) for this book is called Garamond Light. It is a fine, standard choice for situations where there is a lot of reading to do, as in a book. We use a different font (Futura) in different sizes and styles (called a font family) for the headings that divide sections and for the identifying headers at the top of the page.

The body paragraphs are printed in 10-point Garamond, a standard point size for body text. (**Point** is a printer's measure. Seventy-two points equal approximately one inch.)

Just for contrast, this sentence is in 8-point Garamond. Text set in 8-point type is still quite readable but will produce pages that are a bit denser looking. An 8-point type can be opened by using extra leading, say by printing 8-point type on 12-point leading, which would leave a little extra space between each line, as in this paragraph.

Going down even further, in this case to 6-point type, we approach the limits of legibility. Printing close-spaced text in 6-point type on standard leading is one way to print a lot of text in a short space. It might be appropriate in a legal document that no one is expected to read. It might also be a good way to torture any reader over age forty-five, for whom small text becomes increasingly illegible. As you can tell as you strain to read this paragraph, type size and line length are correlated variables: as type becomes smaller, lines should become shorter to aid readability. People find it difficult to track line-by-line when type is small and closely spaced. A rule of thumb says that line length should be about forty to sixty characters.

Garamond is a **serif** font, meaning that it has little extensions from the tops and bottoms of the characters, mimicking the characteristic strokes of an ink pen. This paragraph, in contrast, is printed in 10-point Helvetica, which is a **sans serif** font (without serifs). These letter forms are clean and straight. There is some debate about whether serif or sans serif type is easier to read; it may simply be a matter of what people are accustomed to. Boldface Helvetica does make a very good choice for headings, where large, bold type sets off a section of a report. A traditional design for a document prints headings in boldface sans serif, such as Helvetica, and body type in a serif font, such as Times. These two fonts have the virtue of being on most computer systems and resident in most laser printers, so they make fairly safe choices when you are unsure about where a document will be printed.

Popular serif fonts include Palatino, Bookman, and New Century Schoolbook (a very round, open form that makes good children's books). Popular sans serif fonts include Arial, AvantGarde, and MS Sans Serif. You will notice that some of these are more readable on your computer screen than others, and being able to read your work easily on screen is certainly one factor in deciding which fonts you like to use.

Most of the fonts you will find on your word processor are proportionally spaced. This means that a letter with a thin profile like an *i* or an *l* will take less printing width than a wide profile letter like an *m* or a *w*. **Proportionally spacing** letters gives the printed text a professional, typeset look.

Some fonts are **monospaced** (spaced evenly for each letter) and meant to look like typewritten text; Courier is an example. Each letter gets the same amount of space. This can be handy when you want type to line up vertically in columns. If you compare the letters in this paragraph, you will notice that the letters and spaces line up vertically with each other, in a sort of matrix. With a proportional font, it is impossible to get strings of letters to line up vertically without using tabs. Some people always choose to create tables with proportional fonts because they know that what they see on the screen will come out the same on the printer.

We chose Futura as the font for our exercise and example paragraphs because it is so obviously different from Garamond that it stands out. Also, there is little risk of mistaking a sample of language in an exercise for an explanation as part of the text. You can probably think of other situations in which there are different types of language in a text and a change in font could help you cue the reader. For example, in a computer tutorial, you might want a font that looks like text on a computer screen to indicate the exact, letter-for-letter commands that someone enters. In such a situation, it is important to distinguish text as action (input) from text as explanation.

Some fonts have been designed for special purposes. On a Macintosh, the fonts with city names (New York, Chicago, Monaco, etc.) were designed to be highly readable on a computer screen. On an IBM-type personal computer, System is a font meant for screens, a heavy, sans serif font like the one that you see at the top of your screen on the menu bar. These are called **screen fonts,** and though they were never intended to be printed, people frequently do. On paper, they look somewhat heavy and clunky because they have heavy strokes that use a lot of ink or toner. Font designers are just now beginning to invent font sets that work well with photocopy and fax machines, where the letter form must be robust enough to be legible after poor reproduction or repeated copying.

Typefaces are interesting for the variety and elegance of their design. On some typefaces, the **ascenders** (the vertical strokes that extend beyond the basic height of most letters; the letters *b, d,* and *h* have ascenders) project well above the **x-height** (the horizontal line that can be drawn through a line of type along the tops of lowercase letters). Some typefaces use very round letter forms, with the letter *o* being perfectly round. Such fonts are said to have *open counters;* counter refers to the white space enclosed by certain letter shapes (a, b, d, e, g, o, p, q).

This is 11-point AvantGarde, which is on most *Windows* systems. With a light, even stroke, modern letter forms, high x-height, and very round, open forms, it is not well suited to extended reading but makes a good display font for posters or invitations. As its name suggests, AvantGarde suggests trendy design, not serious reading. With some fonts like this one, smaller point sizes may look large, because their forms are open and light.

Some typefaces have an oblique lean to the letters, as though the forms were tilted forward slightly. Some typefaces have bold, heavy strokes, as if written with a thick pen nib, while some use a combination of thick and thin strokes to mimic the flow of ink from a pen as it goes down, up, or across the paper to form the letters. Some typefaces look as if a machine had stamped them out, with smudgy ink like a stencil might produce; others look as though a computer line printer had spewed them out at one thousand lines per minute. Individual reactions to specific typefaces vary widely, and we can't pretend to be too sure about how a given typeface will color a reader's reaction to a document. When used effectively, typefaces can signal subtle meanings while offering readable and pleasingly designed text.

EXERCISE 24-3

For each of the sample fonts printed in the left column, identify possible uses in the right column. Where would you expect to see such a font? In what kind of document? For what function in a given document type? This is obviously a highly subjective exercise, meant to stimulate discussion, not arrive at correct answers. When you finish, compare your suggestions with those of other people around you.

Opti Valley Forge Compressed is a font with a very low x-height: the ascenders on the letters tower over the lowercase letters that do not have ascenders.	
Bookman's name gives away its design function: a serifed font for extended reading.	
AvantGarde is a sans serif font with a light stroke and a high x-height (the ascenders do not go much above the lower x-line). It has very open counters, the internal spaces in letters like o and a.	
Brush Script MT mimics handwriting strokes. Notice the ligatures, the connecting strokes on letters like T and L, and the variation in stroke width, meant to suggest the flow of ink from a pen.	
Braggadoccio in its plain style looks like a stenciled typeface with very heavy vertical strokes and a very high x-height.	
Book Antiqua has traditional letter forms, as in the letter *g* or *Q*, a relatively low x-height, and uses oblique strokes.	
DESDEMONA HAS ONLY CAPITAL LETTERS WITH SINUOUS LINES AND COUNTERS THAT SAG.	

Work with a Style Sheet

A **style sheet** is a set of format and typographic definitions for the various elements in a document. Word processors allow an author to define and tag the various elements so that a document can be easily and consistently formatted.

In this book, for example, we defined three levels of headings, and when we created a new section, we labeled the heading H1, H2, or H3. This section is level one, so the leading was formatted H1, which was defined as extra bold 12-point Futura, set centered and underlined. The first paragraph under the heading is our normal paragraph style, which is 10-point Garamond Light on 12-point leading. We have other definitions for indented paragraphs, bulleted lists, exercise paragraphs, answers to exercises, odd and even headers and footers, and so on.

The style sheet helps us control and keep consistent the formatting of each chapter and the whole book. As long as all the elements are correctly tagged, all body paragraphs will be formatted exactly the same, all bulleted lists will look the same, all page numbers will be in the right places. If we decide we don't like the look of, say, a level-three heading, we can go into our style sheet and change its definition. Every level-three heading in the document will then change along with our change of definition.

The styles you define for one document can be set as defaults for any new files you create or can establish a style sheet as part of the template for a given type of document: a memo, a letter, a proposal, or a sales report. It takes some time to learn to use style sheets and to set them up, but there is a big payoff when they start working for you. Style sheets are a powerful tool for creating a professional look in your own documents.

At one time, a company that was concerned about producing quality documents would create a publications group through which documents would be routed for formatting, revision, final editing, and printing. This way of working doesn't make as much sense as it used to, because now most people have formatting and printing tools on their desktop, and most computers are connected to high-quality printers. Style sheets can help create a company "look," so all documents appear to have been produced by the same group, following the same principles of thoughtful design.

Style sheets are increasingly being used by complex document publishing systems, both for paper and electronic documents. What you learn about using style sheets within your own word processor will usefully transfer to other situations if you find yourself working with document mark-up for electronic publishing systems, for publishing on the World Wide Web, or for creating document databases. Documents that can easily be imported or exported across different hardware and software systems are often formatted with style sheets defined by the Standard Generalized Markup Language (SGML), and the electronic documents you see on the Web are formatted in Hypertext Markup Language (HTML), a subset of SGML.

It is beyond our ability to teach you specifically how to set up a style sheet for your particular word processor. The best we can do is to tell you that if you are serious about creating good-looking documents, a style sheet is a powerful tool for achieving this effect. Check it out: most word processors have help files that will give you tips; many have short tutorials or sections in the manual that show you how to set up a style sheet.

Refinements

Here is a list of refinements that can dress up a document with a professional designer's touch. You might experiment with these design variables and see which you would like to use in your own texts.

- *Small Caps:* This type style can give an interesting highlighting effect in headers or headings, or they can call attention to words or phrases.
- *No indent after headings:* The first paragraph following a heading does not need to be indented in texts that indent each body paragraph. The spacing of the heading and the initial position of the first paragraph provide all the signals a reader needs.
- *Rules at the top or bottom of pages or to set off text:* A **rule** is a horizontal line across a page, either above or below a line of text. We use them to set off our exercise sections. A rule that sets off a header or footer can give an elegant look to a document.
- *Tabs and indents:* Left, right, center, and decimal tabs can be used to line up information in tables or columns. Data displays benefit immensely from columns with right or decimal justification. Right-justified tabs are the only good way to create a table of contents. A refinement here is to create right tabs with leader dots, a dotted line that helps a reader track from chapter to page number.
- *Vertical alignment:* The ruler bar of your word processor allows you to fine-tune the lines of text so that information lines up vertically with a clean look. In this list, for example, the bullets stand out, with each bulleted paragraph lining up cleanly with the first line.
- *Borders and shading:* Your word processor gives you many choices of rule thickness, borders, and shading. Judicious choices and a light touch with the right amount of ink on a page can contribute to a professional look, especially in tables and diagrams.
- *Text flow:* Many word processors now give you the ability to place frames around graphic objects, so you can flow text around tables or diagrams or create pages with multiple columns.
- *Large margins with embedded callouts or graphs:* An effective report style has large margins, in which text boxes or graphic objects can be inserted that call out key ideas in the text or provide supporting data.
- *Run-in headings:* This bulleted list uses run-in headings, formatted here as italicized phrases that identify what each bullet discusses.

In Summary

Creating professional-looking documents involves more than just making a document "pretty." Well-designed documents show their structures; they guide readers toward what to read, in what order, to find specific kinds of information as quickly as possible. They highlight key information in long documents: the main messages, the important findings, the conclusions, the important issues.

Well-designed documents show respect for the reader. They put your work in the best light and create a positive image for your company. A good design, however, can't fix poorly written text; at best, it may distract a reader briefly. A professional text will have a balance of good writing and good presentation. If you have decided to be careful about your writing, you will want to be careful both about how your text is written and how it is presented.

EXERCISE 24-4

The modified passage on the following pages is from a product manual for a database program called *DataStar*. Skim the whole passage first and then edit it, applying what you have learned in this unit by paying special attention to:

- Eliminating unnecessary grammatical structures
- Subordinating less important ideas
- Keeping parallel ideas in parallel grammatical structures
- Controlling sentence emphasis and flow from sentence to sentence
- Introducing visual emphasis

Keep in mind that the purpose of this passage is to provide general background about *DataStar*. Don't worry too much about explaining technical or scientific terms, since your readers are data-processing professionals.

A Word to the Data-Processing Professional

DataStar is a highly integrated fourth-generation language that makes it easier for you to work with end users. Users can do many things for themselves. These things are things that traditionally have been done by data-processing professionals.

Users utilize the same product for personal computing that you use to create corporate applications. You share with the user a set of common tools and a vocabulary that is shared.

You provide the expertise to design applications and also the database is managed by you. Users write their own reports. Designing their own data-entry screens is something else users can do themselves. You manage data from the corporate database and the interface with data held in other applications that are not in the corporate database. Users maintain their own data, and they also keep their own files current. While at the same time they manage their own data files.

Because DataStar is flexible, it works well as a prototyping tool for corporate applications. You can create prototype screens and reports for users to work with. Seeing their reports and their screens, and also trying them out in various kinds of ways are other things users can do with the DataStar, rather than simply seeing their reports on paper for approval as is often the case where data-processing services are supplied by data-processing professionals for end users.

Because presentation methods are not controlled by the physical layout of the data, departmental applications are easy to maintain. When report requirements change, extensively recoding departmental applications is something you do not have to do.

You can easily add new fields to your DataStar database because DataStar applications depend on field names rather than record layout, making it easy to do this without changing existing applications.

For you to maintain the integrity of the corporate database is easy. You can copy files to departmental or personal data libraries without threatening the integrity of the corporate database. And the process of updating corporate data from user data is a more easily managed process.

Exercise 24-1 Answers

Answers will vary.

Exercise 24-2 Answers

Answers will vary.

Exercise 24-3 Answers

Answers will vary. Below are some sample answers.

Opti Valley Forge Compressed:	Announcements, headings, posters, ads
Bookman:	Children's books, classroom handouts, scripts, documentation, procedures
AvantGarde:	Party invitations, posters, ads, headings
Brush Script MT:	*To suggest handwriting, signatures, personal appeals*
Braggadoccio:	**To suggest stenciled letters, shipping news, circus posters**
Book Antiqua:	To suggest older, fancy, set type in books, ads, extended reading
DESDEMONA:	PRODUCT NAMES, SPECIAL EVENTS ANNOUNCEMENTS

Exercise 24-4 Answers

Below is a marked-up version of the original passage, edited for unnecessary grammatical structures, faulty parallelism, and poor sentence emphasis. See the two possible "cleaned-up" versions that follow for formatting ideas.

A WORD TO THE DATA-PROCESSING PROFESSIONAL

DataStar is a highly integrated, fourth-generation language that makes it easier for you to work with end users. *With DataStar,* ~~U~~users can do many things for themselves. ~~These things are things~~ that traditionally have been done by data-processing professionals.

Users *use* ~~utilize~~ the same product for personal computing that you use *for creating* ~~to create~~ corporate applications. You *and* ~~share with~~ the user *share* a set of common tools and a vocabulary ~~that is shared~~.

You provide the expertise to design applications and *to manage* ~~also~~ the data base ~~is managed by you~~. Users write their own reports~~:~~ *and* d~~Designing~~ their own data-entry screens ~~is something else users can do themselves~~. You manage data from the corporate database and the interface with data held in other applications ~~which are not in the corporate database~~. Users maintain their own data and ~~they also~~ keep their own files current. ~~While at the same time they manage their own data files.~~

Because DataStar is flexible, it works well as a prototyping tool for corporate applications. You can create prototype screens and reports for users to work with. *Users can* S~~seeing~~ their reports and ~~their~~ screens and also try~~ing~~ them out in various kinds of ways ~~are other things users can do with the DataStar, rather than simply seeing their reports on paper for approval as is often the case where data processing services are supplied by data processing professionals for end users~~.

Because presentation methods are not controlled by the physical layout of the data, departmental applications are easy to maintain. When report requirements change, *you do not have to* extensively re-cod~~eing~~ departmental applications ~~is something you do not have to do~~.

Because DataStar applications depend on field names rather than record layout, y~~You~~ can easily add new fields to your DataStar data base without changing existing applications.

With DataStar, you can easily ~~For you to~~ maintain the integrity of the corporate database ~~is easy~~. You can copy files *between* ~~to~~ departmental *and* ~~or~~ personal data libraries without threatening the integrity of the corporate database. ~~And the process of updating corporate data from user data is a more easily managed process.~~

A WORD TO THE DATA-PROCESSING PROFESSIONAL

DataStar is a highly integrated, fourth-generation language that makes it easier for you to work with end users. With DataStar, users can do many things for themselves that traditionally have been done by data-processing professionals:

- Users use the same product for personal computing that you use for creating corporate applications. You and the user share a set of common tools and a vocabulary.

- You provide the expertise to design applications and to manage the database. Users write their own reports and design their own data-entry screens. You manage data from the corporate database and the interface with data held in other applications. Users maintain their own data and keep their own files current.

- Because DataStar is flexible, it works well as a prototyping tool for corporate applications. You can create prototype screens and reports for users to work with. Users can see their reports and screens and also try them out in various kinds of ways.

- Because presentation methods are not controlled by the physical layout of the data, departmental applications are easy to maintain. When report requirements change, you do not have to extensively recode departmental applications.

- Because DataStar applications depend on field names rather than record layout, you can easily add new fields to your DataStar database without changing existing applications.

- With DataStar, you can easily maintain the integrity of the corporate database. You can copy files between departmental and personal data libraries without threatening the integrity of the corporate database.

A WORD TO THE DATA-PROCESSING PROFESSIONAL

DataStar is a highly integrated, fourth-generation language that makes it easier for you to work with end users. With DataStar, users can do many things for themselves that traditionally have been done by data-processing professionals:

Data-Processing Professionals

- Use DataStar for creating corporate applications
- Share a set of common tools and vocabulary
- Design applications and manage the database
- Manage data from the corporate data base and the interface with data held in other applications
- Create prototype screens and reports for users to work with

End Users

- Use the same product for personal computing
- Share a set of common tools and vocabulary
- Write their own reports and design their own data-entry screens
- Maintain their own data and keep their own files current
- See their reports and screens and also try them out in various kinds of ways

Other Advantages for the Data-Processing Professional

- Because presentation methods are not controlled by the physical layout of the data, departmental applications are easy to maintain. When report requirements change, you do not have to extensively recode departmental applications.

- Because DataStar applications depend on field names rather than record layout, you can easily add new fields to your DataStar database without changing existing applications.

- With DataStar, you can easily maintain the integrity of the corporate database. You can copy files between departmental and personal data libraries without threatening the integrity of the corporate database.

chapter 25

Conclusion:
The Marks
of a
Professional Style

In This Chapter

Helping you develop a professional style is the goal of this book, and we assume that it is your goal as a reader of this book. In many ways, style is choice. Style depends on making appropriate choices from a language system that always presents a writer with alternate words and structures. It is not so much a matter of learning what is right and what is wrong but of recognizing and making intelligent, principled choices.

We have given you six principles to consider in making choices, and those six principles have been the organizing device around which this book is ordered. It might be useful to reconsider those principles now:

1. Professional writing is *appropriate* to the situation.
2. Professional writing is grammatically *correct.*
3. Professional writing uses punctuation to show what *is*—and what is *not*—important.
4. Professional writing uses a *clear* and *concise* vocabulary.
5. Professional writing is appropriately *active* and *personal,* rather than passive and impersonal.
6. Professional writing *emphasizes* what is important—and downplays what is *not.*

Each of these principles is the topic of one of the sections that follows.

"Professional writing is appropriate to the situation."

The first questions you should ask about a document are the large ones:

1. Is the writing clear in its purpose: in the messages it sends, the issues it raises, the actions it requests?
2. Is it appropriate to the audience? Does it encourage collaboration rather than conflict?
3. Is it emphatic and persuasive? Will it get the job done?
4. Does it provide appropriate support? Are evidence and data lined up logically?

These are the most important questions you can ask about your writing; everything we say about clarity, consistency, conciseness, coherence, and correctness are subordinate to the large issues of whether your writing is appropriate to the situation. Chapter 1, "Writing on the Job," and Chapter 2, "A Model of the Writing Process," both encourage you to ask the right questions before you begin writing and to take strategic control over your writing process.

Also in the first unit, we went over some kinds of "errors" that are more like preferences than rules (Chapter 3, "Real Rules, Nonrules, and House Rules"). You always have choices of usage, ranging from slangy and colloquial to highly formal (Chapter 20, "Projecting Personality"). It is not that one style is wrong and another right; rather, it is a matter of what is appropriate to a situation. If you learned the lessons presented here, you will be less likely to follow such nonrules as "Never split an infinitive" or "Never begin a sentence with *but* or *and*." You will recognize that these are fairly trivial matters, bothersome to some people, but more on the order of manners than rules.

"Professional writing is grammatically correct."

Throughout the chapters on grammar and style, we tried to identify various grammatical structures that tend to produce errors. We argued that it is important to recognize and avoid certain kinds of errors. These errors include agreement between pronouns and nouns and between subjects and verbs (Chapter 6, "Common Problems with Verbs," Chapter 7, "Placing Modifiers Effectively," and Chapter 8, "Pronoun Problems"). Such errors tend to be quickly noticed: they call attention to themselves, and it is not the kind of attention you want your writing to receive. It takes some specific learning about grammar and control of a vocabulary (*clause, object, agreement,* etc.) to understand errors and to explain them to your-self or others (Chapter 4, "Parts of Sentences and Parts of Speech").

In practice, such clear-cut errors are relatively infrequent in most writers' work. More common are "errors" such as sentence fragments (Chapter 5, "Sentence Completeness"). Fragments are considered out of place in formal writing, but they appear everywhere in advertising, reference works, and lists in scientific and technical prose. The idea presented in this chapter was to recognize what a fragment is and to decide when to use one and when not. When you do use fragments, you can make deliberate choices and thereby gain control, expressiveness, and economy. If you see a list, for example, that contains full clauses, some noun phrases, and some verb phrases, you can decide to bring parallel structure to the coordinate items in the list by making them, say, all verb phrases with objects (Chapter 22, "Parallel Structure"). It is far better to think about fragments as useful in some situations like lists than to have a faulty rule in your head that says, "Never use sentence fragments."

More important to you will be exercising *meaningful* control over grammatical options. For example, you might be more careful about choosing verb forms, knowing that you can make subtle distinctions concerning what you know, when you learned it, and how much confidence you have in the claim (Chapter 6, "Common Problems with Verbs"). The systems of tense, mood, and aspect in the verb are immensely complicated, involving subtle suggestions from the writer to a reader, who may or may not be attuned to the signal system. You have thousands of choices of verb forms, and when you toss in the combinations that are possible in going from sentence to sentence across a paragraph of reasoning, the choices are boggling. So there is no simple rule to follow about switching tenses. The rule is more a suggestion: "Pay attention to the meanings expressed by verbs and make motivated choices when you choose to phrase a verb in past tense or to use an auxiliary like *to have.*" There are important differences, not having to do with time but with confidence, among such phrases as these:

Studies show...

Studies showed...

Studies have shown...

Studies had shown...

Linguists can spend their lifetimes attempting to explain how language systems (like verbs) work, so there is little hope that workplace writers can gain full and systematic control. Luckily, you don't need a formal, systematic understanding. Your language instincts will help you out if you pay attention to your choices, avoid adopting faulty rules, and work through various phrasings and consistencies until you recognize a good choice for the meaning you wish to express.

"Professional writing uses punctuation to show what *is*—and what is *not*—important."

It is important to see punctuation as a resource in written English that helps you convey to your readers how a sentence is to be read.

Punctuation shows voicing and intonation. It shows your reader which words go together—by a hyphen between the words or by no space at all (Chapter 11, "Hyphens"). Punctuation can also separate words or phrases from each other and show to what degree they are separated. We identified various degrees of separation, from slight pauses (Chapter 9, "Commas") to more significant breaks (Chapter 10, "Semicolons and Colons"), leading up to the full-stop period.

In this respect, punctuation is a valuable signal to your reader of the *structural* relation between words or groups of words. Even when using punctuation to join two clauses together within a single sentence, you have punctuation choices about whether to subordinate them (through dependent clauses set off with commas) or to coordinate them. And when coordinating independent clauses, you have the option of showing that the two clauses are balanced (through semicolons or through coordinating conjunctions preceded by a comma) or progressive, with one clause pointing to the next (punctuated with a colon).

Punctuation helps you cue your readers on how to read your sentences. You have no doubt had the experience as a reader of getting halfway into a sentence only to realize that you were going down the wrong path, grouping the wrong words as phrases. And so you backed up and recovered the intended meaning, putting the right groups of words together in your mind as you figured out the grammar of the sentence.

Good punctuation will help you avoid sending readers down the wrong path. For example, punctuation can show your readers where to lower their voices in order to set off less important information (Chapter 12, "Dashes and Parentheses"). Here, too, you have choices: You can use pairs of parentheses, commas, or dashes to set off interrupting comments, with varying degrees of emphasis on the interrupting information. Or you can use single commas or dashes (but still paired parentheses) to set off information at the ends of sentences. The important point is that you have a system at your disposal that gives you choices and allows you to help the reader to read your phrases appropriately, with the subtle meanings and voicings that you intend.

Finally, punctuation can be used to mark an individual style. Because of the various choices that punctuation gives you, you can begin to create an individual style—and to recognize the individual style of other writers—through distinctive patterns of joining phrases and clauses together. You may choose to use lots of coordinate structures, joined by coordinating conjunctions and commas. Or you may choose to coordinate information through the use of semicolons. Another writer may favor subordinate constructions, punctuated with commas. Another may write in a style of almost all simple sentences. You may set off interrupters primarily with commas, while another writer may use parentheses for the same function. Some expressive writers even like dashes and exclamation points!

Not *all* grammatically correct punctuation choices will be equally effective, however. We encourage you, for example, to avoid *either* subordinating *or* coordinating everything. And we certainly advise you to avoid making every sentence a simple structure of only one, independent clause. Such a style sounds choppy and monotonous. Effective style in professional writing is a matter of *rhythm* and *variation*. You create a rhythm through your consistent choices (in this case, choices of punctuation), and then vary that rhythm occasionally to avoid boring your reader while signaling subtle meanings. The most effective rhythms in professional writing are those that combine coordinate and subordinate structures (punctuated appropriately), with the occasional single-clause sentence thrown in for variation.

"Professional writing uses a *clear* and *concise* vocabulary."

There are two words that always arise when praising a strong professional style: *clear* and *concise*. Readers say, "Don't confuse me and don't waste words. My time is too valuable." Good writers send clear messages and do so with economy.

No one would dispute that it is good to be clear (except for those situations in which you can't reveal details or want to leave some ambiguity or "wiggle room"). One source of clarity in professional writing comes from strong underlying sentence structures, often centered on strong S-V-O patterning.

You can also go a long way toward gaining clarity by being alert to patterns of reference within sentences and across sequences of sentences (Chapter 13, "Clear Reference"). Reference is a fundamental property of language—words are always referring to other words or to events in the world. Being clear means thinking about the frames of reference in your readers' heads and doing what you can to make sure your frame of reference is the same as theirs. This concern for readers works at both large levels and small. At the large level, it means giving readers sufficient context and background information to allow them to understand the subject and form logical inferences. At the small level, reference demands that words have clear antecedents. Certain words are born troublemakers: *This*, in particular, always begs the question, "This what?" You can help your readers by answering this question before it arises. Just use a full phrase to delimit the reference, rather than a single word that forces readers to fill in the reference.

At both large and small levels, being clear means coming to terms with what is understood or presupposed by you, the writer, versus what is understood or presupposed by the readers. Your uses of big words, special terms, acronyms, jargon, technobabble, nominal style, and strings of nouns are conditioned by how you wish to be understood and perceived by your reader (Chapter 15, "Technical Vocabulary versus Jargon"; Chapter 16, "Preferring a Verbal Style"; and Chapter 17, "Unpacking Noun Compounds"). A writer with a strong professional style uses specialized terms when appropriate, making careful choices that reflect and respond to the readers' levels of understanding.

In a most particular way, a writer with a strong sense of style chooses individual words for good reason. Words have a way of flowing out in preformed phrases, with too many words for the meaning conveyed. Most writers can go a long way toward having a strong style by pruning the overgrowth, eliminating redundancies, sharpening the focus of sentences, and recognizing wordy constructions (Chapter 14, "Lean Words versus Redundant Words"). A strong style can emerge through revision. Early drafts are inherently wordy and unfocused. Revision tightens prose, bringing economy and precision to the loose structures of early drafts.

"Professional writing is appropriately *active* and *personal,* rather than passive and impersonal."

Cultivating an active and personal style is not a simple matter. Even when workplace writers recognize an active and personal style, they may not be comfortable using one. Bureaucracies tend to encourage writers to develop camouflage; wordy, impersonal styles may flourish because they offer writers a place to hide. Style can reflect a writer's situation, and when situations are tense or uneasy, writing frequently moves toward the passive and impersonal.

An active and personal style stands in the open (Chapter 18, "Recognizing Active and Passive Voice" and Chapter 19, "When to Prefer the Passive Voice"). It projects self-confidence. It directly tells who is doing what, and it may tell who should be doing something they are not. An active and personal style can be a bully style, but it doesn't have to be. It can simply reflect a person who is not afraid to be personally present in a document, a person making clear statements about who should do what.

An active style emerges from using the various elements of style discussed in this book. In some ways, if you clear away the undergrowth, an active and personal style can emerge. Sentences with S-V-O patterns make prose more vigorous, and this pattern only emerges when passive voice, nominal constructions, and wordiness are removed.

The next step is to begin thinking about who you are as a writer: how you want to sound, what kind of tone you are comfortable with, and how you want to project your authority. Of course, who you are is only constituted in the presence of a reader. In writing, you cannot so much *dictate* as *suggest* who you are. And while you can project a role for your readers, readers are notoriously independent. It is a complex and interesting game, in which your job is to project roles that you and your readers can comfortably accept. In the process, when you are successful, you gain understanding and cooperation, because you have learned to use writing as a way of working.

There's a certain comfort that comes from finding one's own voice in prose. Even in serious business settings, it is possible to project personality, to find pleasure in careful turns of language or subtle plays on words (Chapter 20, "Projecting Personality"). When you have found your voice, the words flow and the work gets done.

"Professional writing *emphasizes* what is important—and downplays what is *not*."

In a way, writing is all about emphasis. Communicating is about emphatic messages, helping busy readers separate important from unimportant details. Emphatic writing immediately cues readers as to what is important. They locate necessary actions, get the picture, understand the steps, or accept the argument.

There is a general principle in writing that stresses the importance of first and last. Beginnings of sentences orient readers to the topic; endings deliver the new, crucial information. The same principle of beginning and ending strong is true at larger levels, in paragraphs or in whole documents. Patterns of head-to-head linkage and tail-to-head linkage help you maintain focus on emphatic information across sentence boundaries (Chapter 21, "Managing Sentence Emphasis" and Chapter 23, "Maintaining Flow from Sentence to Sentence"). An alternation between subordinate and coordinate, or parallel structures, not only creates rhythm in prose but also shows readers how ideas line up. The grammatical form reflects the underlying meaning. (See also Chapter 22, "Parallel Structure.")

There's a deep principle at work in sentences, paragraphs, and documents that writers must anticipate and satisfy the readers' information needs. Writers can begin with shared information—background that the writer and readers need to have—before moving on to new information. This way, readers get information in context and can understand it.

This doesn't mean, however, that writers should hold all important information until the end of a document. At the sentence level, shared information announces the subject while new information is offered in the predicate, so the process of offering new information begins with the first sentence. It usually helps readers to know where the writer is going by having writing organized deductively, with findings, messages, actions, and issues addressed up front and then argued for and supported in the passages that follow.

The careful writer attends to what readers already know, establishing a shared context and leading readers coherently through the information. The emphatic writer delivers key messages and issues up front and returns to these key messages throughout the document, wrapping them up at the end. Emphasis is derived from focus, from a clear sense of the purpose of a document and the desired understanding and action the writer wishes to bring about.

You also create emphasis with the *visual* format of a document (Chapter 24, "Defining a Professional Look"). You signal the hierarchical organization of a document by using headings and subheadings that visually reinforce that hierarchy. You show readers what's important by using white space to set off important information or by indenting subordinate information. You emphasize various headings or words within the text with CAPITAL LETTERS, **boldface,** *italics,* or underlining. A style sheet—either one supplied with your word processor or one you create yourself—can ensure that you use visual emphasis in a consistent way.

A Checklist for Professional Writing

The best thing you can do now is to apply the principles of effective grammar and style to your own writing. Applying the particulars of the six principles discussed in this book cannot be done all at once. In actuality, it takes several *passes* through your draft, looking for one or two types of stylistic choices per pass.

Below is a list of these stylistic choices in a convenient order of application.[1] We don't claim that this is the *only* good order of application, but it is one that has worked for us as we have edited the drafts of the various chapters in this book. You might find it useful to copy this checklist and keep it handy when you write.

---

[1] We are indebted to our colleague Lucia McKay for her idea of the "5 Cs" in this list.

Is it clear?
1. Are the sentences understandable? Are sentences formed around strong S-V-O patterning?
2. Are the sentences emphatic and direct?
3. Does the visual format help the reader understand the structure of the document?

Is it grammatically correct?
1. Are all the sentences complete (at least one independent clause)? Have you avoided run-on sentences and fragments (except when intentionally used for lists, etc.)?
2. Are modifiers placed as close as possible to what they modify? Are modifiers of time, purpose, and condition placed up front? Have you avoided long subject modifiers?
3. Do pronouns agree with their antecedent nouns? Do subjects agree with their verbs?
4. Have you used punctuation correctly to signal your intended meaning in how the document is to be read?

Is it concise?
1. Have you avoided unnecessarily complex sentences and clause structures?
2. Have you used short, familiar words in preference to long, complex ones?
3. Have you used only those technical terms that are necessary, and have you defined terms and acronyms that may not be familiar to your various audiences?

Is it coherent?
1. Is the point of each sentence made at the end (rather than the beginning)?
2. Does each paragraph flow from sentence to sentence? Is there a consistent topic for each paragraph?

Is it consistent?
1. Is passive voice used appropriately and consistently to signal special meanings?
2. Have you used parallel structure, especially for lists?
3. Is the voice of the writer appropriate and consistent, especially in terms of how you refer to yourself and your readers?
4. Is there a consistent level of formality in the sentence structures and vocabulary choices?
5. Is the visual formatting for such elements as headings and specialized terms logical and consistent?

Is it correctly spelled?
1. Have you checked your spelling to assure a professional impression?

Please don't infer from the order of the categories that one category is any more important than the other. We have listed these categories in the order of easiest application, not greatest importance. Spelling, for example, is listed last because of the tendency of most writers to introduce spelling or typing errors in correcting other problems. So, for efficiency's sake, it is more practical to check spelling last. But spelling is by no means unimportant. Indeed, spelling errors are one of the *first* things readers will notice. And misspelled words convey an impression of sloppiness, not professionalism.

It is helpful in the first several passes to read your draft out loud and to mark it up on hard copy. (On-line versions are hard to revise when you're trying to get a sense of the *whole* document.)

On Continued Growth as a Professional Writer

Growth in writing style takes time, instruction, attention, and practice. If you have worked carefully through the lessons in this book, your style is probably more professional than when you began. But the real payoff will come as you apply the understanding gained in this book to the various kinds of writing you do at work.

Pay attention to language and style! This book takes a direct approach to instruction, assuming that you can study grammar, usage, and style and take away valuable lessons for your own writing. If you have mastered the vocabulary and grammar presented here, you are ready to think about your writing in these terms and to develop your style over time. You should be able to make better use of the style manuals and reference handbooks on grammar that can be found in many workplaces and in all bookstores. You should be able to identify both the strong aspects of your style and your weaknesses, so you can continue to improve.

You are also now prepared to be more alert to the style of others, describing and naming what you like or don't like about the style of those around you. You should have more to say to a co-worker who asks you to take a look at a report or a proposal. You should be a better coach or mentor to co-workers, able to understand the ways that sentences and style work. This doesn't mean you should play the "gotcha game" with grammar, pointing out other people's errors and making people nervous about their style. Style is interesting; you can share your interest in style with others. Talk about what is interesting or good in someone's writing. When the situation is right, you can be helpful to others. When people seek your advice, you can offer them what you know in ways that are truly helpful. Teaching the principles of style and grammar to others is the best way to reinforce what you know.

Improving one's own language skills can also be a very indirect process. People who read tend to be better writers. People who put themselves in various language situations and begin to feel comfortable with different communicative tasks inevitably improve their language abilities. You can take on a variety of writing assignments at work, volunteering to do the minutes, to draft the report, or to develop a set of procedures. Practicing different kinds of writing will improve your style and versatility.

With writing, as with most important activities, you need to stay the course. Writing has its own rewards: there is satisfaction in getting action from writing, changing work processes, or documenting accomplishments. There is satisfaction and reward, too, in finding that you are willing to have a strong, personal voice. Your writing can project a confidence in who you are as a person. There is no reason that any piece of writing should sound as though it were written by a committee. You can be willing to play and experiment, to show a sense of humor, to take risks, and to be creative.

Creativity underlies all language use. Most of the sentences you speak and write are novel, never having been uttered by anyone else. There's creativity in working with complicated systems, and language is one of our most complicated. There's creativity in figuring out how to use writing at work: how to be efficient, effective, respected, or liked through the documents you create and send to others in a work setting. If this book has helped you to do those things better, then we judge it a success.

Appendix

For Further Work

We assume that this book has taught you certain principles about writing and style, encouraged you to recognize and control some of the choices that language gives you, and increased your confidence in your own writing abilities. We also assume that if you are serious about developing your writing skills, you will want to keep learning. Listed below are the best books we know to help you keep learning. These are the books we use in our classes, encourage our students and friends to buy, and use for our own reference.

There is no single book that will cover everything. The notes under each title give you some idea of what you can expect. Many professions (like biologists, psychologists, or chemists) have their own style guides, somewhat like house rules for professional groups. These guides are not covered here, but your librarian could help you locate such references for your particular field. Beyond the specific books we mention here, we encourage you to develop an interest in language in general. Pay attention to how language is used, whether oral or written. Read for pleasure some of the many books about communication at work. These are good ways to work on your writing indirectly.

Barry, Robert E., and Loretta Scholten. *Applied English: Language Skills for Business & Everyday Use.* Englewood Cliffs, NJ: Prentice-Hall, 1995.

This useful text covers many of the same subjects as *Writing at Work* but with less emphasis on appropriateness and effectiveness and more emphasis on grammatical correctness. This would be a good book if you wanted more practice with the topics covered in Units One and Two in *Writing at Work.*

Bell, Arthur H. *NTC's Business Writer's Handbook: Business Communication from A to Z.* Lincolnwood, IL: NTC Publishing Group, 1996.

This is a highly useful, encyclopedic reference, covering everything from punctuation and style, to writing process, to documentation, to visuals, to publishing. Especially useful are the models of various kinds of reports, proposals, letters, and memos.

The Chicago Manual of Style. 14th ed. Chicago: University of Chicago Press, 1993.

The number of editions tells you something about the status of this work, a tremendous resource on all the hard questions of style, punctuation, usage, editing, referencing, typography, number, foreign words, printing and binding, and more. It is inexhaustible as a reference book—great for settling arguments.

Kosslyn, Stephen. *Elements of Graph Design.* Cambridge: W. H. Freeman and Company, 1995.

This approachable book focuses on reworking charts, graphs, tables, and diagrams to increase their clarity and effectiveness. The author is a Harvard professor of psychology, who is interested in how people perceive data relationships. This book is very useful for those writers who want to improve written reports or oral presentations by improving visuals.

Lanham, Richard. *Revising Business Prose.* 3rd ed. New York: Macmillan Publishing, 1992.

This is a fresh and lively approach to revising prose that reflects many of the principles found in *Writing at Work.* The author shows step-by-step how to rewrite baggy, flabby prose into clear, hardworking, and lively writing.

Strunk, William, Jr., and E. B. White. *The Elements of Style.* 7th ed. Englewood Cliffs, NJ: Allyn and Bacon, 1995.

This small book has had a huge effect on many writers from all fields. It will change the way you think and write, and it will help you find pleasure in choosing words and finding a comfortable prose style that suits your personality.

Williams, Joseph. *Style: Ten Lessons in Clarity and Grace.* 4th ed. Chicago: University of Chicago Press, 1995.

This is a wonderful book that will help you develop your prose style by exercising many of the principles found in *Writing at Work.* The author is a professor of English at the University of Chicago and has a distinguished career of careful research on style and its consequences. The lessons in *Style* are based on the author's work as a consultant to medical, legal, accounting, and government organizations. Although the exercises in the book are difficult, they are valuable, and an answer key can help you if you are studying on your own.

Woolston, Donald C., Patricia A. Robinson, and Gisela Kutzbach. *Effective Writing Strategies for Engineers and Scientists.* Boca Raton, FL: Lewis Publishers, 1988.

This book contains an excellent discussion of the writing process and its stages, as applied to technical writing.

Glossary

acronym: A new word invented by combining the initial letters of the name of an object, project, agency, or entity—e.g., *NASA, radar, scuba.*

action verb: A verb that expresses or contains some action as opposed to a linking verb.

active voice: A clause in which the subject is the doer of the action; *see also* **passive voice.**

actor: The person or thing in a clause that has the role of acting; sometimes but not always the subject of the clause.

adjective/adjectival: A modifier that describes a noun; characterizes properties or qualities of things.

adverb/adverbial: A modifier that describes a verb or other modifier and characterizes actions, telling when, how, or in what manner.

agreement: Sometimes called *concord,* the necessary relations of word to word or phrase to phrase—e.g., plural subjects are used with plural verbs; masculine pronouns, to refer to masculine nouns.

ambiguity: A construction with more than one meaning.

antecedent: The preceding noun or pronoun that a pronoun refers to.

antonym: A word with the opposite meaning of an identified word.

appropriateness: The suitability of a word, phrase, or passage to the particular situation in which it is used.

article: A word that helps form a noun phrase; includes only three words: *a, an,* and *the.*

ascender: The top part of a letter that extends above the x-height. *See also* **descender.**

aspect: Category of verb inflection that shows the degree of completeness of an action. There are three such degrees:

simple: treating action as single point in time

progressive: ongoing action

perfective: completed action

audience: The person or group to whom a piece of writing or a speech is addressed.

auxiliary: A word that is part of the verb phrase in some clauses and that may carry tense, aspect, or mood; also called *helping verb*.

back-formations: New words derived from longer words, frequently shifting their part of speech—e.g., the verb *to donate* is derived from the noun *donation*.

blends: New words formed by combining parts (or all) of other words—e.g., *bookstore, motel, teleconference.*

case: The role a noun or pronoun plays in a sentence—i.e., *subject, object, possessive.*

circumlocution: A long way of saying something; going around a topic with words that add bulk but not muscle to writing; *see also* **redundancy.**

class shifter: A word that can function as different parts of speech in different constructions.

clause: A group of words or phrases, with at least one word or phrase acting as the subject and one word or phrase acting as the predicate (in a finite, time-bound relation).

clincher sentence: A final sentence that summarizes or makes the point of a passage.

clipped forms: Words that are formed by clipping longer words—e.g., *bus* clipped from *omnibus.*

coherence: A desired quality of writing in which sentences and paragraphs are logically sequenced and maintain focus and emphasis across the text.

collective nouns: Nouns referring to a plurality of individuals or things—e.g., *committee, company, army.*

colon (:): A mark of punctuation introducing a list or pointing toward a phrase or clause that amplifies a clause.

comma (,): A mark of punctuation that sets off, balances, or separates words or parts of sentences.

comma splice: Two independent clauses joined (incorrectly) with only a comma; sometimes called a *run-on sentence.*

Communication Triangle: A diagram representing at each corner those factors that most influence a written message: the writer, the reader, and the subject. The connecting sides of the triangle suggest the relationships among the factors.

complement: The part of the clause that works with the verb to form a complete predicate.

complete predicate: A term referring to the whole verb phrase including the main verb and any objects, complements or modifiers.

complete subject: A term referring to the whole subject phrase including the main word (the head noun) and its modifiers.

complex sentence: A sentence that contains at least one dependent clause attached to an independent clause.

compound construction: Any grammatical construction that is composed of two or more parallel parts, as a clause with two, conjoined subject phrases or a verb phrase with two objects.

compound sentence: A sentence that contains two or more independent clauses.

conciseness: A desired quality of writing in which something is said in as few words as possible.

conjunction: A word that ties together words, phrases, or clauses.

conjunctive adverb: An adverb that tends to modify whole clauses or that shows the relation of one clause to another.

connotation: A meaning that comes to be associated with a word and its contexts of use but is not necessarily part of a dictionary definition. *See also* **denotation.**

contraction/contracted form: A verb form that combines two words by dropping or changing one or more letters and uses an apostrophe to signal missing letter(s)—e.g., *can't, hasn't, won't.*

coordinate: Of equal importance, either grammatically or in terms of meaning; *see also* **subordinate.**

coordinate clauses or **phrases:** Two or more clauses or phrases joined as parallel elements by *for, and, nor, but, or, yet, so.*

coordinate phrasing: Phrasing two or more elements (subjects, verbs, objects, modifiers) so that they have parallel roles and grammatical constructions in a clause or sentence.

coordinating conjunction: A conjunction that ties together any two equivalent grammatical elements—*for, and, nor, but, or, yet, so.*

correlative conjunction: A conjunction that works in pairs—e.g., *either/or, not only/but also, neither/nor.*

correctness: Observing the rules of standard English.

count noun: A common noun naming things that can be counted—e.g., *hat, motel, holiday;* has both singular and plural forms.

cumulative (loose) construction: A style of modification, clause, or sentence structure that adds details loosely at the end of the construction.

dangling modifier: A modifier that is not clearly attached to a specific word or phrase in the clause.

dash (—): A mark of punctuation that sets off phrases that interrupt the clause; used in pairs except when the interruption comes at the end of the sentence; longer than a hyphen.

decimal alignment: Vertical alignment of a column of figures on the figures' decimal points.

definite article: An element of grammar with only one member—*the. See also* **article.**

demonstrative pronoun: A pronoun form that points—e.g., *this, that, these, those.*

denotation: The dictionary definition of a word; *see also* **connotation.**

dependent clause: A clause that is unable to stand alone (also called *subordinate clause* and *relative clause*); must be attached to an independent clause or edited to make it a full sentence or an independent clause.

descender: The part of a letter that extends below the line. *See also* **ascender.**

direct address: Writing that directly refers to the reader by name or as *you.*

direct object: A part of some clauses that tells who or what received the action; together with a verb, forms a complete predicate.

discourse reference: Word(s) that refers to place and time within a text, rather than place and time within the "real" world surrounding the text.

discourse roles: The ways in which a text refers to the writer, the readers, and any other involved people.

drafter-rewriter: Writers who begin writing almost immediately with little planning time, who instead do a lot of planning work in the process of refining their drafts. *See also* **planner-drafter.**

drafting stage: Getting words on paper, without necessarily worrying too much about a document's final form.

dummy subject: A word that stands in for the true subject of a clause, an empty filler in the subject slot; typically: *It is . . .* or *There are . . .* constructions.

editing: Rewriting to make sentences and word choice correct and effective.

expletive constructions: Sentences that begin with a dummy subject: *It is . . .* and *There are. . . .*

finite verb: A verb that is "in time" with the subject of a clause; a verb that is tied in a relation of tense to the subject.

first person: The person or persons speaking—*I, me, my, mine; we, us, our, ours.*

floating modifier: A modifier that can move freely before, within, or after a clause.

focus: The starting point or topic of a sentence; also the point or topic that extends across sentences and paragraphs.

font: A typeface family.

footer: Information appearing in the bottom margin of each page of a text; may contain the page number, a date, a document title, a section title, file information, copyright notice; *see also* **header.**

fragment: A group of words that doesn't form a sentence although it is punctuated as one.

full justification: Text that is set so that each printed line aligns evenly on both left and right margins.

future tense: The form of a verb that signals action taking place in the future.

gender: Distinction of nouns or pronouns as *masculine (he, man, actor), feminine (her, actress, girl),* or *neuter (it, picture, table).*

gerund: A nominalization using the *-ing* form of a verb in the role of a noun— e.g., *swimming.*

gobbledygook: The stringing together of long or pompous words that don't mean much. (Named after the sound a turkey makes.)

header: Information printed in the margin area at the top of each page of text; may contain the page number, a date, a document title, a section title, file information, copyright notice. *See also* **footer.**

headings: Labels that show the structure of a text by marking sections and subsections.

headline style: Style of writing that omits all the "little" words in an attempt to save space and to sound more direct; *see also* **telegraphic style.**

head-to-head focus: Maintaining the same grammatical subject across sentences or clauses within a paragraph. *See also* **tail-to-head focus.**

head word: The main word around which a phrase is built.

helping verb: A word that is part of a verb phrase in some clauses and that may carry tense, aspect, or mood; also called *auxiliary* verb.

house rules: Particular principles that a business establishes for the style and format of its documents.

hypercorrection: Creating an error by overgeneralizing a rule; following a rule where it does not apply.

hyphen (-): A mark of punctuation that shows when a word is broken at the end of a line or that joins closely related words that work as a unit.

imperative mood: Grammatical structure that forms commands; *see also* **mood.**

indefinite article: A grammatical element with only two members, *a* and *an; see also* **definite article.**

indefinite pronoun: A pronoun that allows reference to a group or an individual without specifically naming someone or something—e.g., *each, any, everybody.*

independent clause: A clause that may be punctuated to stand alone as a full sentence.

indicative mood: Grammatical structure that makes a statement (as opposed to asking a question or giving an order); the "normal" sentence structure; *see also* **mood.**

indirect object: Part of the clause that tells who benefited from the action expressed by the verb and direct object.

infinitive: The *to* form of a verb (also called *nonfinite*); a verb that is nontensed.

inflection: Endings on words that mark such distinctions as singular vs. plural or present vs. past.

intensifier: A type of adverb that adds intensity to the word or phrase it modifies—e.g., *very, terribly, awfully.*

interjection: A part of speech that interjects an exclamation into a sentence such as *aha, oops,* or *yikes.*

interrogative mood: Grammatical structure that asks a question; *see also* **mood.**

interrogative pronoun: A pronoun that helps form a question—e.g., *who, what, where, when, why, how.*

irregular verb: Verb that forms the past tense by some inflection to the root, infinitive form, rather than by the addition of *-ed.*

jargon: Specialized term(s) useful to insiders but confusing to outsiders.

justification: The way the lines of a text are vertically aligned on a page: to the left, right, center, or to a decimal point.

leading: The white space between each printed line of a paragraph.

linking sentence: A sentence formed with a linking verb that links the subject with the subject complement. Linking sentences have neither passive nor active voice because there is no action expressed in the verb.

linking verb: A verb that does not express an action but simply describes a state of being; includes forms of *to be* and a few other verbs—e.g., *to seem, to feel, to appear.*

loose (cumulative) construction: A style of modification, clause, or sentence structure that adds details loosely at the end of the construction.

loose modifier: A modifier, typically attached to the end of a clause or sentence, that adds details without being integral to the clause. Also called *cumulative modifier.*

mass noun: A noun that refers to substances that exist as quantities that cannot be counted; a mass noun has only a singular form—e.g., *milk, dirt, air.*

medium: The form of delivery a text takes: e-mail, paper, on-line file, radio script, televised program, presentation overhead.

metaphor: A word used in figurative senses in which something is described as something else.

modifier: A general term for all the words, phrases, and clauses that are added to a sentence for descriptive purposes.

monospaced font: A font that gives the same amount of space to each character, whether it is wide (like an *m*) or narrow (like an *l*).

mood: A grammatical category that shows the degree of certainty carried by the verb's action. There are four such degrees:

indicative: stating

interrogative: asking

imperative: commanding

subjunctive: expressing a wish or hypothetical statement

nominalizations: Noun forms of verbs and adjectives—e.g., *disposition* is the nominalized form of the verb *dispose.*

nominal style: Writing that captures actions in nouns, overrelies on prepositional phrases, and feels ponderous.

nonrestrictive modifier: A modifier that is not essential to the word or phrase it modifies and that should be set off by commas or other punctuation.

nonrules: Stylistic preferences that change from one person, time, or place to another; usually only noticed when they are followed.

noun: Traditionally defined, the name of a person, place, or thing; also called *substantive*.

noun compound: Nouns that work as a unit (n+n+n)—e.g., *unit price target* or *elimination round*.

noun phrase: The main word (the head noun), frequently an article, and any modifiers that form the complete noun phrase.

number: Distinctions of singular vs. plural in nouns, pronouns, and verbs.

object: Receiver of the action within the predicate.

object case: The role of a noun or pronoun when used as the object of a verb phrase or as the object of a preposition. *See also* **subject** or **possessive case.**

object of preposition: Noun found at the end of a prepositional phrase; the head word of a prepositional phrase.

parallel structure: Stylistic principle of putting similar ideas in similar form.

parentheses (): Marks of punctuation always used in pairs to set off a phrase that adds a detail or interrupts a clause or clauses.

parenthetical modifiers: Modifying elements that interrupt a clause and are set off by parentheses, dashes, or commas.

participle: The progressive or perfective form of a verb corresponding to the *-ing* and *-en* verb forms, respectively.

parts of sentences: The units that make up clauses—i.e., subjects, predicates, objects, complements, modifiers.

parts of speech: One of the eight categories of words that makes up parts of sentences: *noun, pronoun, verb, adjective, adverb, conjunction, interjection,* and *preposition*.

passive voice: A clause construction wherein the subject is being acted upon rather than doing the action. *See also* **active voice.**

past participle: The *-en* or *-ed* form of a verb; occurs in passive voice with some form of *to be;* functions as a modifier.

past tense: The form of a verb that signals an action in the past.

patterns of reference: A chain of links from sentence to sentence or from text to context that builds coherence.

perfect(ive) aspect: A degree of aspect that shows a completed action.

periodic sentence: A sentence with a climactic pattern that begins with subordinate elements and ends with an independent clause.

person: The distinctions among the person(s) speaking *(first person)* vs. the person(s) spoken to *(second person)* vs. the person(s) spoken about *(third person)*.

personal pronoun: A word used in place of or in reference to nouns or pronouns that refer to people or animate beings.

phrase: A group of words built around a main word and joined to form parts of sentences.

planner-drafter: Writers who do their planning all at once up front and, with very little rewriting, produce their text in almost final form. *See also* **drafter-rewriter.**

planning stage: The idea-gathering stage of writing; the first, or prewriting, stage of the writing process.

plural: A characteristic of verbs, count nouns and pronouns, indicating more than one; *see also* **singular.**

point size: A measure of the size of a letter; the larger the point size, the larger the letter; a 72-point letter would be approximately one inch tall.

possessive case: The case that shows ownership; nouns typically show possessive case by adding *-s* or *-es*; pronouns have possessive forms—e.g., *his, her, their, our, your. See also* **subject** or **object case.**

possessive pronoun: Pronoun that shows ownership.

predicate: The part of a clause that expresses an action, presents new information, or says something about the subject; includes the verb phrase and any accompanying complements, objects, and modifiers.

predicate adjective: A subject complement that works as an adjective modifying the subject.

predicate nominative: A subject complement that is a noun identifying the subject.

preposition: A part of speech that helps show relations and qualities; a word that combines with a head word and modifiers to form modifying phrases—e.g., *in the banking community, around the next bend, at an earlier date.*

prepositional phrase: A modifying phrase formed by a preposition and a head word plus internal modifiers—e.g., *in the banking community, around the next bend.*

present tense: The form of a verb that signals action currently taking place.

progressive aspect: A degree of aspect carried by English verbs that shows ongoing action.

pronoun: A word that usually stands for nouns or other pronouns.

pronoun-antecedent agreement: The grammatical rule that calls for a pronoun to agree in number, gender, and person with the word that comes before it and that it refers to (its antecedent).

proportional font: A font that gives different amounts of space to each character, with more space to wide characters like an *m* than to narrow ones like an *l*.

purpose: The reason one writes or communicates—e.g., *to persuade, to move, to entertain, to express.*

ragged-right justification: Describes a text that is justified on the left margin but ragged on the right, with lines breaking wherever words end.

real rules: The underlying language principles governing word endings, word order, negative constructions, etc.; noticed mainly when they are violated; *see also* **house rules** and **nonrules.**

receiver: The person or thing who is the object of a verb phrase, the one receiving the action.

reduced phrases: Shortened phrases that refer to longer preceding phrases; sometimes whole clauses are reduced to phrases.

redundancy: Unnecessary wordiness in sentence construction that does not add to meaning; *see also* **circumlocution.**

reference: Use of words to refer to other words in the text or to things in the world.

reflexive pronoun: A pronoun form (e.g., *myself, herself, themselves*) that is used when the subject of a clause acts upon itself—e.g., *He gave himself a pat on the back.*

regular verb: A verb that forms the past tense by adding *-ed* to the infinitive form.

relative clause: A clause beginning with a relative pronoun.

relative pronoun: A pronoun that creates relative clauses and ties them to independent clauses—e.g., *who, which, that.*

repetition: The use of the same term to refer to something previously mentioned; useful in maintaining focus.

restrictive modification: Modification that is essential to the meaning of the word or phrase it modifies; often takes the form of a relative clause; should not be set off with commas.

revising: Rewriting for large concerns like appropriateness for the audience, clarity of purpose, and overall organization.

rewriting stage: Stage of the writing process where revising and editing take prominence.

role: The part a word plays in a clause: actor, receiver, action.

root: The simplest form of a word, stripped of any inflections—e.g., *derive* is the root of *derivational*.

rule: In text design, a horizontal line that runs across a page to separate or highlight elements.

rules: The underlying language principles governing word endings, word order, negative constructions, etc.; noticed when they are violated.

run-on sentence: Two independent clauses incorrectly punctuated as a single sentence, or incorrectly joined with only a comma; also called a *comma splice.*

sans serif font: Used to describe a font that has simple letter strokes with no small curls on the tops, bottoms, or ends of letters. *See also* **serif font.**

scope of document: How broadly or narrowly a topic is covered; the range of content in a document.

screen font: A font designed to be legible on a computer screen.

second person: The person or persons being addressed—*you, your, yours.*

semicolon (;): A mark of punctuation that balances clauses or phrases; stronger than a comma but weaker than a period.

sentence: One or more clauses that can stand alone—or everything between a capital letter and a mark of final punctuation such as a period, question mark, or exclamation mark.

sentence emphasis: What a sentence appears to be giving the most weight or meaning; the combined effects of structural emphasis and speech emphasis.

serif font: Used to describe a font that has small curls on the tops, bottoms, or ends of letters; *see also* **sans serif font.**

sexism or **sexist language:** Language that excludes or belittles people based on their gender— e.g., using *he* to refer to either a male or female referent or using *stewardess* as opposed to *flight attendant.*

simple sentence: A sentence composed of a single independent clause.

simple subject: A term referring to the single main word of the subject phrase.

singular: A characteristic of verbs, count nouns, and pronouns, indicating not more than one.

situation: A general term for the larger context that surrounds writing, including purpose and audience but also political or social reasons for writing. The situation often includes constraints that affect writing: time, cost, job definitions, etc.

speech emphasis: The place in the clause or sentence receiving emphatic, voiced stress; typically the beginning and ending of a clause, not the middle.

structural emphasis: Grammatical patterns in sentences or clauses that bring ideas into prominence.

style sheet: A list of format and typographic definitions for elements of a document; can be defined statically on paper or dynamically as part of an electronic file.

subject: Who or what is being talked about; the beginning point within a clause about which something is said.

subject case: The role of a noun or pronoun when used in the subject position of a clause; *see also* **object** or **possessive case.**

subject complement: Part of sentence that follows a linking verb and identifies or describes the subject.

subject phrase: The group of words that forms the subject construction, including the head word plus any modifiers.

subject-verb agreement: The necessary relations of a subject to its finite predicate: *number, person, tense.*

subject-verb-object pattern (S-V-O): A common and powerful sentence structure built around a subject that is doing the acting, an action verb, and a direct object.

subjunctive mood: Grammatical form for statements expressing wishes, hypotheses, or contrary-to-fact meanings; *see also* **mood.**

subordinate: Of lesser importance, either grammatically (as a dependent clause) or in terms of meaning; *see also* **coordinate.**

subordinate clause: A clause that is unable to stand alone; also called *dependent clause.*

subordinating conjunction: A word that introduces and makes a clause dependent—e.g., *because, since, as soon as, whenever.*

suffix: An inflection added to the end of a word that changes its part of speech or adds some quality to the word.

synonym: A word with a similar meaning to an identified word.

tail-to-head focus: Chains of clauses or sentences that achieve focus by linking the end of one sentence to the beginning of the next; *see also* **head-to-head focus.**

telegraphic style: Writing style that omits all the "little" words in an attempt to save space and to sound more direct. *See also* **headline style.**

tense: A grammatical category, expressed in the verb, associated with time: *past, present,* and *future.*

third person: The person or persons being talked about—e.g., *they, them, their.*

topic sentence: A sentence providing a generalization for the paragraph or section that follows.

verb: The head word of a predicate; the core word(s) of a clause that expresses action or characterizes the subjects and objects of the clause; the part of the clause that carries tense, aspect, and mood.

verbal emphasis: The voice inflection placed on words to show emphasis, often represented in writing by italics—e.g., a *critically important* step in the process; *see also* **structural emphasis.**

verbal style: Writing that captures actions in verbs and relies on subject-verb-object (S-V-O) patterning.

verb phrase: A phrase formed by a verb and any accompanying modifiers.

verb tense: The meaning expressed in the verb indicating time: *past, present,* or *future* in the English language.

vertical list: A list that displays itself by breaking elements out of paragraph form into a list structure, typically numbered or bulleted.

voice: Grammatical system that indicates who is doing what in a text—i.e., whether the subject is doing the action or is being acted upon; *active* and *passive* are the two types of grammatical voice.

white space: The portion of the page not covered by ink; used to show divisions and to make text open and inviting.

word-order rules: Rules of English that require a certain word order in phrases—e.g., for adjectives, the more inherent qualities of a thing are to be placed nearer the head noun, while the less inherent qualities are placed farther away.

x-height: The height of the horizontal line that can be drawn across the top of lower case letters; fonts can be distinguished by their high or low x-heights; *see also* **ascender** and **descender.**

Index

Bolded page references indicate defining discussions.